FREDERICK COUNTY, VIRGINIA

Wills & Administrations
1795–1816

INTRODUCTION

These records were digested from microfilm reels Nos. 53 and 54 held by the Virginia State Library, Richmond, Virginia, listing all entries contained in Will Books Nos. 6, 7, 8 and 9 of Frederick County, Virginia, covering the years 1795 to 1816.

Particular attention was given to references to land ownership, which was located in various Virginia counties as well as in Pennsylvania, Maryland, Kentucky, Tennessee, Ohio, and references to North and South Carolina.

Interpreting the handwriting often resulted in questions regarding the spelling of proper names. Several standard reference works were consulted to determine the most accurate usage and variants. The county clerks were not averse to using two or more spellings within the same record, and signers often abbreviated their given names.

Frederick County's early records will be found in Orange County, which was formed from Spotsylvania County in 1734. At the time it was formed, the Virginia Assembly described it as "bounden southerly by the line of Hanover County, northerly by the grant of Lord Fairfax and westerly by the utmost limits of Virginia." The western boundary was the Mississippi River. Lord Fairfax's grant was not surveyed until shortly before he personally appeared in Virginia, in 1749. Although its boundaries were defined in 1738, at which time the Assembly also set off Augusta County, neither new county was financially able to function. Frederick County organized its court in 1743; Augusta began its court in 1745. For that reason, many records of these two counties will be found in Orange County. In 1744, another large area was set off from Orange County on the south side of the Rappahannock River, Culpeper County.

In 1754, the Assembly directed: "Whereas part of the county and parish of Augusta lies within the bounds of the territory or tract of land called the Northern Neck belong(ing) to the right honorable Thomas, Lord Fairfax, Baron of Cameron, and it will be more convenient if the dividing line between the said territory and the other part of this colony be established as the line of the said county and that part of the said county be added to the county and parish of Frederick," it was enacted therefore that the part of Augusta above mentioned be added to Frederick which should then be divided into two counties and "all that part thereof lying to the westward of the ridge of mountains commonly called and known by the name of the Great North or Cape Capon mountains and Warin spring mountain extending to the Potomac River be one distinct county and called and known by the name of Hampshire." Thus Augusta County was removed from the proprietary of Lord Fairfax's Northern Neck Grant. This county is now in West Virginia, as well as the county later formed from it, Hardy County. In 1772, Frederick County was again divided, resulting in the creation of Berkeley and Dunmore Counties. Six years later, Governor John Murray, Earl of Dunmore, had so enraged the people of Virginia that they changed the name of Dunmore County to Shenandoah County. Berkeley County gave up the area then called Jefferson County in 1801; and in 1820 Morgan County was created from Berkeley and Hampshire Counties. So many boundary changes occurred over so short a time that it becomes important to review the origin of the county during the time when it was granted, purchased or sold. Properties which appeared as being located in Frederick County between the years 1795 and 1816 could later be found in another county formed later. Shenandoah County, once part of Frederick, was shorn of part of its land which was combined with part of Rockingham County to form Page County in 1831. Clarke County and Warren County were later created from Shenandoah and Frederick Counties.

Some of the counties originally part of old Frederick County are now in West Virginia, which was formed in 1863.

A great deal of genealogical information may be gleaned from the more or less standard references, the histories of the Shenandoah Valley by Kercheval, Cartmell and Norris, as well as the Hopewell Friends History, 1734-1934, Frederick County, Virginia. Histories of adjacent counties should not be ignored. The references used by the compilers were as follows:

Shenandoah Valley Pioneers and Their Descendants, by T. K. Cartmell; History of the Lower Shenandoah Valley, by J. E. Norris; Winchester, Virginia, and Its Beginnings, 1743-1814, by Katherine Glass Greene; Frederick County Wills and Administrations, 1743-1800, by J. Estelle Stewart King; Frederick County, Virginia, Marriages 1781-1854, by Eliza Timberlake Davis; Berkeley County, Virginia, Marriages, 1781-1854, by Guy L. Keesecker; and the 1800 Frederick County, Virginia, Tax List, printed in The Virginia Genealogist, and the 1810 census index for Frederick County. Two additional sources were not consulted but are called to the attention of readers, i.e.: Frederick County Superior Court Will Books, Nos. 1 and 2, covering the years 1790 to 1815, and the Frederick County Court Minutes. These are on microfilm in the Virginia State Library in Richmond.

Simple abbreviations have been used: exr, exrx; executor, executrix; admr, admx; administrator, administratrix; sec, security; wit, witness.

Arlington, Virginia
November 1982

FREDERICK COUNTY, VIRGINIA

Wills & Administrations
1795–1816

WILL BOOK NO. 6, 1795-1802

BROWN, RICHARD
Inventory & Appraisal. 6 Jan 1795
Appraisers: John Bozea, George Brown, Abel Janny (p. 1)

GLASS, JOSEPH
Will. 23 Jan 1792/ 6 Jan 1795
Wife: Elizabeth Glass
Children: Samuel, Robert, Joseph, David, Sarah, Elizabeth, Martha, Ruth, Nancy, Sophia, Mary Hoge, Georgetta Wilson. Land and negroes benefit of wife and eight youngest children, Joseph, Sarah, Elizabeth, Martha, Ruth, David, Nancy, Sophia. Movable estate to be sold and divided among four sons, except wearing apparel. To each child, varying amounts of money.
Exrs: Samuel and Robert Glass, William Vance
Sec: James David Vance, Solomon Hoge, Ł 1,000
Samuel Glass permitted to decline. (p. 2

HOTSENPELAR, GEORGE
Appraisal. 18 Nov 1794/ 6 Jan 1795
Widow's dowry, Ł 18.5.6
Appraisers: John Orndorff, James Fox
Submitted to court by John Orndorff, Jacob Fry, Jr., Robert Jameson. (p. 6

BEVERLY, JAMES
Estate Sale. 1782/ payment approved 7 Oct 1783
Admr: James Wilson. Sec: David Niswander. Bond Ł 43.14.8
(See Order Book 25, page 372) (p. 7

LITTLER, SAMUEL
Appraisal. 3 May 1778/ 3 Feb 1795
Exr: John Littler
Appraisers: George F. Norton, Meredith Helm

LITTLER, MARY
Account. 3 Feb 1795/ 3 Apr 1795
(One of heirs named, Samuel Littler) (p. 12-13)

ALLEN, JOHN
Inventory & Appraisal. 4 Feb 1795
Appraisers: Joseph Longacre, William Marques, James O. Vance (p. 13-1)

LINDSAY, JAMES
Will. 5 Jan 1786/ 3 Feb 1795
Children: Michael, Thomas, Elizabeth, Margaret (under 18)
Land on Abrams Creek and in Winchester to each of four children; if Margaret dies before 18, divide share among surviving children. Elizabeth's land "paid for by Mrs. Mary Wood."
Exrs: James Gunnell Dowdall, John Peyton, Robert Wood, James Walker
Wit: Edward McGuire, Edward McGuire, Jr., Edward Power
Sec: John Duffield, Edward Powers, James Eagan, Ł 1,000. (p. 17-19)

SMITH, JEREMIAH
Appraisal. Oct 1794/ 8 Apr 1795
Appraisers: Richard Taylor, Joseph Boley, William Taylor (p. 20

DAUGHTY/DOUGHTY, DANIEL
Appraisal. Oct 1794/ 8 Apr 1795
Appraisers: William Headley, J. Allensworth, Solomon Van Meter (p. 22

MARQUIS, JOHN
Inventory. Jan 1795/ 8 Apr 1795
Appraisers: John Miller, Thomas Berry, Adam Aldridge
(p. 26)

WILLIAMS, BARNETT
Will. 10 Mar 1795/ 8 Apr 1795
Children: Charles, Charlotte, Ann, Marget
One fourth share to each child after sale of all estate, except negroes Bob and Lindy and Bed and Bedding, which go to daughter Charlotte and deduct therefor Ł 74. Deductions itemized for other children.
Exrs: Samuel Littler, Elijah Littler, sons-in-law
Wit: John Littler, Jr., John Littler, Sr., Isaac Hill, Hughey Meredith. [Nancy (Ann) Williams m Samuel Littler 18 Oct 1792; Fdk.Co.Marrs.] (p. 26

OLIVER, JAMES
Will. 20 Feb 1795/ 8 Apr 1795
Wife: Nancy. Children not named.
"Bring up and educate my daughters in a becoming and decent manner." John Tompkins and William Thistle testify that "the above record be the work of Mr. Oliver when in his proper senses although the signing was put off until it was too late." Will proved by oath of John Mason who deposed he heard will read to deceased who agreed to contents but postponed signing until morning, but died at 2:00 A.M. of that morning.
Exrx: Wife Nancy
Sec: Ann Oliver, Nathaniel Oliver (p. 27-28)

GLASS, JOSEPH
Appraisal. 17 Jan 1795/ 8 Apr 1795
Appraisers: William Marquis, Joseph Wood, Robert P. Allen
(p. 29-30)

NICHOLSON, GEORGE
Will. 15 July 1793/ 9 Apr 1795
Wife: Martha
Legatee: William Reilly
To wife, all personal estate and land on which he lives for use and disposal upon her decease. To friend, William Reilly, part of lot as long as lease lasts, paying half yearly rent.
Exrs: William Helm, Daniel Thornbrugh
Wit: Mary Simpson (p. 31

FRYER, GEORGE
Will. 10 Jan 1795/ 9 Apr 1795
Wife: Mary
Children: George, Thomas, Joan, Margaret, Mary
To wife, all personal estate. To each child, one shilling and one penny.
Exrx: Wife Mary Fryer, gives bond
Wit: Alexander Potter, James --- (illegible), Edward Power, John Campbell (p. 32

FETHERLING, JACOB
Appraisal. 5 May 1795
"Four years' rent, Ł 5 a year, due 1 Jan 1796-7-8-9."
Appraisers: Frederick Schlosser (Slusher), Daniel Gardner, Jacob Kline, George Good, Sr.
Admx: Widow (unnamed) [Polly Featherling m Philip Kline 24 Oct 1799, Fdk.Co.Marrs.] (p. 33-34)

LINDSAY, JAMES
Appraisal. 9 Apr 1795/ 5 May 1795
Appraisers: Abraham Neile, Thomas Deaderick, R. Wood(p. 35)

RIDGWAY, JOSIAH
Estate Settlement. (Dec'd 1783)/ 5 May 1795
Exrx Mercy Ridgway paid debts of Ł145.16.6, exceeding appraisal by Ł 8.16.2.
Sec: Meredith Helm, Amos Jolliffe (p. 36)

WILLIAMS, BARNETT
Account. 20 Apr 1795/ 5 May 1795
Examiners: Meredith Helm, William Tyler, Roger Barton (p. 37

STUBBLEFIELD, BENJAMIN
Inventory. 26 Feb 1795/ 5 May 1795 (p. 39)

OLIVER, JAMES
Appraisal & Account. 27 Feb 1795/ 5 May 1795
Appraisers: Isaac Littler, William Vintrom, Albert Eagan (p. 32-42)

GILKESON, JOHN
Appraisal & Account. 5 May 1795
Appraisers: John Blakemore, James Blakemore, James Russell (p. 43)

OLIVER, JAMES
Appraisal & Account. 13 Apr 1795/ 6 May 1795
Appraisers: Isaac Littler, William Vintrom, Albert Eagan (p. 43-45)

GILKESON, JOHN
Inventory & Appraisal. 24 May 1794/ 8 July 1795
Appraisers: Stephen Pritchard, James Bell, Daniel Brown (p. 45-48)

CURLET, JOSEPH
Will. 14 May 1795/ 7 July 1795
Mother: Rachel Curlet
Sisters: Margaret Green, Jane Curlet, Rachel Cock (Cochran), Mrs. Elizabeth Brown, Sarah Curlet, Rebecca Curlet
Plantation on which I live to be sold and proceeds divided among sisters after decease of mother, as agreed by my mother, sisters and sisters' husbands. Personal estate to be sold, expenses paid, and remainder to mother.
Exrs: Brother (in-law) William Cochran, mother Rachel Curlet
Wit: Daniel Thornbrugh, John Taylor, Joseph McCartney. [William Cochran m Rachel Curlett, 27 Sep 1789, Fdk.Co.Marrs.](p. 49

ROBERDEAU, DANIEL (of Alexandria, Va.)
Will. 29 Apr 1794-5 Feb 1795/ July 1795
Wife: Jane
Children: Isaac, Anne, Mary, Salina, Jane, James, Harriet.
To wife, all household and kitchen furniture and utensils, dwelling house and lot during life. Provision for educating younger children until 21. Wife appointed guardian of Jane, James and Harriet, three youngest. Property to be divided among seven children.
Exrs: Wife Jane, Charles Simms
Codicil: 1 May 1794. To wife, negro woman Saskey and remainder of time servant William has to serve. Mentions rents from properties in Alexandria and directs executors to make deed to Richard Locke for land in Pa. sold him when he discharges mortgage "given by me on land to James Muligan." Additional executor named, Alexander Smith
Wit: Andrew Jamieson, Arch McLean

Witnesses to confirmation: J. A. Keith, Lemuel Bent, James Muir, Arch McClean
Alexander Smith, exr., gives bond (p. 50-54)

HITE, ISAAC
Will. 4 Jan 1794/ Codicil 16 Oct 1794/ 6 Oct 1795
Children: Isaac, Ann Buchanan, Rebecca Booth, Sarah Clarke
Gr. ch: Isaac Hite Williams, John C. Williams, Eleanor Long
Principal beneficiary, son Isaac. Will identifies and distributes thousands of acres of lands in various counties in Maryland, Virginia and Kentucky, U. S. Treasury certificates, slaves, and land and claims recovered in suit against Lord Fairfax. Testator provides support for life for five "old and infirm" negro slaves, by son Isaac; directs that negro women whose husbands belong to him are to be sold with their husbands; and where such women have young children the child is to be sold with its mother. In addition to real estate and investments divided among children and grandchildren, Isaac is given a wagon, gears, horses, household furnishings - tables, looking glasses, desk, bookcase, buffet, two stills, rifle and brass pistols, negro David a blacksmith with all smith tools belonging to the shop. Isaac, Rebecca and Sarah are to divide all his books among them, and all fowls on the farm on which he lives, among other items.
Wit: William C. Williams, Charles Beale, Alexander Hite, William H. Booth, Andrew Forsyth, William Hinson (Stinson?), Christopher Mack, Isaac Hite
Exrs: Son Isaac Hite, sons-in-law William A. Booth and Jonathan Clarke. Sec: John Milton, Matthew Page, £ 20,000.
[NOTE: Isaac Hite was third son of Jost Hite and Anna Maria Merkle, born 12 May 1721. His wife, Eleanor Eltinge, he married 12 Apr 1745; she died 10 Nov 1792. Another daughter, Mary McDonald, born 25 Aug 1748, married Dr. John McDonald, left a will dated 18 Aug 1788, probated April 1789 in Frederick County, Virginia, surviving her husband, and had no surviving children. Daughter Ann Buchanan, born 8 Jan 1746, no issue, died 9 Aug 1816, wife of James Buchanan of Falmouth, Va. Daughter Rebecca Booth, born 19 Jan 1754, was wife of Gen. William Aylett Booth. Sarah Clarke, born 11 May 1758, died Oct 1818, was wife of Gen. Jonathan Clarke, brother of George Rogers Clarke. Eleanor Williams, born 27 Oct 1750, died 24 Oct 1781, was wife of Major John Williams, were parents of the three grandchildren. Some of the properties devised in this lengthy and detailed will were originally patented in the name of Isaac by Jost Hite when his son was still a minor. Vital dates from Cartmell's history, which gives Isaac's birth date as 7 Feb 1758; however, Sarah Hite Clarke's headstone in the cemetery in Louisville, Ky., where she is buried, states she was born 11 May 1758.] (p. 55-63)

CARTMILL, NATHANIEL
Will. 7 Feb 1795/ 6 Oct 1795
Wife: Sarah
Children: Thomas, Nathaniel, Nathan, John, Jacob, Elijah, Solomon, Martin (youngest), Elizabeth, wife of Dr. Michael Archdeacon, Eleanor wife of James Cochrane, Rachell wife of Henry Crist, Mary wife of Nathaniel Willis.
To wife, all slaves, personal estate and plantation, to be held in common with youngest son Martin. If they do not so choose, property to be divided into thirds by commissioners of Frederick Co. Court, third to wife during her natural life, at her death to Martin. "Wishing wife to be as independent of children as possible, power given her to dispose of part of estate. Three named slaves to wife. All bonds, notes, book debts and cash on hand at time of death to payment of debts.

To sons Thomas, Nathaniel, Nathan, John and Jacob, each one shilling, having given each heretofore as much as the situation of my estate would admit of in justice to my other children. To son Elijah, Ŀ 200 in addition to sum previously given him. To support and maintenance of daughter Elizabeth, a negro wench and Ŀ 100 to be held by son Thomas in trust, to be applied by him as necessities of daughter Elizabeth shall require, "fully relying this son Thomas will do her justice to be expected from an affectionate brother." Slave and increase and unexpended balance of Ŀ 100 to be disposed of by Elizabeth in her last will and testament. To daughters Eleanor, Rachell and Mary, each Ŀ 100. Plantation where I now live to be divided, half to son Solomon; also tract on North Mountain, slave, livestock and fifth part of grain crop now in the ground.
Exrs: Sons Thomas and Martin
Wit: Aquilla Dyson, Nathaniel Cartmill, J. G. Peyton
Sec: Henry Baylis, William Eskridge, Solomon Cartmill.
Bond Ŀ 5,000. (p. 64-67)

HARRELL, JOHN
Estate settlement. 10 Jan 1792-14 Apr 1795/ 7 Oct 1795
Admx: Sarah Harrall. Bonds to assignee, Mr. Isaac,Ŀ30.2.3;
By sundries sold at vendue, Ŀ 30.2.3. (p. 68)

ROBERDEAU, DANIEL (GENERAL)
Appraisal. 8 July 1795/ 1 Dec 1795
Appraisers: Adam Douglass, Goldsmith Chandlee, William Gloverman. (p. 69-75)

THOMAS, RACHEL
Appraisal. 1 Dec 1795.
Appraisers: David Ridgway, Nathan Littler, George Bruce, Jr. (p. 75-76)

SMITH, JERE
Sale Account. 1 Dec 1795 (p. 76-78)

HOLMES, JOSEPH (COL)
Appraisal & distribution, negroes of estate. 26 Sep 1794/1 Dec 1795. Distributees: Mrs. Holmes, Andrew Hunter Holmes, Hugh Holmes, Alexander Legrand, Miss Nancy Holmes, Joseph Holmes, Eliza Holmes, Miss Rebecca Holmes, Erlinda Holmes, Mrs. Legrand, Miss Gertrude Holmes. (p. 79-80)

MARQUIS, JOHN
Distribution of slaves per will. 16 Apr 1795/ 1 Dec 1795
Distributees: Billy Marquis, William Wyley, Hutchins, Blundell, Lipscomb, Nelly Marquis. (p. 81)

COCHRAN, WILLIAM
Will. 10 Jan 1795/ 1 Dec 1795
Children: James, Robert, William, Ann wife of William McKean, Margaret wife of Isaiah Curlett, Martha wife of Benjamin Langley, Agnes, Elizabeth, Mary, Rachell.
Second wife: Mary
Plantation rent until sold to maintain unmarried daughters.
Exrs: James & William Cochrane, sons; William Curlett, son-in-law
Wit: Simon Lauck, Henry Moor, Frederick Kurtz, William Moor
Sec: William Touchstone, Jesse Pugh, $2,000. (p. 82-83)

ROBERDEAU, JANE (boro of Winchester)
Renunciation of will. 5 Nov 1795/ 1 Dec 1795
Widow and relict of Gen. Daniel Roberdeau
Wit: David Carlile, Charles Brent, Jr. (p. 84)

CLARE, EDMUND
Will. 2 Oct 1795/ 2 Dec 1795
Children: James, Mary Helen, Eliza Gibbs Clare
Sister: Hannah Brady
To son James, plantation on Long Marsh where I now live and certain slaves and their increase. To daughter Mary Helen, half of plantation at head of falling waters in Berkeley County (half of 345-acre tract) and certain slaves. To daughter Eliza Gibbs Clare, other half of plantation and certain slaves. Life estate to sister Hannah Brady; daughters may sell after her death. Personal property to be sold and proceeds divided among three children. If Mrs. Ann Gibbs dies before Elisa is of age, son James to have use of negro Nathan until she is of age. Pay executors Ł 20 annually to bring up and educate her.
Exrs: Thomas Throckmorton, Sr., John Milton, James Gibbs, and James Clare
Wit: James Stuart, Abraham Davenport, M(athias) Frame
Sec: Thomas Throckmorton, James Gibbs, William Throckmorton, James McCormick. Ł 2,000 (p.84-87)

BLACKFORD, PETER
Administration. 29 Oct 1792/ 2 Dec 1795
Widow, Prudence Blackford, guardian of Joseph Blackford
Admr: William Boyd
Examiners: James Dowdall, George F. Norton. Unpaid balance, Ł 79.17.0. (p. 87-88)

MARKER, JACOB
Account; Sale of personal property & lot. 6 June 1795/ 5 Jan 1796
Admrs: Elisha Williams, A. Bainbridge (p. 89

HOGE, JAMES
Will. 18 Mar 1793/ 5 Jan 1795
Wife: Agnus Hoge
Children: Moses, James, Solomon, John, Edward (dec'd), Martha Allen, Mary Evans, Barbara Reed.
Gr. ch: Moses and Edward Hoge, sons of son Edward, dec'd.
To wife, negro Jude beside her thirds. Personal estate to be appraised except the still; remainder to children as wife decides. If she marries, all but widow's thirds to be divided, half to son Moses, quarter to son James, quarter to daughter Martha Allen. To grandsons Moses and Edward Hoge, land in survey made by Thomas Buck, 186 acres, Moses to enjoy whole until brother Edward is 21. If one dies, survivor to have whole. Son Solomon Hoge to have all the rest of land, conditioned on his payment of legacies: to John Hoge, son, to Mary Evans, to Barbara Reed - 5 shillings sterling if they come to demand it; to son James, Ł 20; to daughter Martha Allen, Ł 15. Wife and Solomon to share plantation as outlined.
Exr: Wife Agnes Hoge
Wit: John Setzer, Philip Barr, Mary Setzer
Sec: Peter Senseney- John Setzer. Bond Ł 2,000 (p. 90-92)

COCHRAN, WILLIAM
Appraisal. 11 Dec 1795/ 5 Jan 1796
Appraisers: Daniel Thornbrugh, Samuel Griffin, John McLure (p. 93-95)

BEARD, JUSTICE (Recorded as Barnes)
Appraisal. 8 Dec 1795/ 6 Jan 1796
Appraisers: George Stubblefield, John Blakemore, George Barnett, Achilles Barnett (p. 95-96)
Sale Account. 15 Dec 1795/ 6 Jan 1796
(Joanna Beard Lindsay, household furniture, Ł 25) (p. 96-97)

CRAIGON, ROBERT, SR.
Will. 8 Feb. 1796
Wife: Susanna
Children: Robert (eldest), John (youngest)
To wife, life estate in house and lot where I live, with all appurtenances; reversions, negroes Toby and Hannah, personal estate. To Robert, 115-acre tract in Hampshire Co., wagon and team, and stock of horses except mare and colt; has received part.
To John, reversion of house and lot after death of wife, 5-acre lot in the commons, tract near Parkins purchased from William Cochran, 17 acres called No. 3; also tract in Hampshire Co., 315 acres, to be surrendered to him at age 21; also young mare and colt after widow's decease. Personalty to be sold and divided between sons when wife dies.
Exrs: Wife Susanna, Henry Beatty
Wit: James Newham, Marmaduke Magson, John Peyton
Henry Beatty refuses executorship; John Craigon to obtain letters of administration with will annexed.
Sec: Isaac Littler, Jacob Hager (p. 97-99)

HAINES, ROBERT
Will. 9 Jan 1796/ 3 Feb 1796
Wife: Margaret
Children: John, Amos, Robert, Noah, Nathan, Mary, Margaret
To wife, half of movable estate; other half to children as they arrive at age 21, to defray cost of education of "4 youngest sons," remainder to be divided among children after decease or marriage of widow. To three youngest sons, Amos, Robert and Nathan, whole plantation where I live, 300 acres; to John, plantation where he now lives, 143 acres. To John, Amos, Robert and Nathan, parcel of State land west side of Crooked Run, about 488 acres, equally. To son Noah, plantation where John Smith now lives, 125 acres, brothers John and Robert to pay him Ƚ 140 curr. within three years of 21st birthday. To daughters Mary and Margaret, lots in Front Royal, Lot 28, 200 acres, and lot of 67 acres rented to Abraham Supinger, divided equally when Mary is 21, to be rented before and daughters to begin collecting rents as they come of age. Noah, Amos and Nathan, land to be rented by executors until they are 21, then to be paid rent by exrs.
Exrs: Wife Margaret, Thomas Fawcett, Thomas Smith
Wit: Joshua Swayne, John Clevenger, John Haines
Sec: Isaac Painter, Joshua Swayne. Ƚ 2,000 (p. 99-103)

THROCKMORTON, ALBION
Will. 17 Aug 1795/ 3 Feb 1796
Wife: Mildred
Children: Warner Washington, Hannah Fairfax
To wife, life estate in tract where I now live. At her death to Warner Washington, to be equally divided if now pregnant wife has a son. Son to be bound out to a trade; also four negro boys to be bound out, then to son. Negroes to Hannah Fairfax. If unborn child is a daughter, 8 negroes. Personal estate to son, but to be equally divided if unborn child is a son. (Added: If Warner should die before 21 and unborn child is a son, he is to take Warner's legacy; if child dies before 21, Warner to take his legacy. Hannah Fairfax to receive property at 18. If unborn child is daughter, to inherit at 18 or marriage. Daughter's inheritance not to be sold, if possible, to protect it.)
Exr: Friend Warner Washington
Wit: William Snickers, Robert Throckmorton, Catherina Nelson, John Nelson.
Sec: Robert and William Throckmorton. Ƚ 10,000 (p. 103-105)

OLIVER, JAMES
Sale Account. 3 Feb 1796 (p. 106-108)

COCHRAN, WILLIAM, SR.
Sale Account. 12 Dec 1795/ 3 Feb 1796
Exrs: James Cochran, William Cochran, Thomas Curlett
Among buyers: William Cochran, Mary Cochran, James Cochran, Elizabeth Cochran. (p. 109-112)

RIDGWAY, JOSIAH
Appraisal. 2 Feb 1795/ 3 Feb 1796
Appraisers: James Steer, William Reed, Joshua Coop. (Cooper?), Amos Jolliffe (p. 112-113)

BOSTEYOUN, JOHN (BASTION)
Appraisal. 3 Feb 1796
Appraisers: James Simrall, John Schultz, Nicholas Mesmore (p. 113-114)

NEWBOROUGH, JOHN
Appraisal. 4 Feb 1796
Smith and carpenter's tools left by exrs to be sold.
Appraisers: William Cochran, William Van Horn, Robert Cochran (p. 114-116)

BRITTON, JOSEPH (BRITAIN)
Appraisal. 16 Oct 1795/ 7 Apr 1796
(Bonds of Amos Albright, Jacob Landiss, for Ⱡ 320 Pa. money; Jacob Grimes note; notes on Adam Albert & McMunn, Wilson Britton, totaling Ⱡ 484.9.6-1/2)
Appraisers: Robert Wood, Sampson Thomas, Jacob Rinker, James Smith (p. 116-117)

SEEVAR/SEAVER, JOHN
Will. 29 Feb 1796/ 7 Apr 1796
Brother: Henry
Sister: Elizabeth
Father: Caspar/Gaspar
Legatees: William McGahan son of Elizabeth; John Seaver son of Henry
Accounting with brother to be prepared. To the poor, $20. To sister Elizabeth to compensate for care during illness. Remainder to be held by father for William McGahan and John Seaver until they reach 21.
Exrs: Father Caspar Seaver, brother Henry
Wit: Thomas O. Williams, Benjamin Ober, Thomas Aldridge
Gaspar Seaver refused to act.
Sec. for Henry Seaver: Nathan Anderson, William Throckmorton, Ⱡ 2,000. (p. 118-119)

STEPHENS, JOSEPH (of Stephensburg)
Will. 1 Feb 1796/ 7 Apr 1796
Wife: Not named
Children: Joseph, John, Tabitha wife of Joshua Myers, Athilia, Elizabeth, Rebecca, Deborah
To wife, life estate, to sell whatever she pleases. Two best out lots reserved for sons Joseph and John. Divide estate after wife's death among seven children, deducting $100 already received from share of Tabitha Moyers and value of wood lots, after appraisal, from sons' shares.
Exrs: Wife and Joshua Moyers
Wit: Elij. Sparks, Henry Weavor, John McGinnis. (p. 119-120)

CONRAD, JOHN
Inventory. 24 Sep 1794/ 7 Apr 1796
Large merchandise inventory of trading establishment.
Appraisers: Joseph Tidball, Abraham Naile, J. Weaver
(p. 121-151)

NEILL, JOSEPH
Will. 12 Feb 1796/ 7 Apr 1796
Wife: Rebecca
Children: Lydia, Lewis, unborn child
Brother: Lewis Neill
Brother-in-law: John McPherson
To wife, during widowhood, specified household items, three milk cows, and income from land rentals for support and maintenance of children until 21 or married. Remainder personal property to be sold, proceeds to be put out to interest together with all money and bonds owned at death. Executors to lease out all lands including mill. If wife marries before children reach majority, executors to deliver to her fourth of all personal and real estate. Children to hold property as tenants in common, not joint tenants. Four negroes to be manumitted, males at 21 and females at 18.
Exrs: Brother Lewis Neill, brother-in-law John McPherson
Wit: Arch'd Magill, Robert Miller, Jane McPherson
Sec: Thomas Neill, Joseph Bond. $12,000 (p. 151-153)

CYPHERS, PHILIP
Orphan of Laurence Cyphers
Guardianship. 7 Dec 1796
Guardian: Peter Senseney, Arch'd Magill. Bond $300. (p. 153-154)

JOLIFFE, ELIZABETH, DEC'D, EXCX OF WILLIAM JOLLIFFE
Account & Estate Settlement. 11 Sep 1783/ 7 Dec 1796
Exr: Lewis Walker
Legatees: J. Bruce, Mary Jolliffe, Amos Jolliffe, Polly, Amos and Eliza Jolliffe; "bequest for keeping Crispin." Settlement agreed to for Eliza and Mary Jolliffe, Archibald W. Cagill, James Bruce, Amos Jolliffe. Settlement of estate of Elizabeth Jolliffe, dec'd, approved. (p. 154-156)

STRIBLING, WILLIAM
Inventory & Account. 19 Dec 1793/ 19 Dec 1796
Admr: W. Hodgson of Alexandria, Va.
Statement of financial situation pending suits. (p. 156-163)

HITE, ISAAC
Appraisal (exclusive of bonds). 5 Nov 1795/ 7 Dec 1796
Exr: Isaac Hite
Appraisers: Edward Howe, Vance Bush, M. Richardson. (p. 164-175)

HOLMES, JOSEPH
Appraisal. 1 Feb 1794/ 7 Dec 1796
"Taken at Holmes Grove Farm" 22 Jan 1793
Appraisers: O. Samuel Dowdall, George A. Briscoe, Joseph Tidball. (p. 176-186)

STEPHENS, JOSEPH
Appraisal. 1 June 1796/ 7 Dec 1796
Appraisers: David Wilson, Jacob Moirs, Stephen Moirs, John Groves. (p. 186-187)

CYPHER, LAURENCE
Sale Account. 7 Dec 1796
Among buyers: George Sifret (Cifret), Andrew Cyfret/Cyphret, Fanny Cyfret. (p. 187-190)

CARTER, BENJAMIN
Will. 13 Dec 1795/ 7 Apr 1796
Wife: Rachel
Children: Edmund, Joseph, William, Isaac, Mary, Jemima, Phebe, Benjamin, James, Ann, Jonathan, David
Brother: James Carter
To wife, entire use of plantation until youngest child is 12 years old (now aged 3). If wife marries, plantation to be rented until youngest child is 12, then children put out to trades, and plantation to be sold and divided. To wife, two shares in lieu of dower, remainder among children except Edmund. Refers to contract with Edmund for land on Opequon Creek at mouth of Marsh Run, about 20 acres, for Ł 100, half to be discharged from payment, his full share of estate, unless he chooses to give up land and share with other children, money paid to be refunded when land is sold. Book debt owed by son Joseph cancelled, to receive Ł 20 from sale of land and division of proceeds. Land sold to brother James requires deed from executors.
Exrs: Wife Rachel Carter, son Joseph
Wit: Joseph Carter, James Carter, Jr., James Carter.
Sec: Joseph Carter, Sr., James Carter. Ł 1,000. (p. 191-194)

SWORDS, WILLIAM (Borough of Winchester)
Will. 14 Apr 1796/ 3 May 1796
No wife named
Son: William (under age)
Grandson: James Storrow
Legatee: Sarah Peeling
To son William, all real and personal property. To grandson, Ł 100 at age 21, to be held for him by son William. To Sarah Peeling, for care during illness, permit her to occupy back room in lower end of my house rent free, exclusive of wages now due her. Pay Ł 100 to persons to superintend leveling of market house. Archibald Magill appointed guardian of William until 21. Executors authorized to repair properties. Lots in Knaves Town may be sold.
Wit: Isaac Skiles, Peter Senseney, Joshua Hunt
Exrs: Conrad Kremer, James Simrall, Archibald Magill
Sec: James Glenholmes, William Richardson, Thomas Baldwin.
Bond Ł 2,000. (p. 194-196)

SYFRETT (CYPHRET/CYPHER), LAURENCE
Inventory. 7 July 1795/ 3 May 1796
Appraisers: Samuel Briarley, Philip Carper, William Carper. (p. 196-199)

RUSH, WILLIAM
Inventory. 23 Apr 1796/ 3 May 1796
Appraisers: Robert Livright, Joseph Longacre, Jr., Joseph Snapp. (p. 199)

HOGE, JAMES
Appraisal. 26 Sep 1795/ 4 May 1796
Appraisers: Alexander Feely, William Barrow, John Barrow. (p. 200-203)

STIGLER, JAMES
Appraisal. 8 Mar 1796/ 11 May 1796

FULLERTON, HUMPHREY
Account. 1782/ 4 May 1796
Excx: Ann Fullerton. Due Ł 150.2.7, 10 May 1796 (p. 205-206)

BROWN, JAMES
Appraisal. 10 Oct 1795/ 4 May 1796 (p. 206-207)

MURRAY, GEORGE
Appraisal. 8 Oct 1794/ 5 July 1796 (p. 207-208)

CLARE, EDMUND (of Berkeley County)
Appraisal. 22 Apr 1796/ 5 July 1796
Appraisers: James Anderson, Richard Ransome, Richard McKnight
Appraisal in Frederick Co. Recorded 5 June 1796
Appraisers: Robert Hollingsworth, Thomas Lindsey, Thomas M. McCormick, John Lindsey (p. 210-214)

BALL, WILLIAM
Will. 14 May 1796/ 6 Sep 1796
Wife: Not named; refers to "present wife"
Children: William Payne Ball, Thomas Kemp Ball, Nancy, Judith Throckmorton, Betsy Henry
Trustee: Samuel Pittinger, indenture dated 12 July 1790 on part of plantation in trust for wife during her life in lieu of dower, reversion to sons when wife dies; residue of land and rents to be divided when Thomas becomes 21. Whole tract may be sold upon reversion.
To son Thomas, daughters Judith, Betsy and Nancy, named slaves.
Residue to be divided among children, of which the "two younger children are by my present wife."
William and Thomas to be bound out to trade; also negroes given to them.
Wit: F. Harrison, Robert Page
Exrs and guardians: Francis Whiting of Fauquier Co., Thomas Parker, Laurence Butler (p. 214-217)

WHITE, MARY
Appraisal. 15 Aug 1796/ 1 Sep 1796
Appraisers: George Ball, Henry Catlett, Samuel Kercheval (p. 217-219)

PICKERING, JOHN
Will. 20 Sep 1796/ 4 Oct 1796
Wife: Jane Pickering
Children: William, Enos (eldest sons), John, Joshua, unnamed infant, Sarah, Elizabeth, Rachel, Rebekah, Mary and Jane
Brother: Jonathan Pickering
To wife, one third estate for life, reversion to children at her death. To eldest sons William and Enos, land in Harrison County. To sons John and Joshua, tract where I live. If either dies before age 21, portion to infant brother. If both survive, each to give infant brother bond for Ł 50 payable when he is 21.
Daughters to have equal parts of proceeds of personal estate.
Remainder, real and personal, to be sold and equally divided among all children.
Exrs: Brother Jonathan Pickering, John McCoole
Wit: Jacob Pickering, Danniel Collett, Lydia Adams
Sec: John Wright, Jacob Pickering. $3,000
(John McCoole refused executorship) (p. 219-223)

BAKER, SAMUEL
Will. 1 Sep 1796/ 4 Oct 1796
Wife: Not named
Children: James, Samuel, Elizabeth
All estate, including that in possession of son James, to be sold and money equally divided. All money to be used to purchase land. "My wife knows the contract between us. I wish not to leave a wife to suffer or want." To son Samuel, a young mare colt called Kit. Negroes falling to two young children, Samuel

and Elizabeth, to be hired out for their support and to put Samuel to school; then at discretion of executors.
Exrs: Major Thomas Massie, John S. Woodcock, William Davis and son James Baker
Wit: William Davis, George Brown (p. 223-224)

SIMPSON, THOMAS
Will. 1 Apr 1796/ 4 Oct 1796
Wife: Ann
Children: Andrew (refers to "children" but no others named)
To wife, reversion of tract in Frederick County leased of George Alen, and rest of personal estate during her life. After her decease, estate to be equally divided among children.
Exrs: Wife Ann and son Andrew Simpson
Wit: Francis Gilbert, John O'Bannon (p. 224-225)

JOHNSTON, GEORGE (of Stephensburg)
Will. 22 Sep 1796/ 4 Oct 1796
Wife: Margaret
Children: John, Charles, David (dec'd), Samuel (dec'd), George (dec'd), Mary Johnston, Jean, Ann, Elizabeth
Gr. ch: Children of son David, dec'd; children of son Samuel, dec'd; children of son George, dec'd.
Exrs sell at public vendue full lot of ground in this town where I live, with all buildings and improvements, together with out lot having five acres of enclosed land; also all stock of cattle, whole household furniture, wheat, rie(sic), hay, flax and cabbage. Proceeds to be divided into four shares and paid to wife Margaret, sons John and Charles and daughter Mary. Wife's share to remaining three legatees at her death. One shilling sterling to each: daughters Jean, Ann and Elizabeth, children of dec'd son David (unnamed), children of dec'd son Samuel (unnamed), children of dec'd son George (unnamed).
Exrs: James Reed, Sr., John Tedford, son Charles Johnston
Wit: George Lamley (Lemley?), John Smith, George Somerville, John Tedford
Sec: Thomas Cartmill, John T<u>a</u>dford. $3,000. (p. 225-228)

JOHNSTON, GEORGE
Appraisal. 11 Oct 1796/ 6 Dec 1796
Appraisers: Vance Bush, William McLeod, Jacob Miers (Moiers), Gent'm. (p. 231-232)

BRITTON, JOSEPH
Sale Account. 29 Oct 1795/ 6 Dec 1796
Admr: Jesse Britton
Among buyers: Abigail Britton, Joseph Britton, Jesse Britton (p. 233-236)

SEEVER, JOHN
Appraisal & Sale Account. 12 Apr-22 Apr 1796/ 6 Dec 1796
Exr: Henry Seever
Appraisers: Jacob Sperry, John Littler, Thomas Brown
Noted - moiety to partner, Henry Seevers
Among buyers: Henry Seevers (p. 236-241)

PURTLE, NICHOLAS
Appraisal. 18 Oct 1796/ 6 Dec 1796
Admx: Elisabeth Purtle
Appraisers: David Faulkner, John Dillon, Joseph Hackney (p. 241-243)

RINKER, HENRY (of Town of Winchester)
Will. 9 Feb 1770; memo 6 Dec 1796/ 3 Jan 1797
Wife: Mary Rinker

Brother: Gasper Rinker
To wife, house and part of lot in Loudden (sic) St.; house and lot in Woods' new addition No. 6 to Town of Winchester. A black cow, feather bed and silverware now in possession of brother Gasper, household furnishings, and cordwainer utensils.
Exx: Wife Mary Rinker
Wit: William Green, Charles Rodden, James Lindsey
Wit to memo: Michael Aldred (p. 243-244)

SHERIFF, JOHN
Will. 8 Dec 1796/ 3 Jan 1797
No wife named
Children: William, Benjamin, Ann, Elenor
All personal estate to be equally divided; sons to pay each of their two sisters 10 shillings lawful money of Virginia.
Exrs: Sons William and Benjamin
Wit: Josiah Rogers, Peter Dick

BALL, WILLIAM and GREEN, ANN
Orphans of Jesse Ball
Sale Account & Settlement. Jan 1797/ 7 Feb 1797
Order of Lancaster (Pa.) Court dated Jan 1797 to settle estate of Ann Green and William Ball, orphans of Jesse Ball, which was in hands of Capt. Richard Seldon. Balance due William Ball of Ŀ 9.9.6. Appraisal of negroes by William Yerby, William Davis, and Sever Galles recorded Fdk. Co. Ct. 7 Feb 1797.(p. 245-246)

RUTTER, MATTHIAS
Appraisal. 2 Aug 1794/ 7 Feb 1797
Appraisers: John & William Kerfoot, John Grove. (p. 246-248)

HOTT, GEORGE
Will. 22 Mar 1791/ 7 Feb 1797
Wife: Magdalen
Children: George, Samuel, John, Henry
Sons to support wife during her life per their contract and bond. After wife's death, divide all movable estate among sons or their heirs. To son George, one shilling, "he having had his portion heretofore in lands." To Samuel, John and Henry, tract where I live purchased from Jacob Sowers, except part sold to George.
Exrs: Sons George, Samuel, John and Henry Hott
Wit: Richard Barrett, Thomas Barrett, Samuel Hott, Jr., William James. (Martin Frees not named as witness in will but testified at probate of will in court as witness)
Sec: Thomas Barrett, Richard Barrett, Ŀ 500. (p. 248-250)

GLASS, ROBERT, SR.
Will. 13 July 1796/ 7 Feb 1797
Wife: Sarah
Children: Samuel, James, Joseph, Robert, Elizabeth, Ann, Mary, Sarah, Susannah, Ruth, Margaret, Martha wife of Henry Sherer.
Gr ch: Robert Vance
To son Samuel, 200-acre tract where he lives; to daughter Elizabeth, full amount of Col. Cox's bond sent to her husband in Kentucky; to daughter Ann, Ŀ 10 curr. money; daughter Mary and grandson Robert Vance, each Ŀ 5 curr. money. Residue of plantation, about 344 acres, to be sold and money divided among children: sons Robert, James and Joseph, each two full shares; wife, one share; daughters Sarah, Susannah, Ruth and Margaret, each one share; to son Robert in trust for daughter Martha wife of Henry Sherer, one share, but if Martha receives reasonable allowance from husband from whom she is now separated within 7 years of my decease, then deduct Ŀ 50 curr. money from this one

share and divide among sons Robert, James and Joseph. Trust to end when Henry Sherer dies. To wife during widowhood, negroes to work for her and daughters living with her. After her marriage or decease, negroes to sons Robert and Joseph, they paying then value to son James, daughters Sarah, Susannah, Ruth, Margaret, and trust for Martha, Robert and Joseph to share equally in distribution. To Robert, James and Joseph, all land in Kentucky, deeded, patented or not, to hold as tenants in common. All residue to be sold and money equally to wife and children.
Wit: Archibald Magill, Joseph Wood, Elisha Moore
Exrs: Robert Glass, James Vance
[Martha Glass m 2 June 1785 Henry Sherrard; Ann Glass m William Vance 18 Aug 1791. Fdk.Co.Marrs.] (p.250-252)

ROGERS, JAMES
Appraisal. 13 Jan 1797/ 7 Feb 1797
Appraisers: George Bell, John Kerfoot, Samuel Kerfoot
(p. 252-253)

GLASS, JOSEPH, JR.
Orphan of Joseph Glass
Guardianship bond. 7 Feb 1797
Distribution when Joseph Glass, Jr., is of legal age.
Bondsmen: Robert Glass, John Wilson, Ŀ 5,000. (p. 253-254)

WILLIAMS, BARNETT
Sale Account. 8 Feb 1797
Among buyers: Samuel Littler
[Nancy Williams m Samuel Littler 18 Oct 1792, Fdk.Co.Marrs.]
(p. 254)

PICKERING, JOHN - ORPHANS
John, Eliza., Joshua, Rachel, Rebecca, Mary, Jane, Jonathan.
Guardianship bond. 7 Feb 1797
Bondsmen: Robert Rodgers, James McDonald, Joseph Steer, Ŀ 1,000 curr. money. (p. 254-255)

BRIDGES, JOSEPH
Appraisal. 20th da, 2d mo, 1796/ 8 Feb 1797
Admr: George Rubles
Appraisers: Joseph Hackney, David Faulkner, John Griffith
(p. 255-256)

CLARE, EDMUND
Orphan of Elizabeth Gibbs Clare
Guardianship bond. 8 Feb 1797
Bondsmen: James Gibbs, John Peyton, Ŀ 2,000
[Edward Clair m Eliza Gibbs 29 May 1790, Fdk.Co.Marrs.]
(p. 256-257)

MOYERS (MOIERS), STEPHEN
Will. 11 Feb 1797/ 3 Apr 1797
Wife: Not named
Children: John (under 21), Elizabeth (under 18), Catherine
Legatee: Mrs. Cabbage (relationship not stated)
All lands to be sold on north side of Stephens Run except house and 30 yards below it to be kept in estate for wife and Mrs. Cabbage jointly. House and lot in Stephensburg during their lives, then to daughter Catherine. To wife, rents from unsold part of plantation until son John is 21, then title to him on condition he pays Ŀ 200 to daughter Elizabeth when she is 18. If he does not, land to be sold, payment of Ŀ 200 made, and balance paid to son John. Personal estate to be sold and divided among named legatees. "The bed my wife commonly uses to be kept for her without appraisement."

Exrs: Wife and Capt. Jacob Moyers
Wit: J. McGinnis, Daniel Mytinger
[Henry Lewis appeared as witness at probate although signature not shown as witness to will.]
Sec: Daniel Mytinger, Henry Lewis. $3,000 (p. 257-258)

PICKETT, HENRY
Appraisal. 25 da, 2d mo, 1797/ 4 Apr 1797
Appraisers: Abraham Bronson, Isaac Steer, Joseph Steer (p. 259)

DONALDSON, JOHN
Will. 17 Jan 1797/ 7 Feb 1797
Wife: Hannah
Children: Mentioned, names not given
To wife Hannah, one third of real estate and child's part of personal estate, or part entitled to by law. Two mills to be rented for five years and money used to pay debts and support children. After five years, mills and adjoining lands to be sold for specie only, proceeds divided among children. If mill rentals are insufficient to support children, Kentucky lands to be sold as necessary. Balance of Kentucky lands to be equally divided among children and heirs. All negroes and other personal property to be sold immediately and money divided among children as they come of age. All estate to Hannah, my wife, to be equally divided among children after her death.
Exrs: Archibald McGill, George Bruce, James McDannold, William Donaldson, George Blakemore
Wit: George Blakemore, John Littler, Joseph Metcalf
Codicil: Testator to have, by agreement, 500 acres of land from Capt. James McDanold (sic) which he was paid for. Patent to be issued immediately in children's names and equally divided.
Wit: George Blakemore, John Littler
Sec: Angus McDonald, James Edmonson, $20,000 (p. 259-261)

HITE, ISAAC
Account. May 1797
Payments to legatees and other accounts submitted by son Isaac Hite, Exr.
Examiners: Charles Buck, Sr., John Buck, Alexander Hite (p. 262-277)

PICKETT, HENRY
Account. May 1797
Estate settlement by admx.
Examiners: Abraham Neill, William Helm (p. 277)

PIGGOTT, HENRY
Vendue Account. 5 Apr 1797/ 1 May 1797
Among buyers: Hannah Piggott, Moses Piggott, Nathan Piggott, John Piggott (p. 277)

GRAPES, ABRAHAM
Appraisal. 5 May 1797
Appraisers: Thomas Likan, Abraham Taylor, Thomas Brown (p. 278-279)

ALEXANDER, WILLIAM
Will. 27 Feb 1796/ 1 May 1797
Wife: Dorcas
Dau: Hannah
Gr. ch: Thomas Shepherd, son of Hannah
To wife, all personal and real estate and any residue. To grandson Thomas Shepherd, all goods and chattels daughter Hannah has belonging to me.
Excx: Wife, Dorcas Alexander

Wit: Benjamin Orear, Moses Green, Jesse Orear, Jr.
Sec: Benjamin Orear, Moses Green. $1,000
[Hannah Alexander m Presley Shepherd 5 Aug 1790, Fdk.Co.Marrs.]
(p. 279-280)

DONALDSON, JOHN - ORPHANS
Mary, Rebecca, Rachel
Guardianship bond. 2 May 1797
Bondsmen: George Bruce, Jr., William Pyatt/Pyett. $3,000.
(p. 281)

RICE, EDMUND
Will. 20 Apr 1796/ 4 Apr 1797
No wife named.
Mother: Betty Rice
Sister: Betty Rice
Nephew: John Rice, son of sister Betty Rice
Brother: George Rice
To John Rice, son of my sister Betty, all landed property in Frederick County to which I am entitled by will of my father (unnamed), and all landed property in Kentucky and elsewhere. To mother Betty Rice, mare and colt; to brother George Rice, increase of mare given to mother.
Exrs: Micajah Roach, James McDonald, Joshua Wilson
Wit: James Jones, William McCormick
Sec: William McCormick, $5,000.
[Eliza Rice m William McCormick 10 Jan 1795, Fdk.Co.Marrs. Also see will of George Rice 2 Oct 1792/ 9 July 1795.] (p. 281-283]

NORTON, JOHN HATLEY (of Town of Winchester)
Will. 19 Nov 1792/ 3 July 1797
Wife: Catherine Norton
Children: George Hatley Norton, Edmund Randolph Norton, Daniel Norborne Norton
To wife, annual income of £150 during her life; full use of mansion house and other houses where I live, my garden, stable and stable lot; use of all furniture, household properties, pictures, books, carriage, horses, cattle and house servants; mulatto Hannah and her issue on condition she leaves them at her death to child or children by me.
Exrs: Robert White, Jr., of Town of Winchester, Edward Smith, of County of Frederick, Warner Lewis of Warner Hall in County of Gloucester, Virginia.
Wit: John Conrad, Robert H. Little, Daniel Kelleher
Codicil dated 6 Jan 1794, recorded 13 Oct 1795: Wife's annual allowance increased to £ 200 for life; she to have black Betty and her issue provided she leaves them at her death to any children by me. My children to be properly educated and maintained, expense to be paid by estate.
Wit: Mary Smith
Codicil dated 6 Jan 1794, recorded 13 Oct 1795: All plate to which I am entitled at death of Mrs. Mary Prescott of Butrim to my wife and at her death to my children by her. Proved by oaths of Hugh Holmes, Charles Magill, Archibald Magill. Exrs. Robert White, Jr. and Edward Smith refused executorship. Warner Lewis refused executorship and agreed to appointment of Hugh Holmes of Borough of Winchester as administrator with will annexed, 11 Jan 1798.
Sec: Philip Bush, Joseph Tidball, James Singleton, William McGuire, Robert Wood. $15,000. (p. 283-285)

NEILL, JOHN
Will. 11 May 1796/ 4 Sep 1797
Wife: Ann
Children: Lewis, Isaac, Thomas, Abraham, William, John, Rachel, Lydia, Ruth, Phebe, Mary

To wife, all personal estate for raising and educating children. Tract I live on to be equally divided among five sons Lewis, Isaac, Thomas, Abraham and William, they to pay for support of son John Ŀ 120 Va. curr. or interest therefrom yearly till paid, beginning when they arrive at age of 21 or when estate comes into their hands as they reach 21. Friends William McPherson, Joseph Steer, Lewis Neill, Thomas Neill to divide tract among sons. Pay from personal estate when they become 21 to daughters Rachel, Lydia, Ruth, Phebe and Mary, Ŀ 5 each. Testator and wife have agreed to divide tract adjoining Winchester equally among five daughters. Son John to have lot in Winchester.
Exrs: Wife Ann, son Lewis
Wit: David Lupton, Isaac Steer, Rachell Neill, Mary Lupton.
Sec: David Lupton, Isaac Steer, Lewis Neill, Sr., Thomas Neill. $10,000. (p. 285-287)

GLASS, ROBERT
Inventory & Sale Account. 4 Sep 1797 (p. 287-296

CATLETT, JAMES, SR.
Will. 27 Mar 1797/ 4 Sep 1797
No wife named
Children: John, James, Charles, Peter (dec'd), Betsey McPherson, Jane Gosney
Gr. ch: Granddaughter Eady Catlett
Legatee: Charles McPherson (relationship not shown)
To son John, 100-acre tract with improvements known as Fork plantation; road wagon and iron grey stud horse; to son James, tract where I live, not surveyed but laid out to him, bounded by Carter and Haines; 106-acre tract in Frederick Co. on branch of Cedar Creek; grey mare Pegg and her colt; my old desk, hair trunk, one case bottles, silver watch, wearing apparel; to son Charles, all remainder of plantation in this county with improvements, any remaining surplus land, bay horse Pompey, one case bottles, he to pay from legacies for covering barn 30' long x 20' wide, new desk; to daughter Betsey McPherson, 150 acres in Shenandoah Co., leather trunk; to daughter Jane Gosney, 150 acres in Shenandoah Co., negro wench Mary and her child Will, riding horse Wallis, one case bottles. To Charles McPherson, grey mare Grey and her colt. To granddaughter Eady Catlett, debt of Ŀ 21 due me from estate of my son Peter Catlett, dec'd, with interest from 1774, lent to Peter in gold and silver coin. Lot and houses in Front Royal to be disposed of and money equally divided among five children; feather bed to each of five children; negroes given to children in their possession to be kept as they are.
Exrs: John and James Catlett, sons
Wit: Edward Cary, William Gosney, John Gosney
Sec: Joseph Pollard, Robert Ware Peacock. Ŀ 10,000. (p. 296-298)

GRIFFITH, SAMUEL
Account & Sale Account. 1 Sep 1797/ 4 Sep 1797
(mentions Gibbs est., John Joliffe's est., Long's est., "balance due Samuel Griffith's est. from Thomas Butterfield, Admr.")
Examiners: Elijah Littler, Meredith Helms
Among buyers: John Griffith, Sr., Mary Griffith, John Griffith, Jr., Richard Griffith. (p. 299-303

GRAPES, JACOB
Appraisal. 29 July 1797/ 4 Sep 1797
Appraisers: Jonas Lykans, John Milburn, Thomas Brown (p. 303-305)

CORNWELL, ELIZABETH
Orphan of (no name given)
Guardianship bond. 5 Sep 1797
Bondsmen: John Groves and John Groves, Jr., $300 (p. 306)

WILSON, JAMES
Account. 18 Mar 1793/ 2 Oct 1797
Exrs: Robert Lockart and Margt (Margery), his wife. (p. 307)

GARDNER, LUKE
Account. 6 Oct 1797/ 2 Oct 1797
Admr: Samuel Mounts - balance due him £ 7.9.6 (p. 307-309)
Among names: Sarah Gardner

CHAPMAN, CAPT. THOMAS
Appraisal. 1 Sep 1797/ 2 Oct 1797
Appraisers: Benedict Rust, Mikel Everhart, John Lefevre (p. 309-310)

BROWN, WILLIAM (minor)
Guardianship bond. 2 Oct 1797
Bondsmen: Alexander White 3d, Amos Joliffe. $5,000 (p. 310-311)

ALEXANDER, WILLIAM
Appraisal. 12 May 1797/ 2 Oct 1797
Appraisers: John Morgan, Jesse Orear, John Dyer (p. 311-312)

RAVENHILL, FRANCIS
Appraisal & Sale Account. 7 Oct 1797/ 4 Dec 1797
Appraisers: Jacob Moiers, Daniel Mytinger, Casper Kline
Among buyers: Thomas Ravenhill (p. 312-313)

PRICE, GEORGE
Will. 21 Oct 1797/ 4 Dec 1797
Wife: Catherine
Children: Mentioned, not named.
To wife, plantation with appurtenances for five years, then one-third undivided part; 1 mare colt, two cows, 1 heifer, 3-year-old bay horse, all stock of hogs, all stock of sheep, all grain wheat and rye in barn, all crop of Indian corn in ground, all threshed buckwheat, all household goods or such as she chooses before estate sale date, until end of five years; and after, she is to have one equal third of household goods absolutely, also hay and fodder. To all my children born and begotten of my body by wife Catherine, equal shares after payment of debts. All boys to be bound to trades. Executors to divide estate among children, to sell plantation at public sale after youngest child born or begotten of my body attains 20, then divide estate.
Exrs: Henry Seevers, Michael Price, John Pearle
Wit: Jonathan Brady, Thomas Dunn, John Shipe, James Day
Sec: William Van Horn, Thomas Neill, Joseph Smith. $6,000. (p. 314-316)

BRYAN, SYLVESTER
Appraisal. 15 Oct 1796/ 4 Dec 1797
Appraisers: Joseph Snapp, John Fawcett, Thomas Fawcett.
"To his adjusted account with the estate of General Isaac Zane, dec'd, for balance due for books at Marlbro Iron Works."

GRAPES, JACOB
Sale Account (public vendue). 4 Dec 1797
Among buyers: Jacob Grapes, Sarah Grapes, David Grapes, Solomon Grapes. (p. 317-319)

WILL BOOK NO. 6, 1795-1802

BARTON, UNDRIT
Appraisal. 5 May 1797/ 4 Dec 1797
Appraisers: John Dilon, John Bowen, John McLean (p. 320-322)

ROBERDEAU, DANIEL (GENERAL)
Sale Account. 5 Nov 1795/ 4 Dec 1797
Most items purchased by Mrs. Daniel Roberdeau; some by estate attorney, Alexander Smith. (p. 322-329)

TAYLOR, BENJAMIN, SR.
Will. 19 Jan 1798/ 6 Feb 1798
Wife: Sarah
Children: George, Jacob, Benjamin, William, Susannah, Elizabeth
Son's wife: Elizabeth Taylor
Son-in-law: David Cole
To wife, one-third of all estate during widowhood; divide linsey yarn with son's wife Elizabeth. To daughters Elizabeth and Susannah and son-in-law David Cole, 10 shillings each. After three years, sell land and divide proceeds equally among sons, they to reside in houses where they now reside during interim. Various land parcels to sons. Appraise all stock and movables and divide agreeable to law. Divide all clothes among sons. Wife to have new cloak from new cloth; remainder of cloth to sons.
Exrs: Jacob Taylor, Benjamin Taylor, sons
Wit: Sarah Cochran, Edward Holland
Sec: John Milburn and Jacob Grapes. $2,000.
[William Taylor m Elizabeth Dunlap 19 Oct 1797, surety Benjamin Taylor, Fdk. Co. Marrs.] (p. 330-331)

PICKERING, JOHN
Appraisal. 10 Nov 1796/ 7 Feb 1798
Appraisers: John McCoole, Walter Denny, Casper Rinker (p. 331-333)

HOTSABILLAR, STEPHEN
Sale Account. 1789-5 Dec 1797/ 6 Feb 1798
Exrs: Jacob Hotsabillar and Valentine Switzer
Balance due Valentine Switzer, exr., £ 43.0.6-1/2
Examiners: Joseph Caldwell, Goldsmith Chandlee (p. 333-334)

PRICE, GEORGE
Appraisal. 15 Dec 1797/ 6 Feb 1798
Appraisers: Thomas Brown, William Tyler, Thos.Helm(p. 334-335)

NEILL, JOHN
Appraisal. 14 da of 9th mo 1797/ 6 Feb 1798
Appraisers: Isaac Brown, Jonathan Wright (p. 335-338

CONRAD, FREDERICK
Appraisal. 10 Jan 1794; Acct. current. 1794/8 Feb 1798
Appraisers: Philip Bush, Jacob Sen (?), Frederick Haas, Edward McGuire
Exrs: John and Frederick Conrad
Examiners: Joseph Tidball, Abraham Neill
Sale Account. 7 Feb 1798
Among buyers: Mary Conrad, Frederick Conrad, John Conrad, Daniel Conrad (p. 338-360)

DEALE, JAMES (Manor of Leeds)
Appraisal. 15 Feb 1798; Sale Acct. 17 Feb 1798/ 3 Apr 1798
Admr: Jeremiah Leetch
Appraisers: John Stribling, Richard Turner, Jacob Halley (p. 360-363)

LOYD, JAMES
Appraisal 17 Feb 1797; Sale Acct. Mar 1797/ 3 Apr 1798
Appraisers: John McCoole, Conrad Heironymus, William Adams
(p. 363-365)

ROBERTSON, WILLIAM
Will. 1 Dec 1797/ 3 Apr 1798
Wife: Frances Ann Robertson
Children: James, William, John, Elender, Hannah; mentions "all married daughters" but does not name them.
After legacies, all estate to be divided among wife, Frances Ann Robertson, son James, and daughters Elender and Hannah.
To daughter Elender, grey horse Rock and new hunting saddle.
To daughter Hannah, bay horse Noland and new hunting saddle,etc.
To sons William and John, and to all married daughters, each one shilling sterling.
Exrs: Wife and son James
Wit: Jeremiah Basye, Nancy Martin, William Flynn
Sec: Jeremiah Basye and James Silvio. $2,000 (p. 366-367)

HALL, JAMES
Will. 29 Jan 1798/ 3 Apr 1798
Wife: None shown
Children: Bennett, Caleb, James, William, Sarah Adduddel, Martha Denny, Elizabeth Hill, Mary Speer
Gr. ch: James Speer, son of dau Mary; Elizabeth, Mary and Sarah Hill.
To son Bennett, whole plantation and appurtenances and all personal estate if he promptly pays legacies. To son Caleb, Ł 200 curr. money in one year after decease; to James, Ł 200 in two years; to William, Ł 200 in three years after decease. To Sarah Adduddel, Ł 20 curr. money 3 months after decease; to Martha Denny, Ł 15 curr. money 3 months after decease; to Elizabeth, Ł 5 curr. money 3 months after decease, she also to have a negro boy; to granddaughters Elizabeth, Mary and Sarah Hill, each Ł 10 curr. money.
Codicil: To grandson James Speer, son of dau Mary, Ł 5 when he is 21.
Exrs: Bennett and Caleb Hall, sons
Wit: Joseph Longacre, Mordecai Bean, Ezekiel Cleaver
Sec: Mordecai Bean, Ezekiel Cleaver. $20,000
[Mary Hall m Moses Speer 8 Apr 1794; Martha Hall m John Denny 7 Apr 1789; Fdk.Co.Marrs.] (p. 367-368)

STRIBLING, WILLIAM
Account. 1793-20 Feb 1798/ 3 Apr 1798
Admr: William Hodgson of Alexandria, Va.
Examiners: John Potts, John Gill, Thomas Williams(p. 368-373)

RICE, JOHN
Appraisal 24 May 1785; Sale Acct. 24 May 1785; Acct. Curr., Dec 1783/ All recorded 3 Apr 1798
Appraisers: Lewis Hollingsworth, Robert Hollingsworth, Michael Lefevre.
Examiners: Matthew Wright, Thomas Stribling
Among buyers: George Rice, Hannah Rice (p. 374-376)

HAMMOCK, RUDOLPH
Appraisal 4 Apr 1798; Sale Acct. 28 May 1787; Acct. Curr., 28 May 1787-27 Mar 1798/ 4 Apr 1798
Appraisers: William Barrow, Geo. Warth(?), James Wilson, John Larrick
Admrs: Elizabeth Hammock, widow, and John Hammock, son
Examiners: Elisha Williams, Isaac Hite
Among buyers: Jacob, Rudolph, John, Elizabeth Hammock
(p. 377-383)

TAYLOR, BENJAMIN
Appraisal. 22 Jan 1796/ 4 Apr 1798
Appraisers: James Smith, Thomas Lloyd (p. 385-386)

BALL, WILLIAM
Division of negroes. 2 Jan 1798
Statement of payments to equalize division.
To William Ball, Nancy Ball, Betsey Ball, Mrs. Judith Singleton, Thomas Ball. [Judith Ball m James Singleton 26 Oct 1797; Fdk. Co. Marrs.] (p. 385-386

ALLNUTT, JAMES (Probated Montgomery Co., Md.)
Will. 17 May 1786/ 1 May 1798
Wife: Jane
Children: Jesse, William, Lawrence, James, John, Joseph, Talbart, Daniel, Ann Coats wife of Charles Coats, Sarah Price wife of William Price, dec'd, Mary Peck wife of Richard Peck, Susannah Allnutt, Rebecca Allnut
To wife during life, one third part of property called Thomas's Discovery including dwelling house where I now live and adjoining land. After wife's decease, to be divided equally among five daughters. To son Jesse Allnutt "I have given all I intend to give him" To son William Allnut I have given 100 acres called Thomas's Discovery which he has sold to Samuel Dyson, also other things, "which is all I intend to give him." To sons Lawrence and James, all the remaining part of Thomas's Discovery, equally divided. To sons John, Joseph, Talbart and Daniel, 400 acres known as Mercer's, being 13th part of 15th lot on Buck Marsh in Frederick County, equally divided. Should any die without issue, share to be divided among survivors. "If I get a patent on land in Kaintucke on the western waters of Virginia when a warrant was located for me there," to be divided equally among four youngest sons and two youngest daughters after daughters Susannah and Rebecca each has a bed and furniture, 1 cow and calf, 1 pewter dish, 6 plates, half dozen knives and forks.
Admr: Wife Jane
Wit: Samuel Dyson, Maddox Dyson, Elijah Voiars(?)
Proved Montgomery Co., Md., 22 Dec 1794, certified by Samuel Turner, Reg'r; will copy recorded Frederick Co., Va., 1 May 1798. (p. 387-388

GOOSE, GEORGE
Will. 4 Mar 1798/ 2 July 1798
Wife: Fanny
Children: John, Andrew, George, Jacob, Mary Gardner wife of Daniel Gardner, Elizabeth, Margaret D. Long wife of Nicholas D. Long (DeLong?), Sarah Simmers, Elizabeth Goose, Susannah.
To wife: $100 in silver, crops, and all her goods and chattels brought with her when I married her; also, to live in house and have her creatures cared for until sold or division made. Remainder to be divided equally among children. To sons George and Jacob Goose, land to be divided and deeds given by executors provided they pay equal dividend to other legatees in four equal annual installments. If they do not, executors to sell land and distribute equally among nine children. Any remaining personal estate equally divided but no legacy to be claimed before settlement of my book accounts against legatees.
Exrs: Jacob Kline, John McGinnis
Wit: Jacob Moirs (Moyers?), Jacob V-----(?), Adam Stahl
Sec: Jacob Myers (Moyers), John Barrow, George Gardner.
$2,000. (p. 388-389)

BOWMAN, GEORGE
Distribution under will. 1769/ 3 Sep 1798
Distributees: John Bowman, Abram Bowman, Joseph Bowman, Mary Stephens, Elizabeth Ruddle, Sarah Wright, Regina Dyerley(?), Rebecca Brinker. (p. 389-391)

STEPHENS, LAWRENCE
Accounting. 1769/ 1798
Mary Stephens' acct. for Lawrence Stephens' bond. (p. 392)

BOWMAN, JOSEPH
Settlement of estate. 3 Sep 1798
Exr: Abraham Bowman
Mentions redivision of land, land on Cedar Creek. Examiners approve and submit final settlement of accounts of Joseph and George Bowman, 20 Jan 1798.
Examiners: A. Bainbridge, James Singleton

WALL, WILLIAM, ORPHAN OF JESSE BALL
Guardianship Acct. Feb 1797-July 1798/ 3 Sep 1798
Guardian: Augustine Green
Among items: "Expense of his negroes from Lancaster to Frederick; Clerks of Lancaster against me as guardian." Balance due William Wall, £ 7.13.6.
Examiners: Abram Neill, H. Ruth (p. 394-395)

SIMRALL, JAMES
Will. 22 Aug 1797/ 3 Sep 1798
Wife: Sarah Simrall
Children: Alexander, William Ferguson, James, Joseph, Frances Meem
To wife, whole lot I live on during life as widow, also personal estate except specific legacies to children; negro Nancy during widowhood. If wife marries, she is to have a horse and saddle, furniture for one room, choice of beds and furniture, and other household items. Remainder of personal estate divided between wife and our children by three reputable neighbors mutually chosen. To sons Alexander Simrall and William Ferguson Simrall my Kentucky lands, but if one dies without heirs, to be divided among remaining brothers. To son James Simrall the whole water lot in Kernstown purchased from Adam Kern, Jr., with lot lately purchased from John Mark, possession at 22. Also to have north part of lot purchased from Adam Kern, Sr. To son Joseph Simrall lot where I live after wife's death or remarriage, possession at 22. Also division of out lot purchased from Adam Kern, Sr. To sons William Ferguson Simrall, James Simrall and Joseph Simrall, at 22, each one feather bed and bedding. To William Ferguson, James, Joseph, daughter Frances Meem (Mimm), negroes. To son Alexander, all my stills in his possession and negro; my silver watch to son William F.; my desk to son James; my clock to son Joseph - all at mother's death or remarriage.
Exrs: Wife Sarah, sons Alexander, William Ferguson Simrall, Archibald McGill, Esq.
Wit: Henry Peters, John Hotsinpillar
Sec: Stephen Pritchard, John Hotsinpillar. $20,000
[Frances Simrall m Gilbert Mimm 1 Aug 1793, Fdk.Co.Marrs.]
(p. 396-397)

MARQUIS, JOHN
Appraisal. 1795; Sale Account. Jan 1795/ 3 Sep 1795
"Sale of land and sundry land in the mountains"
Examiners: Matthew Wright, Thomas Stribling (p. 397-398)

MARQUIS, ELIZABETH and ELEANOR
Orphans of John Marquis
Guardianship Account. 1795/ 30 Aug 1798
Guardian: Francis Hutchins (p. 399)

MARQUIS, JOHN
Sale Account. 1798
Property in Blue Ridge Mountains
Exrs: Francis Hutchins, William Wiley (p. 399-401)

SIMRALL, JAMES
Appraisal. 12 Sep 1798/ 1 Oct 1798
Appraisers: John Brady, James McDonald, Howson Seaton, James D. Vance (p. 401-415)

SYDNOR, SAMUEL
Orphan of William F. Sydnor
Guardianship. 1 Oct 1798
Guardian: Ann Sydnor
Guardianship bond: Robert Livright, Samuel Y. Sydnor (p. 415-416)

GRIFFITH, SAMUEL
Additional accounting.
Omitted from accounting with Thomas Butterfield
Examiners: Meredith Helm, Elijah Littler (p. 416-417)

GREEN, MOSES
Will. 28 Feb 1798/ 3 Dec 1798
Wife: Elizabeth Green
Children: James. Others mentioned but not named
To wife during widowhood, estate for life. To each son, one horse saddle and bridle, at 21. To each daughter, a feather bed and furniture at 21. Divide all estate among children.
Exrs: Wife Elizabeth and son James
Wit: Elijah Coats, John Dyer, Benjamin Orear
Sec: John Dyer, Peter Catlett. $5,000. (p. 417-418)

DRAGGOO, BENJAMIN (Var. Draggio, Dragio, Drage)
Will. 3 Mar 1798/ 3 Dec 1798
Brother: William Dragoo, whole of estate
Nephew: John Jolliffe, negro woman Bell
Niece (not named): Money legacy
Exrs: John Jolliffe, Collin Carroll
Wit: John Jolliffe, Benjamin Fenton, Charles Perry
Sec: Elijah Litler. $4,000. (p. 418)

CARTER, JAMES
Will. 25 Oct 1798/ 3 Dec 1798
Wife: Ann
Children: Joseph, James, Arthur, Katherine, Mary, Sarah, Rachel (dec'd)
Gr ch: Children of deceased daughter Rachel
Brother: Joseph
To wife, one bed and furniture, 2 cows, horse and saddle (her choice) and negro girl, besides what the law allows her. To son Joseph, land on Abraham's Creek with dwelling houses, grist mill, outhouses and other improvements. To son James, land between Redbud and Abraham's Creek with improvements, land on east side of Opeckon Creek, meadow ground on north side of Redbud. To son Arthur, remainder of tract on north side of Redbud Run, also whole tract purchased from my brother Joseph. To sons James and Arthur, equal right to all mills and mill seats within my limits on Redbud. To daughters, Katherine, Mary and Sarah, Ŀ 50 to be paid each by son Joseph two years after he is in possession of

devised premises. Movable estate remaining and negroes equally divided, one share each to three living daughters and fourth to children of deceased daughter Rachel when of age. Negroes to be retained in family if sold, to have liberty to choose masters.
Exrs: Sons Joseph and James and Arthur Carter
Wit: Joseph Perral, Peter McMurry, Cuthbert Hayhurst
Sec: Elijah Littler, Peter McMurry, William Kerfoot. $20,000. (p. 419-420)

MIERS, STEPHEN (late of Stephensburg)
Appraisal. 15 Apr 1797/ 3 Dec 1798
Appraisers: H. Weaver, William McLeod, Daniel Smith, Andre Pitman (p. 420)

HELMS, THOMAS, ESQ.
Sale Account. 15 Oct 1778-15 Mar 1779/ 3 Dec 1798
Included 300 acres land.
Among buyers: Capt James Barnett for Joseph Helms, Meredith Helm, William Helm, Jr., John Helm, Miss Peggy Helm. (p. 421-430)

TAYLOR, BENJAMIN
Renunciation. 15 Aug 1798/ 8 Dec 1798
Sarah Taylor, widow and relict, relinquishes and renounces provisions and legacies in will of husband dated 19 Jan 1798.
Wit: Thomas Brown, William Brown (p. 431)

SYDNOR, RICHARD, WILLIAM and ANNE
Orphans of William Sydnor
Guardianship. 8 Dec 1798
Guardianship bond: Mattie Haynie, John Haynie, George Reynolds. $3,000. (p. 431-432)

HAYNIE, MOLLY
Orphan of George Haynie
Guardianship. 3 Dec 1798
Guardianship bond: Mattie Haynie, John Haynie, George Reynolds. $3,000. (p. 432-433)

HAYNIE, PRESLEY
Orphan of George Haynie
Guardianship. 3 Dec 1798
Guardianship bond: Matty Haynie, John Haynie, George Reynolds. $3,000. (p. 433)

MYERS, STEPHEN
Orphan of Leonard Myers
Guardianship. 3 Dec 1798
Guardianship bond. William Elzey, Jacob Myers, Henry Lewis, $3,000 (p. 434)

MITCHELL, CARY
Appraisal. 24 July 1798; Sale Acct. 15 Aug 1798/ 4 Dec 1798
Appraisers: William Bourn, William Helms, George Clopton (p. 434-435)

LOY, JOHN
Will. 28 Aug 1784/ 4 Dec 1798
Wife: Elizabeth
Children: Daniel, John, Conrad, Maria, Elizabeth wife of Samuel Hott, Christiana wife of Henry Hott, Catherine, Mary Elizabeth, Madline
Gr. ch: Three unnamed children of Mary Loy [Schultz], dec'd
To wife for life, tract where I dwell, 149 acres, and personal estate owned at time of death. After wife's death, executors to sell estate and divide equally among nine children, to receive when of age or married. Funds due minor children to be put to

interest. If John or Conrad die before reaching legal age and without issue, share to be divided among surviving children.
Exrs: Samuel Hott and Henry Hott, sons-in-law
Wit: George F. Norton, D. Norton, George Somerville, John Peyton.
Codicil: 11 June 1790: Daughter Mary, since married to Frederick Schultz and now deceased leaving three children, share to be divided among them or survivors when of age.
Wit: James Gibbs, J. Peyton, Edward Christian. (p. 436-438)

BREAMS, HENRY (HINRY BRIAN)
Appraisal. 5 Dec 1798
Appraisers: Thomas Lewis, William Tyler, John Carter. (p. 438)

TALBOTT, EDWARD
Account. 6 June 1798/ 5 Dec 1798
"Due on settlement, to Levi Smith for land, Ł 18.16.8."
Mentions William Talbott
Admrs: Edward Talbott, Jr., Daniel Magruder
Examiners: John Smith, Meredith Helm (p. 438-444)

BOYD, SAMUEL
Account current. 30 Nov 1798/ 31 Dec 1798
Admr: Robert White (p. 445)

SYDNOR, WILLIAM F.
Appraisal. 17 Aug 1798/ 31 Dec 1798
Appraisers: Edward Howe, John Gordon, Lewis Stephens, Jr. (p. 446-449)

TAYLOR, BENJAMIN
Sale Account. 16 Feb 1798/ 31 Dec 1798
Among buyers: Benjamin Taylor, William Taylor, George Taylor, Jacob Taylor, Abraham Taylor, widow Sarah Taylor (p. 449-452)

CARTER, JAMES
Appraisal. 7 Dec 1798/ 31 Dec 1798
Appraisers: George Clopton, John Brady, Mabra Madden, John Carter (p. 452-454)

ORNDORFF, JOHN, SR.
Will. 17 Nov 1798/ 31 Dec 1798
Wife: Hannah
Children: William, John, Joshua, Jesse, Philip, Samuel, Israel, Benjamin, David, Levi, Phineas, Isaac, Elizabeth, Anne, Rebecca, Eleanor.
To wife, "mother of these last children," to be paid sundry payments. To son William "in consideration of a debt due him," brown horse bought of son John, my saddle and bridle and new blind bridle, wooling yarn for great coats for him and one for son Samuel, and brown heifer bought of Peter (H)Kinkinius(?) on which he is to give up my notes to my executors. All flax and yarn to be left for my children now living with me. Executors to sell estate and pay debts. Pay son Joshua $1.00, all I allow him. To son Jesse, half a dollar for his share. Divide remainder into 16 parts, distributed among sons and daughters: John (including Ł 15 already received); Philip (including Ł 15 already received); Elizabeth (including Ł 6 already received); Anne, also young heifer called her own which is not to be sold; 1/16 part to each William, Samuel, Benjamin, Israel, David, Rebecca, Levi, Phineas, Eleanor and Isaac.
Exrs: Elias Kackley, Jacob White
Wit: Moses Russell, Philip P. Bucher, Peter (H)Kinkinius(?) (p. 454-456)

RICE, PATRICK
Will. 9 June 1798/ 4 Feb 1799
No wife named
Children: Rebecca Connel, Susanna Hollingsworth
Gr. ch: James Rice; sons of Robert Hollingsworth (unnamed); Rebecca Connel; Hester, Elizabeth, Hannah and Susannah Hollingsworth
To daughter Rebecca Connel, Ł 10 Va. curr.; to daughter Susannah Hollingsworth, curr. and "all my outstanding debts by bonds, notes or book accounts not herein mentioned"; to grandson James Rice and granddaughter Rebecca Connel, each Ł 5; to granddaughters Hester, Elizabeth, Hannah and Susannah Hollingsworth, each Ł 10 Va. curr.; in case of death of any of them, to be divided among survivors; to grandsons, sons of Robert Hollingsworth, wearing apparel, goods and chattels, divided among them.
Exrs: Robert Hollingsworth and his son George Hollingsworth
Wit: Elizabeth Rice, Rebekah Rice, George Blackmore
(p. 456-457)

LOYD, JAMES
Account current. Mar 1797; Sale 1797/ 5 Feb 1799
Admr: Joseph Bland
Examiners: Joseph Tidball, Joseph Caldwell (p. 457-459)

CHRISMAN, HENRIETTA (now CLARKE)
Orphan of Isaac Chrisman
Guardianship Acct. & Settlement. May 1796/ 1 Apr 1799
"Paid Jan 1799 to Lewis Stephens, Jr., for six months' board, education &c, Ł 12.0.0"
Examiners: James G. Dowdall, Isaac Woodrow (p. 459-460)

DECKER, HENRY
Appraisal. 2 Apr 1799
Appraisers: William Reynolds, Moses Payne, Edmond Pagett
(p. 460-461)

MOFFITT, JOHN (dec'd Nov 1788)
Appraisal. 6 May 1799
Appraisers: Strother G. Settle, Richard Basye, William Hand
(p. 461-462)

GOSSETT, ABNER
Appraisal. 29 Apr 1799/ 6 May 1799
Appraisers: Joseph Gordon, Thomas Smart, Joseph Baley
(p. 462-463)

DRAGOO, BENJAMIN
Appraisal. 6 May 1799
Appraisers: Lewis Neill, David Ridgway, James Bruce
(p. 463)

McDONALD, ANGUS
Accounting. 4 Apr 1768-15 Nov 1798/ 1 July 1799
"Capt. John Greenfield estate to estate of Angus McDonald." (Hampshire County records show Angus McDonald, John Greenfield and Mayor James Livingston were apparent partners in land dealings in that county.)
Examiners: Meredith Helms, Charles Smith (p. 464)

MARBURGER, JOHN (of Stephensburg)
Will. 25 Feb 1799/ 1 July 1799
Wife: Ann Blauburger (sic)
Bro-in-law: Philip Miller, wife's brother
To wife, two in lots, five out lots and appurtenances, movable furniture, wearing apparel. After her death, to Philip Miller, brother of my wife, of Stephensburg
Exrs: Ann Marburger, Philip Miller
Wit: Daniel Mytinger, Andrew Pitman (p. 465)

MINSOR, JACOB (MINSON?)
Appraisal. May 1799/ 2 July 1799
Appraisers: Jonas Likens, James Steele, William Reed
(p. 466-467)

BALLET, JAMES
Appraisal. 3 July 1798
Appraisers: John Lupton, Joshua Lupton, John Lupton, Jr.
(p. 467-468)

WHITING, HENRY
Appraisal. 25 June 1796/ 2 July 1799
Appraisers: William Castleman, William Frost, Thomas Kinnan
(p. 468-469)

HENDRY/HENRY, DEBORAH
Will. 24 Sep 1796/ 2 July 1799
Husband: George Henry (dec'd)
Children: William, Abraham, Isaac, George, Nancy Worley, Mary umphries (Humphries?), Betty Burden (Borden?), Rebecca Duncan
Brother: Joseph Borden
Gr ch: Mary Ann Hendry; Elizabeth and Mary Worley daughters of Nancy Worley
Land I live on, 200 acres, to be sold and net proceeds divided equally, three parts among sons William, Abraham and Isaac; son George's share equally divided among daughters Betty Borden, Rebecca Duncan, Nancy Worley, Mary Umphries "in accordance with will of my deceased husband, George Henry." My burying ground not to be sold but kept for use of me and my heirs forever, same quantity of land to be taken off my 100-acre tract adjoining above 200 acres. Remainder of 100 acres to be sold and Ŀ 5 paid to son William Henry; remainder equally to two sons Abraham and Isaac and to two granddaughters Elizabeth and Mary Worley. "Whereas a certain Thomas Campbell, Jaler (Jailer) in Winchester, Frederick County, when my husband was in jail, took the advantage of his necessity and he not being in his proper senses, he signed a deed for conveyance of 360 acres of land, which land I give ... all my right, title and claim that my husband gave me" to daughters Nancy Worley and Mary Umphries and to granddaughter Mary Ann Henry equally. Daughters Betty Burden and Rebecca Duncan, only five shillings each, "they being very disobedient children." To Nancy Worley, Mary Umphries, Elizabeth and Mary Worley, daughters of Nancy, wearing apparel. "Whereas I empowered my brother Joseph Borden to sew (sue) for a part of my father's movable estate which I had not received," for which Joseph Borden is to have half for his trouble and cost, the other half I give to sons Abraham and Isaac Henry.
Exrs: William Davis, Thomas Berey
Wit: John Elkins, John Hathaway, Charles Ferguson
(Thomas Berey refused executorship.) (p. 469-472)

WITZELL, CHRISTOPHER (sadler of Boro of Winchester)
Will. 2 Nov 1798/ 2 Sep 1799
Wife: Catharine
Children: John Henry, Christopher, Nancy (eldest); other daughters not named
To wife, household goods and movable effects; last bond due me from William German for Ŀ 35; full possession of house and lot where I live and lot in Cameron Street, during widowhood. To son John Henry, lot in Cameron Street except the quarter adjoining lot of Godfrey Miller. To son Christopher, all remainder real estate and property, all debts, bonds and debts due me immediately, and at decease of wife, house and lot where I live, provided he pays all just debts and, at death of wife, pay each daughter, as they come of age, $66.67, except daughter Nancy (eldest) to be maintained for life and to have the quarter lot

reserved above, her property forever, at decease of wife.
Exrs: Wife Catharine, son Christopher
Wit: Christian Streit, Peter Lauck (p. 472-474)

GREEN, MOSES
Appraisal. Dec 1798-31 May 1799/ 2 Sep 1799
Appraisers: Benjamin Orear, James Walter, James Strother (p. 474-475)

McCAN, DANIEL
Will. 23 May 1799/ 2 Sep 1799
Wife: Catherine; sister: Sarah Malhott and sons
Legatees: (relationship not stated):
Samuel Rogers, uncle of John Carson; Betsy's son Carson; Betsey and her daughter Catherine Carson, her son William Capon(?); Thomas Carson.
To wife Catherine, maintenance for life; to Samuel Rogers, 100 acres of land joining Charles Miers; to John Carson son of Betsey, 50 acres of land joining his uncle Samuel Rogers' 100 acres; to Sarah Malhott, son Daniel Malhott and his youngest brother (unnamed), balance of tract I live on to be divided equally. If no heirs, to Catherine Carson, daughter of Betsey Carson, 1 cow and calf; remainder of movable property to be divided equally between Betsey Carson and Thomas Carson, her son William Capon(?), and Catherine Carson daughter of Betsey Carson.
Exrs: Samuel Rogers, John Catlett
Wit: Ally Catlett, Ann Catlett, Henrietta Catlet
(Widow renounced any claim under will.) (p. 475-477)

MYERS, LEONARD (STEPHEN)
Orphan of Leonard Myers
Guardianship Settlement. Nov 1796/ 2 Sep 1799
Settlement of estate which should have been for Stephen Myers, orphan of Leonard Myers
Examiners: Lewis Stephens, Jr., William McLeod (last signature illegible) (p. 477)

GIBSON, WILLIAM
Nuncupative will. 23 June 1799/ 2 Sep 1799
Deposition of Samuel Turner: On 23rd day of June 1799, being the day on which William Gibson died, Samuel Turner was at the house of John Walters near the dwelling house of William Gibson, who informed deponent he wished his property to be left in house of Capt. Edmond Newman for use of his widow and natural son called Thomas Gibson. The testator died three hours later. (p. 478)

RICHARDS, CAPT. HENRY
Account current. 8 May 1799/ 3 Sep 1799
Exrs: John Richards, Robert Jameson
Examiners: Joseph Longacre, Gerard Briscoe (p. 478-479)

RICE, PATRICK
Appraisal. 3 Aug 1799/ 3 Sep 1799
M. Smith, Daniel Hunsecker, James Thompson (Appraisers)
Names mentioned: George Rice, dec'd; Micajah Roach exr of George Rice; Elizabeth Rice. (p.480)

BOWER, JACOB
Will. 15 July 1799/ 3 Sep 1799
Wife: Barbara
Children: George, Henry, Jacob, John, Eve Feasell, Catharine Wisegarver (Wisecarver)

To wife, for natural life, one third produce, arable land, orchard and meadow, all other stock, household and kitchen furniture; bed and furniture to her, her heirs and assigns forever. To son George, all the tract where I live, 147 acres, with all appurtenances, providing he tills and cultivates all arable land, orchard, meadow, and gives one-third to his mother, Barbara, to keep two cows and a heifer for her during her life; to pay to son Henry Ŀ 10 curr. money within one year of mother's decease; to pay my daughter Catharine Wisecarver Ŀ10 curr. money four years after mother's death; to daughter Eve Feasell Ŀ10 curr. money two years after mother's death; to pay son John Ŀ10 curr. money five years after mother's death.
Exrs: George Hite, Jacob White, John Feasell, George Bowers
Wit: Joseph Longacre, Jacob Spelman, John Witzell. (p. 480-482)

WILSON, JAMES
Account current. 1797- 16 July 1799/ 3 Sep 1799
Exrs: Robert Lockhart and Margery, his wife
"Legacy left above Margery by will, Ŀ 200.0.0." (p. 482-484)

COCHRAN, RACHAEL
Orphan of William Cochran
Guardianship bond. 1 Oct 1799
Bondsmen: William Cochrane, Jesse Brown, Joseph Gill;
$2,000. (p. 484)

JONES, JAMES
Appraisal & Sale Acct. 14 Apr 1797/ 2 Dec 1799
Appraisers: Mabra Madden, William Coe, Samuel Littler
"Clothes delivered to Mr. William Riens." (p. 484)

BOWER, JACOB
Appraisal. 28 Sep 1799/ 2 Dec 1799
Appraisers: Joseph Snapp, Thomas Fawcett, David C. Gilhaus.
(p. 485-487)

WHITE, EDWARD
Will. 27 Nov 1799/ 6 Jan 1800
Wife: (Unnamed)
Children: Lucinda, Joseph; Thornley White, wf's first son
Brother: Jose (Joseph?) White
To wife, personal property divided among wife and children. To children, all land, 153 acres, divided equally. To Thornley White, wife's first son, two full years' schooling.
Exrs: Wife and brother Jose (Joseph?) White
Wit: John Haines, Edward Draper (p. 487-488)

FAUCETT, JOHN (FAWCETT)
Appraisal. 12 Dec 1786/ 8 Jan 1800
Appraisers: Benjamin B. Frye, Jacob Frye, Joseph Snapp
(p. 489-491)

HOLLINGSWORTH, ROBERT
Will. 15 July 1792/ 7 Jan 1800
Wife: Susannah
Children: Joseph, Lewis, Robert, Abraham, Isaac, John, James, Edmond, George, Easter, Elizabeth, Hannah, Susannah
To wife during widowhood, 100 acres of tract where I live. After her death, land to be sold and money divided among sons named above except George. To wife, all personal property for support of family, she to dispose of as she thinks proper. Wife's dower of land to be sold after her death. Executors to sell residue of land, 100 acres, and tract bought of Capt. Rice, 89 acres, and tract adjoining James Thompson and my son George, 30 acres.

Money therefrom to be equally divided among sons Joseph, Lewis, Robert, Abraham, Isaac, John, James and Edmond. To above sons, 2,666-2/3 acres, my part being 1,333-1/3 acres, to be equally divided among above-mentioned sons. To daughters Easter, Elizabeth, Hannah and Susannah, 800 acres on Otter Creek, residue of above 1,333-1/3 acres, equally divided. All remainder of personal estate to be sold and each daughter to have $50 as they come of age or marry, remainder to be equally divided among sons Joseph, Lewis, Robert, Abraham, Isaac, John, James and Edmond. Should any son die without issue before coming of age, surviving sons to divide his share. Same provision as to daughters. To son George, tract I purchased of George Rice on High Land Creek, 200 acres. Executors to make deeds for tract of 1,333-1/3 acres on Otter Creek willed by Capt. George Rice to George Rice and heirs. Approval given should any son desire to be bound to a trade. Should any executor settle on any part of my military land, not to exceed 400 acres in each lot, children shall not intercept, and shall accept the 400 acres as their quota.
Exrs: Joseph Hollingsworth, Lewis Hollingsworth, Robert Hollingsworth, Jr.
Wit: George Blackmore, John Nelson, Michael Smith(p. 491-494)

WHITE, EDWARD
Appraisal. 31 Mar 1800
Appraisers: John Haines, William Timberlick, Thomas Ralph (p. 494-496)

DISBONET, ABRAHAM
Appraisal. 31 Mar 1800
Appraisers: Michael White, William Touchstone. (p. 495-497)

BUCHER, JACOB
Will. 7 Aug 1799/ 31 Mar 1800
Wife: Mary
Sister: Mary
Children: Unnamed, except son John
To wife, household goods, debts due me and movable property; also other house and lot and stable opposite it where my sister is now building, reserving use of house sister Mary is building on it; if she chooses, a small yard adjoining it to sister as long as she lives. At end of widowhood or decease of wife Mary, all real estate to be sold and money equally divided among my children, except son John who, in consideration of expenses I have been at for his education, shall receive only one dollar, he having already received more than the rest.
Exrs: Christopher Witzel, Michael Groves, William Brown
Wit: Christian Streit, Christopher Witzel, Michael Groves, William Brown.
(Christopher Witzel relinquishes executorship) (p. 497-498)

BERRY, JOHN
Will. 26 da of 10 mo called Oct 1792/ 31 Mar 1800
Wife: Patience
Children: Joseph, Samuel, David, John, Adson(?), Lydia, Margaret Tucker, Patience Dick
To wife, maintenance from plantations, use of dwelling and household and kitchen furniture during widowhood and natural life. To son John, all carpenter's tools, plantation tools and all stock except sorrel horse Pompey. To daughter Lydia, sorrel horse Pompey and bed and bedding. To sons Samuel, David, John, Adson(?), and daughters Margaret Tucker and Patience Dick, each 20 shillings to be paid in property one year after my decease.
Exr: Son Joseph Berry
Wit: Jacob Pickering, Moses Royse, Lydia Pickering (p. 499-500)

McCANN, DANIEL
Appraisal & Sale Acct. 18 Sep 1799/ 31 Mar 1800
Appraisers: John Barrow, William Barrow, Christopher Slusher
Among buyers: Catharine McCann (p. 500-502)

SMITH, ISAAC
Appraisal. 7 Jan 1800/ 1 Apr 1800
Names: Due from Christian Smith, son of deceased; due from Philip Leavly, son-in-law; account from Mathias Smith.
(p. 502-504)

WHITE, ANN
Dower partition. 30 April 1800
"In obedience to order of court to lay off 51 acres, third part of tract of Edward White, deceased, as widow's dower.
Subscribers: Asa Clevinger, John Haines, George Ball
(p. 504)

LAWYER, ADAM
Appraisal. 7 Dec 1799/ 6 May 1800
Appraisers. Christopher Moyers, John Moyers, Philip Casper, Thomas Ralph. (p. 505)

McMAHON, TIMOTHY (blacksmith)
Will. 8 Jan 1800/ 6 May 1800
Wife: Sarah
Children: Daniel, John, Michael, Timothy, Mary Ann Juliet
All effects except house, land and household furniture to be sold. Negro man Will to remain with wife and children at my house for their use and benefit. Negro woman Nancy and her children to be sold and negroes about 3 or 4 years old to be purchased and given to daughter. All money from sale of effects to be put at interest and income applied to support of wife and five children. Children to inherit, sons at 21 and daughter at 18. Should any child die, divide among survivors.
Exr: Capt. Thomas Byrd
Wit: Henry Ashburn, Arthur Grimes
Bushrod Taylor given letters of administration with will attached. Bond $2,000
(Thomas Byrd refused executorship) (p. 506-508)

BRUCE, GEORGE
Will. 25 Jan 1797/ 30 June 1800
Wife: Rachel Bruce
Children: George, James, Sarah Walker, Leah Hanry(?), Rebecca Chenowith
To wife for natural life, lot reserved in son George's devise with dwelling house and other houses, with all my goods and chattels, to be disposed of at her discretion at her decease. To son George, part of my plantation where he now lives northwest of the Great Road from Sheppards Town to Winchester, reserving one acre where I now live, not to be conveyed at the expense of George, with the grist mill and all buildings, etc. My clock to him after wife's decease. Son George to pay my wife yearly one-third of profits from the mill and plantation during her life. To son James, all remainder of plantation on southeast of road with grist and saw mill and other improvements, etc., he not to raise water to prejudice of brother George; to him also lands I hold on south side of Mongahalia River and adjoining river with all improvements, he paying wife Rachel £ 10 Va. curr. yearly and every year during her life for use of saw mill. To Sarah Walker and Leah Hanry(?), each 5 shillings. To dau Rebeckah Chinoweth (Chenowith), house I live in after decease of wife with lot devised to wife.
Exrs: Wife Rachel, sons George and James
Wit: John Cowgill, Susannah McKelween, William Piett
Sec: William Piett, $2,000. (p. 508-510)

RENNER, GEORGE
Will. 10 Feb 1800/ 30 June 1800
Wife Barbary
Children: Peter, Barnett (both under 21), Adam, George, Jacob, Isaac, Abraham, John, Mary (handicapped), Barbary, Madeline, Margaret Orendorff, Catherine Nelson
To wife Barbary, old mansion house and plantation where I live and all property, real and personal. Movables to pay expenses. To daughter Mary "unfortunately subject to fits" - if she outlives wife, maintenance and care from sons Peter and Barnett "provided it is adjudged by two or more judicious and candid men she is not capable of maintaining herself during her natural life." Peter to live with mother until 21; Barnett under 21. After wife's death, all personal estate to be divided between these two sons, Peter to have full possession of estate after wife's death until Barnett is 21. Should either son die, survivor inherits. After wife's death, sons to have plantation, 346 acres, resurveyed by Joseph Longacre. Plat of 410 acres to be equally divided between sons, Peter having first choice. Whichever takes the old mansion pays the other Ł 10 within three years. To daughter Margaret Orendorff, son George, son Jacob, each 5 shillings Va. curr; to daughter Catherine Nelson, son Isaac, son Abraham, son John, each 3 shillings Va. curr. To daughter Barbary Ł 5 Va. curr; to daughter Madeline Ł 4 Va. curr.; to son Adam, Ł 3 Va. curr.
Exrs: Wife Barbary Renner, son Peter Renner
Wit: Iona Lupton, George Hite, Stephen Peacock
[Margaret Renner m John Orndorff 5 June 1792; Magdaline Renner m John Pitcock 13 Dec 1804; Jacob Renner m Barbara Wisecarver 4 Nov 1790; Peter Renner m Magdaline Shultz 12 Dec 1811; Fdk. Co.Marrs.] (p. 510-514)

GOSSETT. ABNER
Account current. July 1798/ 30 June 1800
William Gossett, Admr.
Examiners: Joseph Gamble, Nathan Anderson
[Abner Gossett m Mary Mercer 23 Dec 1797, bondsman Wm. Gossett; William Gossett m Nancy Smith, no date shown; Fdk.Co.Marrs.] (p. 514)

TODD, JAMES (of Back Creek)
Will. 17 Apr 1800/ 30 June 1800
Wife: Jane Todd
Son: William Todd
Dau-in-law: Elizabeth, wife of William Todd
Gr. son: James, son of William & Elizabeth Todd
To wife, use and benefit of whole estate except following: To son William, Ł 5 curr. money and all wearing apparel payable one year and one day after decease; to daughter-in-law Elizabeth Todd, Ł 4 curr. money; to grandson James Todd, son of above Ł 5 curr. money.
Wit: Samuel Talbott, Thomas Nesmith, Nathan Littler, Jr.
[James Todd m Jane Lowry 17 June 1794, Fdk.Co.Marrs.] (p. 514-515)

KENDRICKS, ABRAHAM (formerly of Lancaster Co., Pa.)
Will. 16 Aug 1800/ 1 Sep 1800
Eldest brother: John Kendricks of twp of Strasburg, Lancaster Co., Pa.
Exr: friend Elisha Phelps
Wit: John Mason, William McLeod, Henry Walker, John Cryder (p. 515-516)

SMITH, CATHERINE
Appraisal. 18 Apr 1800/ 1 Sep 1800
Appraisers: James Graham, Arthur Graham, Thomas Shepherd, Jr.
(p. 516-517)

PICKERING, SAMUEL
Will. 30 da of 5th mo 1798/ 1 Sep 1800
(No wife mentioned)
Children: Jacob, Samuel, Benjamin, Jonathan, John, Mary, Grace, Marcy, Rachel, Hannah
To sons Jacob and Samuel, plantation I live on, 287 acres divided equitably provided they pay to each of brothers Benjamin, Jonathan and John Ł 60 over three years. To Mary, Grace, Marcy, Rachel, each Ł 20; to Hannah, Ł 30; to Hannah and Marcy each, one feather bed and its furniture. Daughter Rachel has her furniture. To Rachel and Hannah, each one cow. All household property not bequeathed to be equally divided among daughters. Sell at public vendue stock and farming equipment, two looms and their furniture, to pay debts, remainder divided among daughters.
Exrs: Jacob and Samuel Pickering
Wit: Thomas Faucett, Joshua Lupton, Jonathan Taylor.
(p. 517-519)

TALBOTT, ELEANOR (widow of Edward)
Will. 15 Apr 1800/ 1 Sep 1800
Nephews: Archibald Edmondson, Daniel Magruder
Niece: Ann Nichols wife of Samuel Nichols
Brother: Hezekiah Magruder; his children Daniel Magruder, Ann wife of Jonah Harding, and George Magruder
Other legatees: Thomas Edmondson; Theodore Magruder son of Daniel Magruder; Hezekiah Young; Anne Harding wife of Isàiah Harding; Lancelot Lee
To nephew Archibald Edmondson for life, 200 acres formerly in possession of Robert Porterfield. After his demise, to Thomas Edmondson. Payment of half of all money due and owing Lancelot Lee. To nephew Archibald, Ł 75 Va. curr. payable 12 months after decease, my nicest feather bed, green bedstead and all the furniture belonging thereto. To nephew Daniel Magruder for life 200 acres formerly in possession of George Stockton alias Stockden. After decease to Theodore Magruder, son of Daniel Magruder, money to be paid to Lancelot Lee, residue of purchase money due him for said land. To niece Ann Nichols wife of Samuel Nichols, negro woman Aminto. To Hezekiah Young, Ł 20 payable 12 months after my decease. To Ann Harding, wife of Isaiah Harding, four-wheeled riding carriage and Ł 15 Va. curr. 12 months after my decease. Executors to emancipate and free, after my decease, negro woman Hannah. To brother Hezekiah Magruder and his three children Daniel and George Magruder and Ann, wife of Jonah Harding ...
Exr: Hezekiah Magruder
Wit: Benjamin Harris, James Hickman, John Cooper
(Hezekiah Magruder refuses executorship; Daniel Magruder named administrator with will attached)
[Edward Talbott, of Calvert Co., Md., will probated Frederick Co., Va., 9 Feb 1778/ 2 Apr 1793. Archibald Edmundson m Nancy Wrenn 29 Oct 1789; Thomas Edmundson m Ann Cambell 16 Mar 1786; Samuel Nichols m Ann Edmondson 28 Apr 1795; Fdk.Co.Marrs. The Magruder family left records in Prince George's Co., Md.; also Colonial records in Calvert Co., Md., of Edmundson, Harding and Magruder families.] (p.520-522)

JONES, JAMES
Account current. 1797/ 1 Apr 1799
Examiners: Matthew Wright, George Blackmore, Charles Smith
(p. 522-523)

RENNER, GEORGE
Inventory & Appraisal. 5 Aug 1800/ 1 Dec 1800
Appraisers: Joseph Snapp, Jonah Lupton, Henry Shultz, George Hite. (p. 524-526)

PARKINS, ISAAC
Appraisal. 18 Oct 1793/ 1 Dec 1800
Appraisers: William Hoge, Jacob Brbur(?), Casper Rinker, Walter Denny (p. 526-527)

THARP, ISAAC
Will. 1 Sep 1799/ 1 Oct 1800
Wife: Elizabeth
Children: Benjamin (oldest), John, Andrew, Isaac, Jane, Elizabeth, Mary and Sarah (under age)
To wife, her thirds, all personal estate, goods and chattels. To oldest son Benjamin, house with 38 acres of land adjoining; to sons John, Andrew, Isaac, remaining part of tract; to four daughters, land between Jacob Murra(?) and Leonard Weaver to be sold and money equally divided among them. Sons to pay daughters Ł 5 each when they come of age.
Wit: William Taylor, Simon Taylor, John Laney
Exrx: Wife Elizabeth
(Widow refused executorship; John Laney and Jesse Taylor named) (p. 527-528)

MITCHELL, CAREY (administration)
Account current. 6/11/1798-25 Sep 1800/ 6 Oct 1800
Balance due administrator, Ł 4.3.4.
Examiners: J. Milton, William Helm, William Davis (p. 529-530)

BRUCE, GEORGE
Appraisal. 27 Sep 1800/ 6 Oct 1800
Appraisers: Nathan Littler, Robert Hodge, Elijah Littler (p. 531-532)

WALKER, JAMES
Appraisal & Sale Account. July 1799-1 Sep 1800/ 1 Dec 1800
Appraisers: William Ball, Isaac Littler, Lewis Hoff
Among buyers: Rachel Walker

KLINE, ADAM
Will. 9 Dec 1799/ 1 Dec 1800
Children: Michael, John, Susannah wife of Henry Grever, Mary wife of Peter Gilhaus (dec'd), Barbara wife of Abraham Grapes (dec'd), Elizabeth Evans.
Other sons-in-law: Daniel Trout, Michael Ridenour, Jacob Lawyer
Brother: Jacob Kline
Sell all personal estate, lands and appurtenances at public auction, use resulting money as follows: To son-in-law Henry Grever and Susannah his wife, 2 shillings and no more; to son Michael Kline, 5 shillings curr. money and no more. Having heretofore lent and advanced to my son and sons-in-law sums stated, these amounts to be added to return from sale of estate and equally divided into eight parts to be given as follows: Six parts equally divided among son John Kline, sons-in-law Daniel Trout, Michael Ridenour, Jacob Lawyer, and daughters Mary Gilhaus and Barbara Grapes; one part to children of son Michael or survivors equally when they come of age or marry; one part to daughter Elizabeth Evans, abandoned by her husband, Ł 10 annually to be delivered until she has received her share.
Exr: Brother Jacob Kline and Andrew Redd
Wit: John L. Woodcock, Jacob Belin, Peter Helphenstine
Sec: Andrew Redd, $10,000
(Jacob Kline refused executorship)
[Barbara Clyne m Abraham Grapes 19 May 1792; Fdk.Co.Marrs.] (p. 557-558)

ORNDORFF, JOHN
Appraisal. 1 Dec 1800
Appraisers: Michael White, Philip P. Bucher, William Touchstone
(p. 559-561)

BROWN, RICHARD
Appraisal & Sale Acct. 20 Jan 1795 - 18 Dec 1799/ 2 Dec 1800
Appraisers: John Bogan, George Brown, Abel Janney
Examiner: James B. Murray (p. 561-566)

GREENLEE, ELIZABETH
Will. 5 Sep 1800/ 1 Dec 1800
Children: David, Elizabeth
Gr. son: John Greenlee, son of daughter Elizabeth Greenlee
To daughter Elizabeth Greenlee, wearing apparel, beds, bedding and household furnishings of all kinds, also all my share of livestock, all cash, bonds and notes found at my decease, except: To son David Greenlee, bond of Ł 37.10.0 on Thomas Jones bequeathed to me by my deceased husband, John Greenlee. To grandson John Greenlee, son of daughter Elizabeth Greenlee, Ł 10 Va. curr., to be put at interest until of age.
Exrs: Friends Joseph Carter, John Jones
Wit: Mary Harvey, Jane Harvey (p. 566-567)

SHAVER/SHEAVER, CHRISTIAN
Will. 22 Feb 1800/ 5 Jan 1801
Brother: Martin
Bro. Martin's children: Daniel, Robanna, Catherine, Jacob, Bittsey, Peter, John, George, Sarrah
Brother's wife: Elizabeth
Legatee: Lydia Pearce
To brother Martin, one acre and better, grain in the ground; to Martin's wife Elizabeth, my beef in sale; to Martin's son Daniel, Ł 50 at age 21; To Martin's other eight children as they come of age, boys at 21, girls at 18, balance both real and personal. To Lydia Pearce, the third for rent which Martin is to pay her. Executors to pay legacies from collections due me and sale of estate not willed. Also, Ł 0.15.0 payment for burial in graveyard at plantation of Lake George (Price?)
Exrs: Brother Martin Shaver, Daniel Thornburg
Wit: Joseph Harsha, Catherine Sheaver
(Noted in margin: Corrections made from original by County Clerk 3 May 1944.) (p. 567-569)

GREENLEE, JOHN
Greenlee's Division. 28 Apr 1800/ 5 Jan 1801
Estate of John Greenlee devised by last will to wife Elizabeth, son David and daughter Elizabeth, and appointed executors William Bowen and Meredith Helm, "but the witnesses thereto being removed to so great a distance it appears difficult to bring them to court for proof thereof," and heirs being satisfied with terms of the will, Elizabeth, David and Elizabeth, Jr., mutually agree that William Bowen and Meredith Helm proceed to a division as if duly authorized by law. They divide as follows: To widow Elizabeth Greenlee, all cash on hand, bonds, notes, furniture and half the stock except that to David. To David Greenlee, 75+ acres, 3 head cattle, 4 sheep, fruit of 5 rows of apple trees on west side of orchard, for 8 years ... half the farming utensils. To Elizabeth Greenlee, Jr., remainder and western part of said tract, 59+ acres, more or less, half the stock except David's part, and half the farming utensils. David permitted to take extra partition fence between premises and enjoined to keep fence in repair during term of lease. David may also live in house he occupies till Christmas next, and stock of both families to run together as usual til next fall. Agreement authorized and

ratified by heirs 28 Apr 1800; recorded 5 Jan 1801.
Wit: William McPherson, Peter McMurray (p. 569-570)

GREENLEE, ELIZABETH
Appraisal. 8 Dec 1800/ 5 Jan 1801
Appraisers: Peter McMurray, Mabra Madden, Gordon Rowland (p. 571-573)

LONG, PETER
Appraisal & Sale Acct. 5 Jan 1801/ 5 Jan 1801
Appraisers: Jacob Morris(?), Jacob Leonard, Jacob Lawyer
Among buyers: Elizabeth Long (p. 573-576)

MITCHELL, CAREY
Appraisal. 2 Feb 1801 (p. 577-579)

PARKINS, JOSEPH
Will. 20 day 3d mo 1800/ 3 Feb 1801
Wife: Susannah
Children: Alfred (under 10), Maria (under 18), Sarah
Father: Isaac Parkins
To wife, undivided half of 500-acre farm (Paddy's Pond) conveyed to me by David Brown; other half to her during her life; also new frame house I live in and lot it stands on; also meadow and orchard lots as now enclosed. To daughter Sarah, one fourth tract I live on and one fourth mill &c, possession at age 18. To daughter Maria, remaining fourth of tract I live on and one fourth mill property, all undivided, possession at 18, the whole tract of 25 acres conveyed to me by my father, foregoing subject to dividend devised to wife during her widowhood. At wife's decease, half of Paddy's Pond farm to surviving children, equally divided. Encumbrance on wife's land to be released and annual rent payment to be made to my father. When son Alfred is 10 years old, executors and his mother to consult on his education. Children to pay proportionate share of debts as they take possession. Executors may give individual bond.
Exrs: Jonas Potts, Joseph Steer (Sep. bonds, $10,000 each)
Wit: Isaac Hollingsworth, Thomas Hollingsworth, Farling Ball. (p. 579-582)

MILLER, RICHARD
Appraisal. 12 Jan 1801/ 3 Feb 1801
Appraisers: Joseph Fawcett, Jacob Lenard (Leonard?), Goldsmith Chandlee (p. 583-586)

SETTLE, JOHN
Will. 10 Nov 1800/ 2 Feb 1801
Wife: Elizabeth
Children: Vincent, John, Edward, Tracey, Margaret, Elizabeth Williams
All perishable part of estate to be sold immediately after decease, and if inadequate to pay debts executors to sell lease of land, 200 acres, where I live. After satisfaction of debts, to wife during widowhood one third of all personal estate for life, half of lot and house I live in, for life. After her death, to son Vincent; other half to son John. Covenants of lease not to be violated by working more than four persons in the 200 acres. Remaining personal estate to be divided among four children - John, Tracey, Margaret and Vincent, except - to son Edward and daughter Elizabeth Williams, each 3 shillings.
Exr: Son John Settle
Wit: L. G. Settle, Matthew Maddox, Rachel Maddox. (p. 586-588)

McKEE/MACKY, ROBERT
Will. 4 June 1792; Adm 1 Dec 1800/ 6 Apr 1801
Wife: Susannah
Children: William, John, Robert, Joseph, Bartholomew, Mary Hock, Margaret Fisher, Jane, Anne, Elizabeth, Sarah, unnamed infant. "Old and weak." To son William, small parcel land on Opekon Creek adjoining John Hott; to sons Robert, Joseph and Bartholomew plantation I live on, divided equally, first of age to possess it without interest, giving suitable education to youngest; Joseph to enjoy half at age 21 until youngest is of age. To son John and daughter Mary Hock, each 5 shillings Va. curr.; to daughter Margaret Fisher, 3 shillings Va. curr; to daughters Jane, Anne, Elizabeth, Sarah, and infant, each Ł 10 Va. curr. Exrs: Susannah McKee, Benjamin McDonald. Letters of administration with will annexed
Wit: James McGinnis, Thomas Taylor, Robert Lockhart
[Margaret Mackey m Thomas Fisher 4 Dec 1789; Robert McKee m Susannah Dalby 23 Jan 1793; Robert McKee m Jane Cather 5 Sep 1793, Joseph Cather bondsman; Fdk.Co.Marrs.] (p. 588-589)

PAINTER, JOHN
Will. 22d da 7th mo 1799/ 6 Apr 1801
Wife: Susannah
Children: Robert, David, Jacob, John, Susannah(reference to eight children but only five named)
Grandson: Robert Painter
To wife during widowhood, third part movable estate, dwelling house and plantation I live on. At her death, personal estate to be divided among children. To son Robert, plantation; to grandson Robert Painter, gristmill and sawmill on above plantation with water privileges; to son David, 20 shillings; to son Jacob, land on east side of Crooked Run where he lives, part of above plantation bounded by Isaac's, Martin's and Oglesby's lines. To son John, part of tract on Stephensburg Run, 167 acres, granted by proprietor's office. Son Robert to pay brother David Ł 20 four years after my decease. Out of movable estate, son Robert and daughter Susannah to have share equal to other married children. Remainder to be divided among my eight children at my decease.
Exrs: Wife Susannah, sons Jacob and John
Wit: Isaac Painter, Benjamin Ramy, Abraham Painter(p. 590-592)

SMITH, MICHAEL
Will. 28 Jan 1801/ 8 Apr 1801
Wife: Mary
Children: George, Nicholas, Jacob, Margaret, Barbary Everheart (Everhart), Eve
Gr. ch: Children of son Jacob
To wife for life, Specific items of furniture, 1 mare, saddle and bridle, 1 cow. After her death, above items to be equally divided among my children and grandchildren, as follows: To son George, $100 from sale of personal estate; to children and grandchildren, Margaret, George, Nicholas, Barbary, Eve, son Jacob's children, personal estate equally divided. To daughter Barbary, tract where I live, 181 acres, she and husband Michael Everheart to pay Ł 133 curr. money in Ł 20 installments to each legatee - Margaret, George, Nicholas, Eve, son Jacob's children (one legacy among them). Wife Mary to live with daughter Barbary and her husband in the house I now live in during her natural life and to have wheat now on hand of old crop, also crop now growing on meeting house lot, for her support in ensuing year. Thereafter, each legatee, Michael Everheart excepted, to furnish her with five bushels good wheat or money in lieu thereof for her support each year during her natural life;

Barbary and husband to furnish wife forage for horse and cow during her natural life, in lieu of wheat, for her support. My lot in Berryville to be sold and money divided equally among children and grandchildren.
Exrs: Friends George Smith and Peter Hunsicker
Wit: Bartholomew Smith, George Blakemore
Sec: Robert Gray, Bartholomew Smith, $3,000.
[Barbara Smith m Michael Everhart 24 Oct 1786, Fdk.Co.Marrs.]
(p. 592-594

DONALDSON, JOHN
Appraisal. 20 Apr 1797/ 7 Apr 1801
Appraisers: John Littler, Jonas Likins, James Bruce
(p. 594-599)

FROST, WILLIAM
Will. 16 June 1797. Adm 6 July 1801/ 31 Aug 1801
Dau: Frances Hickman alias Frost
Nephew: Isaac McCormick
To daughter Frances Hickman alias Frost, all tract in Frederick County on Long Marsh, 287-3/4 acres, on which I live, conveyed to me by Martin Baker and Elizabeth his wife, of Hanover County, by deed of bargain and sale on 17 Sep 1781. Frances Frost Hickman is base born child that I begot of then Elizabeth Hickman, widow of Isaac Hickman, deceased, which said Elizabeth is now wife of Capt. Peter Rust of Frederick County. "To me the said Frances hath behaved as a dutiful and affectionate child and can not be dearer than she is." To nephew Isaac McCormick, son of Francis McCormick, one third part of tract in Frederick County on Babbs Run, 133-1/3 acres, and £ 50 payable out of my personal estate. All remainder to my daughter Frances. My negro woman Judy to be discharged from servitude, manumitted at my decease. Negroes Tom and Jack to be bound out to good trades by executors until 21, then to be manumitted.
Exrs: John Milton, Archibald Magill, who are also appointed guardian to daughter Frances until 21 or married
Wit: John Butler, Henry J. Luddington, Elijah Quinn.
(p. 599-602)

FROST, WILLIAM
Request for Attestation. 1 June 1801
Request of Commonwealth of Va. to Mayor of City of Baltimore, Md., to procure attestation of signing and witnessing of will of William Frost by Henry G. Luddington, by Clerk of Frederick Co., Va., Court. (p. 603-605)

FROST, WILLIAM
Affidavit of witness. 6 June 1801
Certification of attestation as witness by Henry G. Luddington. Exrs. refused to act. Letters of administration issued with will attached to Bushrod Taylor. (p. 605)

DAVIS, JAMES
Appraisal. 23 Feb 1801/ 7 Apr 1801
Appraisers: Elijah Littler, David Ridgway, Abraham Branson
(p. 605-606)

KERLIN, JOHN
Sale Account. 28 Mar 1801/ 7 Apr 1801
Admr: David Ross (p. 606-607)

CARLIN, JOHN (KERLIN?)
Appraisal. 7 Apr 1801
Appraisers: Daniel Ridgway, George Bruce, John Cowgill
(p. 607-608)

AID, JOHN
Appraisal. 23 May 1796/ 6 Apr 1801
Appraisers: Charles Ferguson, William Hendry, John Smith
(p. 608-609)

PUGH, ANN
Will. 21 da of 2d mo 1797/ 4 May 1801
Children: Jane Denny, Elizabeth Jay, Ann Dillon, Rachael Jenkins
Son-in-law: Walter Denny
Debts to be paid by Walter Denny. To Walter Denny and Jane, his wife, tract where I live, during their lives, and after decease to heirs of Jane Denny. To Jane Denny, my black horse. To daughters Elizabeth Jay and Ann Dillon, each, $5 to be paid by Jane and Walter Denny. To daughter Rachael Jenkins a moiety or part of tract adjoining B. Fisher and John McCoole for which I have Walter Denny's title bond
Exrs: Son-in-law Walter Denny and Jane Denny
Wit: John McCoole, William Adams, Jacob Taylor (p. 609-611)

CLYNE/KLYNE, ADAM
Appraisal & Sale Acct. 4 Dec-12 Dec 1800/ 4 May 1801
Appraisers: Elisha Phelps, William McLeod, David Carlyle
(p. 611-618)

BRUCE, GEORGE
Acct. Settlement. 15 Nov 1800/ 20 Apr 1801
Named in settlement: Rachael Bruce (p. 618)

POE, BALTZER, of Corp. of Winchester
Will. 16 Mar 1800/ 1 July 1801
Children: John, Jacob, Catharine Brown wife of Jesse Brown, Barbara Slote wife of John Slote
Gr. ch: Children of Barbara and John Slote
All estate to be sold by executors at public auction and divided into four equal parts, to be distributed as follows: To son, John Poe; to son Jacob Poe; to daughter Catharine Brown wife of Jesse Brown. Fourth part in trust by executors for daughter Barbara Slote wife of John Slote, for her use, and any residue remaining at her death to be divided among her children when aged 21. Also, to daughter Barbara, $1.
Exrs: Son Jacob Poe, son-in-law Jesse Brown
Wit: Obed Waite, James B. Galloway, William Brown
[Kitty Poe m Jesse Brown 20 Nov 1791; Jacob Poe m Jane Kidd 16 Dec 1792; John Poe m Catherine Borders 26 Nov 1804. Fdk.Co. Marrs.] (p. 619-621)

BERRY, JOHN, JR.
Appraisal. 6 July 1801
Appraisers: George Keeter, Evin Cowgill, Joseph Wall
(p. 621-623)

BALL, CAPTAIN WILLIAM
Sale Account. 19 Dec 1796/ 6 July 1801
Exrs: Thomas Parker, L. Butler
Among buyers: Mrs. Drucilla Ball, Miss Judith Ball

HOTZEPILLAR, STEPHEN (HOTZENPILLER)
Account.
Exr: Vallentine Switzer
Legacies paid: Nicolas Kerns, Elizabeth Kerns, Mary Kerns, Magdalin Kerns, Frederick Kerns, Jacob Kerns, John Kerns, surviving heirs of Catharine Kerns; Rudolf Bumgardner, Rebecca Bumgardner; Peter Switzer; Anna Maria Shoup; Sarah Coffman; Stephen Hotzenpillar, Jacob Hotzenpillar; Susannah Seigler; Elizabeth Hoover; Susannah Hicklind; Jacob Hoster; Abraham

Bernard (wife's legacy); Mary Switzer. Some vouchers found irregular by court. Power of attorney from several heirs to Nicholas Kerns assigned by Mary Kerns, Magdaline Kerns and Frederick Kerns before magistrates of Greenbrier County, Va.
Examiners: W. Harrison, Goldsmith Chandlee (p. 628-630)

PAINTER, JOHN
Appraisal. 16 Apr 1801/ 31 Aug 1801
Appraisers: Moses McKay, John Haines, Jacob McKay, Jr.
(p. 630-634)

BALL, WILLIAM
Memo of valuation of property. 16 Dec 1796/ 15 Aug 1801
Appraisers: George Eckridge, John Hieronimus, William Cook

DEAL, JAMES
Account Current. 30 Aug 1801
Exr: Jeremiah Leach (p. 638-639)

BELL, ANTHONY
Will. 20 July 1801/ 31 Aug 1801
Wife: Mary
Son: James George Bell
Mother: Eisley Bell of Louisa County
Brothers: George, Nathan, Ashby, Pleasant
To wife, best bed, furniture, table, kitchen furniture, three chairs, a cow, one third of personalty. To son, James George Bell, all remaining property. If he dies before age 21, to my mother, Eisley Bell of Louisa Co. Should she also be dead, to my four brothers equally.
Exrs: Jonathan Lovett and John McCoole, to serve on individual bonds.
Wit: Thomas Mitchell, Lewis McCoole, Jesse Pugh, Jr.
[Anthony Bell m Mary McCool, 29 May 1800, Fdk. Co. Marrs.]
(p. 640-641)

McDONEGALL, THOMAS
Will. 18 Dec 1800/ 31 Aug 1801
Wife: Catharine
To wife, house and lot and all pertaining thereto; all personal estate and any other property I have claim to now or hereafter.
Wit: E. Smith (p. 641-642

FRYE, CHRISTOPHER, SR. (of Winchester Town)
Will. 13 Feb 1801/ 31 Aug 1801
Wife: Unnamed
Children: Christopher, Jr., eldest, Michael, Joseph, youngest (under age), Polly Martin
Son-in-law: James V. (Ramey?) Singleton
To wife, house and half of lot we now live on and 5-acre out lot (290 acres), 1 cow, rents for her support for life. To Christopher Frye, Jr., eldest son, to live with parents and care for mother. To son-in-law James V. (Ramey?) Singleton and daughter Polly, 500 acres at Sleepy Creek and house and lot southwest of town. To son Michael, 200 acres on drain of Opekon and 200 acres by survey in town of Monongalia; half lot adjoining Christian Schar, corner lot fronting Cameron St. on tract the market house is in. To son Joseph, youngest son, two tracts on drains of Babb's Run, in all 425 acres; also this house and lot, at decease of self and wife. When of age, full lot at west side of town, No. 79, if not sold. If sold, Joseph to have half the 5-acre out lot in place of Lot 79. When child comes of age, to take such property as not needed for aforementioned support.
Exrs: Christopher Frye, Jr., Peter Senseney, Sr., and "my wife"
Wit: Geo. McCord, Isaac O---, John Haymaker. (p. 642-645)

CUNNINGHAM, JOHN
Will. May 1796/ 31 Aug 1801
Wife: Elizabeth
Children: John, Charles, Thomas
To wife during widowhood, all lands, lots, freehold and lease, all stock (horses, cows, sheep, hogs), implements, household furniture, etc. If she marries, children to be bound out, all estate sold at public auction and funds put at interest, to be equally divided when youngest is of age. If wife marries, sons John and Charles to be bound out as they choose.
Exrs: Wife Elizabeth, son Thomas
Wit: James Brown, William Brown (p. 645-646)

McKEE, ROBERT
Appraisal. 1 Sep 1801
Appraisers: Robert Lockhart, William Gossett, Jr., Jonathin Lovett (p. 647)

EVANS, ELIZABETH
Will. 17 Jan 1801/ proved 6 Jul & 31 Aug 1801/ 1 Sep 1801
To Robert Roach, use of all my negroes after my death; beds and furniture, all household and kitchen furniture; house and lot in Town of Winchester. To Rebecky Roach, wife of Robert, all my clothing.
Exrs: Robert Roach, Abraham Woodrow
Wit: Abraham Woodrow, John Adams
Abraham Woodrow refused executorship. Thomas Evans, husband of decedent, contested recording of will; appealed to next District Court held in Winchester) (p. 647-651)

DONALDSON, JOHN
Accounting. 1795-12 Sep 1801/ 5 Oct 1801
Exr: John McDonald; due from estate Ł 693.11.8
Examiners: P. Smith, Meredith Helm (p. 652-655)

DEAN, RICHARD, of Prince Edward Co., now of Frederick County
Will. 31 Dec 1799/ 30 Nov 1801
Niece: Sarah Woodcock
Husband of niece: James Powers
To James Powers, who married my niece Sarah Woodcock, Ł 400, one mare in my possession, bed and furniture.
Exrs: Friend William Connagy and James Powers
Wit: Archibald Brownley and Samuel Kercheval
(William Connagy refused executorship) (p. 655-657)

STEELE, RICHARD
Appraisal. 6 Dec 1800/ 1 Oct 1801
Appraisers: James Scott, Francis Barker, Levi Smith (p. 657-659)

MOFFETT, JOHN
Account current. 6 Oct 1798-5 Sep 1801/ 30 Nov 1801
Admr: Francis Ash

WHITE, JACOB
Will. 9 Sep 1800/ 30 Nov 1801
Wife: Agnes
Brothers: Michael; half-brother John Shotter(?)
Nephew: John White, son of Michael
Niece: Abigail, "sister's daughter"
Sister: Mary White
Legatees: John Drake; also about seven brothers and sisters of John White, son of Michael, unnamed;
To wife, plantation during widowhood. If she marries, one third of plantation and mansion for life; also two thirds of all house-

hold goods, kitchen furniture, her choice after appraisement, her own property; half stock of horses, third stock of cattle, third stock of sheep and hogs, half of grain now in ground; wagon and farming utensils for plantation use, and at her decease any remainder to be sold. To brother Michael White's son John White (after wife's decease), all the plantation where I now live, 226 acres, John White to pay brothers and sisters Ł 10 annually, payable after wife's decease and he comes to age, in order of age, eldest first, amounting to about Ł 70. To sister Mary White, Ł 20 Va. curr. to be paid within 1-1/2 years after my decease. To John Drake, Ł 15, deducting Ł 7 for price of a horse due me, Ł 8 balance to be paid within three years of my decease. To brother Michael White and to half-brother John Shotter(?), $10 within two years of my decease. To my sister's daughter Abigail, Ł 2, within four years; negro girl to be sold at public sale after my decease, plus rest of movable estate not willed. Balance after payment of debts to widow. If widow marries, the two-thirds of real estate to be rented and money equally divided among brother's and sister's children as they come of age. Also, all farming utensils and stock to be divided among them. If widow dies before John White comes of age, plantation to be rented and money divided among above named children.
Exrs: John Fry, Joseph Snapp, wife Agnes
Wit: Jonas Lupton, John Cackley, Jacob Frye
(Widow refused executorship) (p. 663-666)

SEABERT, JACOB
Will. 20 Jan 1801/ 30 Nov 1801
Wife: Mary
Children: Mentioned; only one named Elizabeth Orndorff
To wife, old mansion house to live in; all plantation where I now live during life; all movable estate and all lands and tenements during life. After her decease, plantation, 202 acres, to be sold and debts paid, balance to be divided among children except daughter Elizabeth Orndorff who shall have only 5 shillings. Movable estate to be sold at wife's decease and money divided among all children except daughter Elizabeth "to whom I have bequeathed 5 shillings from an opinion that she had her greater, or at least what I think she is in justice entitled to, for certain reasons not necessary to insert at large." After my decease, land in Hampshire County, 250 acres, to be sold at private or public sale if not disposed of in my lifetime, monies to be equally divided among all my children except Elizabeth Orndorff.
Exrs: Mordecai Bean, James Bean
Wit: Jona(?) Lupton, Michael White, John Cackley
[Elizabeth Seabert m Philip Orndorf 15 Oct 1782, Fdk.Co.Marrs.]
(p. 666-668)

SMITH, JEREMIAH
Account & Settlement. 21 Nov 1801/ 30 Nov 1801
Exrs: Samuel Smith, Jeremiah Smith
Examiners: Jonathan Lovett, Joseph Baker, Benjamin McDonald, Joseph Baley (p. 669-670)

NICKLIN, JOSEPH
Appraisal. 1 Dec 1801
Appraisers: Francis Stribling, William Talbott, Levi Smith
(p. 670-673)

LARRICK, CASPER
Appraisal. 18 Sep 1801/ 3 Nov 1801
Appraisers: Michael White, Mordecai Bean, Enoch Marple

SHERRIFE, SARAH
Appraisal. 18 Feb 1800/ 30 Nov 1801
Appraisers: William Bayles, Henry Bayles, Martin Cartmell
(p. 675-676)

SMITH, MICHAEL
Appraisal. 18 Apr 1801/ 4 Jan 1802
Appraisers: John Lindsey, John Smith, George Hollingsworth
(p. 676-679)

KENDRICK, ABRAHAM
Appraisal & Sale Acct. 27 Sep 1800/ 4 Jan 1802
Appraisers: William McLeod, John Mason, Daniel Mitinger
(p. 679-686)

HOLMES, ELIZABETH
Orphan of Joseph Holmes
Guardianship Account. 1792-1798/ 4 Jan 1802
Guardian: Rebecca Holmes
Examiners: Elizabeth McGuire, Edward McGuire, Jr.(p. 1-6

HOLMES, REBECCA
Orphan of Joseph Holmes
Guardianship Account. 1792-1798/ 4 Jan 1802
Guardian: Rebecca Holmes
Examiners: Daniel Conrad, Rebecca Conrad (p. 6-11)

HOLMES, NANCY
Orphan of Joseph Holmes
Guardianship Account. 1792-1798/ 4 Jan 1802
Guardian: Rebecca Holmes
Examiners: G. Samuel Dowdall, Abraham Neill (p. 11-13)

HOLMES, NANCY
Guardianship Account. 1798-1801
Proven by Joseph Longacre 26 Oct 1801
Examiners: J. Peyton, W. Davison, 3 Dec 1801 (p. 13-15)

HOLMES, GERTRUDE E.
Orphan of Joseph Holmes
Guardianship Account. 1792-1798/ 4 Feb 1802
Guardian: Rebecca Holmes
Examiners: G. Samuel Dowdall, Abraham Neill (p. 15-17)

HOLMES, GERTRUDE E.
Orphan of Joseph Holmes
Guardianship Account. 1798-1801/ 16 Jan 1802
Guardian: Rebecca Holmes
Proven by Joseph Longacre 4 Jan 1802
Examiners: J. Peyton, W. Davison (p. 18-20)

HOLMES, JOSEPH, JR.
Orphan of Joseph Holmes
Guardianship Account. 1792-1798/ 4 Jan 1802
Guardian: Rebecca Holmes (p. 21)

HOLMES, JOSEPH, JR.
Orphan of Joseph Holmes
Guardianship Account. 1798-1801/ 4 Jan 1802
Guardian: Rebecca Holmes
Proven by Joseph Longacre
Examiners: J. Peyton, W. Davison (p. 22)

HOLMES, ANDREW HUNTER
Orphan of Joseph Holmes
Guardianship Account 1792-1798/ 4 Jan 1802
Guardian: Rebecca Holmes
Examiners: G. Samuel Dowdall, J.P., Abraham Neill(p. 23-24)

HOLMES, ANDREW HUNTER
Orphan of Joseph Holmes
Guardianship Account. 1798-1801/ 4 Jan 1802
Proven 26 Oct 1801 before Joseph Longacre, J.P.
Examiners: J. Peyton, W. Davison (p. 24-25)

ROWLAND (BOWLAND?), GORDON
Will. 20 Dec 1801/ 1 Feb 1802
Wife: Elizabeth
Children: Sarah, Samuel, Rebecca, Mary, Elizabeth, Lucy, Benjamin, Gabriel

Brother: Thomas Rowland
To wife, all estate, personal and real. At her death, all to be sold and monies equally divided among surviving children or their heirs.
To son Samuel, one-year-old mare colt
Exrs: Wife Elizabeth, son Samuel, brother Thomas
Wit: Rezin Duvall, William Jackson, Joseph Carter(p. 26)

BEAN, RICHARD
Appraisal. 1 Feb 1802
Appraisers: Reuben Clarke, Charles Buckley, Peter Helphenstine (p. 27)

COCHRAN, WILLIAM
Account for land sold by exrs of dec'd. 2 Feb 1802
"137 acres to William Cochran"
Examiners: James Cochran, William Cochran, Thomas Curlett (p. 27-28)

COCHRAN, WILLIAM
Account current. 1 Feb 1802/ 2 Feb 1802
Legatees of estate: James Cochran, William Cochran married to Rachel Curlett, Thomas Curlett, Benjamin Langley married to Martha Coc hran, William Langley married to Elizabeth Cochran, Richard Brookover married to Mary Cochran; estate share to ward, Rachel Brookover; Margaret Calvert.
[James Cochran m Mary Hogan 24 Sep 1788; William Cochran m Rachel Curlett 27 Sep 1789; Martha Cochran m Benjamin Langley 21 Sep 1790; Agnes Cochran m Joseph Langley Dec 3, 1795; Susannah Cochran m Thomas Curlett 21 Sep 1790; Fdk.Co.Marrs.]
Examiners: David Conrad, Cornelius Baldwin (p. 29-30)

TALBOTT, BENJAMIN
Appraisal ordered Apr 1791/ 2 Feb 1802
Appraisal of property in Loudoun Co., recorded 9 Apr 1802
Appraisers: Hugh Kennedy, William McLeod, John Milburn (p. 30-32)

TALBOTT, BENJAMIN
Sale Account. 19 Apr 1791/ 6 Apr 1802
Admr: Elisha Phelps
Buyer: Sarah Talbott (p. 32-35)

NOBLE, GEORGE
Appraisal. 17 Feb 1801
Appraisers: J. Milton, John Forster, William Taylor
Addition to Appraisement, 20 Jan 1802
Appraisers: J. Milton, George B. Norkenson(?), John Forster (p. 35-37)

NOBLE, GEORGE
Sale Account Memo; approved & recorded 5 Apr 1803
Admrs: Mary Ann Noble and Eli Swearingen, certify property sold before appraisement by agreement, and appraisers did not attend sale to ascertain value. Signed by Henry Stubblefield; witnessed by John Noble (p. 38-39)

MYERS, STEPHEN, ORPHAN
Guardianship Account. 5 Apr 1802
William Elsia replaces Jacob Lenard as guardian and acknowledges receipt of Ł 30.3.8 estate balance, by court order.
Examiners: J. B. Feldin, William McLeod (p. 40)

LIKENS, HENRY
Appraisal. 10 Dec 1801/ 5 Apr 1802
Appraisers: Joshua Cooke, Nathan Littler, Thomas Lloyd (p. 40-41)

BELL, ANTHONY
Appraisal. 5 Feb 1802/ 5 Apr 1802
Appraisers: Josiah Harding, James Scarff, William Talbott
(p. 41-47)

WHITE, JOSEPH and NATHANIEL
Orphans of Thomas White
Guardianship Account. 15 Mar 1797/ 6 Apr 1802
Guardian: Thomas Brown
Examiners: Joseph Tidball, Robert Mackey, 2 June 1798
(p. 47-48)

GOOSE, GEORGE
Estate Settlement ordered Jan 1802/ 6 Sep 1802
Exrs: Nicholas DeLong, George Goose
Examiners: N. Samuels, Conrad Tebo, 25 May 1802 (p. 48)

PICKERING, SAMUEL
Inventory & Appraisal. 6 da 9 mo 1800/ 6 Sep 1802
Appraisers: Isaac Steer, Joshua Lupton, Nathan Lupton
(p. 49)

PICKERING, SAMUEL
Sale Account. 8 da 9 mo 1800/ 6 Sep 1802
Submitted for recording by Samuel and Jacob Pickering
Among buyers: Hannah Pickering, John Pickering, Jonathan Pickering, Jonas Pickering, Jacob Pickering, Samuel Pickering
(p. 49-53)

ROWLAND, GORDON
Appraisal. 13 Feb 1802/ 6 Sep 1802
Appraisers: George Hollingsworth, Henry Langes(?), Peter McMurray (p. 53-54)

HOLLIDAY, ROBERT
Will. 30 July 1802/ 6 Sep 1802
Mother: Unnamed
Brothers: William, Elijah, Alexander
Sister: Unnamed
To brother William during mother's life, Round Hill tract near Winchester in trust for use of mother, rents and profits to be received by her, "not by her present husband or to his use," to be disposed of "only by an instrument under her hand attested by two credible witnesses and not otherwise." If sale of personal property is insufficient to pay debts, sell lands on Cumberland River or elsewhere than Virginia, also houses and lots in Town of Bath, Berkeley County, Pine Hill land adjoining Joseph Baker. Residue to be equally divided among brothers and sister. After mother's death, Round Hill tract to then surviving brothers and sister, share and share alike, except brother Alexander is to have two shares. To brother William, $284 out of money due me from Robert Lockhart, to be used for payment of my debts; balance due from Lockhart, and any other due me, to brother William to hold in trust for mother, to be paid her and not her husband or his heirs. Father devised me 1500 acres of military land in Kentucky, which would leave only 200 for brother Elijah, a deficiency of 300 out of the 2,000 acres then divided. Elijah to take full 500 acres, attaching loss to my legacy and not to his.
Exr: Archibald Magill
Wit: John Dougherty, Abijah Rigdon, Charles Hoyle, Jr.
Archibald Magill refused executorship
William Holliday, Jr., granted letters of administration with will annexed. [William Holliday, father of Robert, left will dated 17 June 1790, probated 6 Sep 1790, naming wife Jane, sons Robert, William and Elijah, and a daughter, Jane. Son Alexander is not named. Jane Holliday m Joseph Caldwell 18 Dec 1792, but Jane could have been either mother or daughter; Fdk.Co.Marrs.]
(p. 55-56)

BERRY, ENOCH
Will. 8 Jan 1800/ 6 Sep 1802
Wife: Nancy
"To wife Nancy, 'faithful companion,' all property."
Wit: William Helm, Jr., James Hathaway (p. 57)

BROWNLEY, JOHN
Will. 12 May 1801/ 6 Sep 1802
Wife: Betty
Grandson: William Brownley
To grandson William Brownley Ł 500 in specie when aged 20. If deceased before 20, money to return to estate.
Wit: Robert Page, Wyatt Whitehead, William Carnagy
Betty Brownley, widow, granted letters of administration with will annexed, no executor being named'
Sec: Mandley Taylor, William Carnagy, $30,000. (p. 57)

WHITE, JACOB
Appraisal & Sale Account. 4-10 Dec 1801/ 6 Sep 1802
Appraisers: Moses Russell, John Cooper, Elias Kackley
Exrs: John Frye and Joseph Snapp (sold to the highest bidder on 10 Dec 1801)
Examiner: Jonathan Lupton
Among buyers: Agnes White (p. 58-64)

BROWNLEY, JOHN
Appraisal. 16 Sep 1802/ 4 Oct 1802
Appraisers: Richard Meade, William David, Samuel Kercheval, Edward Howe (p. 64-69)

McCOWN, JOHN
Appraisal & Sale Account. 5 Dec 1802/ 6 Dec 1802
Appraisers: George Ritenour, Joseph Fawcett, (?) Graff
Admr: Jacob Leonard
Among buyers: Mrs. McCown, Margaret McCown (p. 69-73)

HENCH, CHARLES FREDERICK (of Corporation of Winchester)
Will. 29 July 1801/ 7 Dec 1802
Wife: Elizabeth Hench
Legatee: Mary Houghman daughter of George Houghman
To wife Elizabeth, 1/2 acre lot in Woods Addition to Corporation of Winchester, No. 23; also all personal estate. To Mary Houghman, daughter of George Houghman, one house Bible and hymn book
Exrs: Wife and Conrad Kreps
Wit: Godfrey Miller, George Wolfe, Conrad Kremer
[Charles Fred Hench m Elizabeth Toomy 28 Oct 1797; Fdk.Co.Marrs.] (p. 74)

PICKERING, SAMUEL
Account. 1800/ 6 Dec 1802
Jonathan Lupton filed for exrs; balance Ł 82.7.10-1/2
Examiners: Jona Lupton, Joseph Longacre (p. 75)

COOPER, JEREMIAH
Appraisal. 21 Oct 1802/ 6 Dec 1802
Appraisers: Jacob Danner, John Senseny, Abraham Niswanger (p. 76-77)

COMBS, MARQUIS C.
Will. 28 July 1802/ 6 Dec 1802
Brothers: John Holden Combs, William Combs, Fielding Combs, Lesly Combs, Samuel B. Combs
Nephew: Marquis Combs, Jr., son of Samuel B. Combs
Aunt: "Aunt Calmes"

To brother John H(olden) Combs, all property held in Virginia with one fourth part of land that I do or will hold (at Aunt Calmes death) in Kentucky. Also all monies due me in this state. To brothers William, Fielding and Lesly, each one fourth of land in Kentucky. If they die without heirs, to be divided among survivors and their children. To Marquis Combs, Jr., son of Samuel B. Combs, money owed me by Samuel B. Combs. If Marquis dies, then to John Hoiden Combs.
Exrs: Brothers John Holden Combs and Samuel B. Combs
Wit: Philip Smith, Daniel Pool (p. 77-78)

SANSBURY, WILLIAM
Will. 24 Aug 1797/ 6 Dec 1802
Daus: Linny, Nancy, Milly, Hanny
Grandson: Reason Randle
Legatee: Idie Reason Randle
To daughter Linny, cow, trunk, chest, mare Fanny, largest pot and pewter dish, 6 plates, all cups and saucers, earthen plates, two teapots, one coffeepot, corner cupboard, bed and furniture, punch bowl, teakettles, and other household items. To daughters Nancy, Milly and Hanny, specific pots, pewter, and other household items. To grandson Reason Randle, the heifer over the river, my bed and bedding. To Idie Reason Randle, my grey horse.
Exrx: Daughter Linny
Wit: Simson Fitch, Charles Cochran, Peter Speers (p. 78-79)

SAMPLE, SAMUEL
Account. 1786-Nov 1802/ 3 Jan 1803
Real estate, 500 acres, partly sold. William Patty, surviving executor, on 21 Aug 1792, settled estate with Elenor Sample, executrix and devisee.
Examiners: Cornelius Baldwin, Joseph Tidball (p. 80-81)

SWORDS, WILLIAM
Estate of James Simrall
Guardianship Account. 23 Apr 1796/ 3 Jan 1803
Examiners: Joseph Tidball, Cornelius Baldwin, 13 Sep 1802 (p. 81-83)

GARROT, JOHN
Appraisal. 28 Apr 1801/ 3 Jan 1803
Appraisers: Richard Briarly, John Self, Francis Ash (p. 83)

ALLENSWORTH, PHILIP
Appraisal. 28 Apr 1801/ 3 Jan 1803
Appraisers: William Headley, Richard Bryarly, Francis Ash

VANCE, SAMUEL
Appraisal. 12 Apr 1802/ 3 Jan 1803
Appraisers: William Chipley, Jonathan Brown, David Carlile, Samuel Kercheval (p. 84-86)

HOLMES, JOSEPH
Account. 1792-Nov 1802/ 31 Jan 1803
Admrs: Rebecca, Hugh and David Holmes
Examiners: Joseph Tidball, J. Peyton (p. 87-90)

GANDER, CASPER and MAXINE, his wife
Account & Settlement. 19 June 1793/ 31 Jan 1803
Admr: George Smith
Examiners: Charles Smith, George Blackmore, Bushrod Taylor (p. 90-92)

LYNN, GEORGE (of Winchester)
Will. 2 May 1802/ 31 Jan 1803
Wife: Anna Mariah

Children: George, John, Mary wife of John Fry, Henry, Daniel, Elizabeth wife of Jacob Fry
To wife, whole estate, real and personal, during life, to support her and my son George until he is 21 or qualified to be bound out as apprentice. If wife remarries, all property to be sold and money divided among children and wife. To son George, my clock. Executors to act with Adam Albert and Thomas Lewis relative to mill land, they to be trustees. One fourth acre to each child of lot adjoining Chissel or Mackey and Hoover. Henry, Daniel and George under 21. Land shares to be sold and money given to sons if they decide not to settle in Winchester.
Exrs: Wife Anna Mariah, son John, Conrad Crebs
Wit: Jacob Kiger, Isaac Busk
Sec: A. Magill, $5,000 (p. 92-94)

BRINKER, CATHERINE
Appraisal. 31 Jan 1803
Appraisers: R. Bowen, William Holliday, (last signature in German, illegible) (p. 95)

BRACKNEY, JOSEPH (dec'd 15 Dec 1802)
Nuncupative will. Recorded 31 Jan 1803
Wife: Rachel Brackney
Children: Mentioned, but unnamed
Statement by Ebenezer Haines: Two days before he died, the deceased told him he wished to leave all property to care of his wife to do with as she thought best, to have care of his children. One or both horses to be sold to pay debts. Statement by Patience Haines: Three or four days before his death, decedent told her he wished wife to have care and management of all his property and wanted horses sold. Statement of Jeremiah Basey: A few days before death, decedent sent for him and made similar declaration.
Widow Rachel Brackney named administrator of estate with will annexed. (p. 95-96)

LEHEU, SPENCER, SR.
Will. 16 Sep 1802/ 1 Feb 1803
Children: John, Moses, Spencer, Jr., William, Mary Pomeroy, Nancy Leheu, Elizabeth, Edia Vannort, Rebecca Leheu, Rachael Wiley
To son John and daughter Mary Pomeroy, land in Blue Ridge; to son Moses, Ŀ 15; to Spencer, Jr., the place I now live on; to son William, balance of plantation; to daughters Nancy, Elizabeth, Edia and Rebecca, each Ŀ 25, Rebecca's money to be put at trust until she becomes of age; to Rachael Wiley, Ŀ 6.
Exr: Son Spencer Leheu
Wit: William Carnavan, William Vanourt, Jr. (p. 96-98)

BROWNLEY, JOHN
Sale Account. 19 Oct 1802/ 1 Feb 1803 (p. 98-103)

GRAYSON, WILLIAM
Sale Account. 1 Feb 1803
Admr: Joseph Tidball
Examiners: Abraham Neill, W. Davison (p. 103-104)

WEAVER, LEONARD
Appraisal. 4 Feb 1803
Appraisers: William Taylor, Christopher Elis, Thomas Davis, Jacob Leonard (p. 105-106)

PITMAN, ANTHONY
Will. 3 Dec 1802/ 5 Apr 1803
Wife: Catharine
Children: Andrew, Catharine, Elizabeth, John, Rosanna
To wife, all estate during her widowhood; at her death or marriage, divide all estate among children.
Exrs: Philip Pitman, Thomas Davis
Wit: David Henning, John Pitman, Thomas Davis (p. 106-107)

COLVIL, JOHN
Will. 2 Nov 1802/ 5 Apr 1803
Sisters: Jennet, Margaret Newell, Martha Colvil, Ann Thompson, Mary Marques
Brother: Samuel (wife Mary, dau Ann)
Legatee: Robert Mattock; John Adams; Presbyterian congregation of Cedar Creek Meeting House; bound boy James Church
To sister Jennet during her natural life, farm on Long Marsh to be divided, valued and reserved for her; reserve for Robert Mattock his weaver's shop and small garden and lodging in the mansion during his natural life. To brother Samuel Colvil, sell him part of the land. All personal property to be sold and the sum of $116.76-2/3 to be placed at interest for support of the gospel in the congregation of Cedar Creek, such interest to be paid annually to the Presbyterian minister officially at the Cedar Creek Meeting House. Upon death of sister Jennet, the principal to return to estate to become part of residue to be willed to nephews and to each of their sons related to me by consanguinity and named after me - to each Ŀ 10 - John Colvil and John Marquis, nephews, their sons John Colvil, sons of Joseph, John Marquis son of John Marquis Sr., John Marquis son of John Marquis, son of James. To John McCauly, son of niece, Ŀ 10. To sister-in-law Mary Colvil, $10. To my friend Robert Mattock, $50. To bound boy James Church, one year's schooling, and if he lives with my sister Jennett to age 21 and behaves dutifully, a horse saddle and bridle of $100 value and $100 in money or bonds. Negro girl Milo, about 8, and negro boy Griff, age 2 years, to be manumitted at age 30, to be property of sister Jennett in interim. Estate residue to brother Samuel Colvil and John Adams, but if they decide not to take it at appraisement, executors to sell within one year of my decease. Residue to be divided into five equal parts: To brother Samuel, less Ŀ 50 to his daughter Ann; to sister Margaret Newell and family; to children of family of sister Martha Colvil; to sister Jennet; to sister Ann Thompson with remainder to her daughters at her death. The family of sister Mary Marques (William Marquis, John Marquis, Thomas Marquis, Sarah Vance, Annie Cowan, Elizabeth McCauly and James Marquis) live a considerable distance away, and I do not know if they are alive.
Exrs: Daniel McCauly, John Adams, Robert Mattock, William Marquis
Wit: Edward Howe, Charles Barris, Jacob Rodes
Sec: James Marquis, David Osborn, Ŀ 2,000 (p. 107-111)

PRICE, GEORGE (GENERAL)
Sale Account. 6 Apr 1803
Among buyers: Catharine Price, Michel Price (p. 112)

HAMMICK (HAMMOCK), RUDOLPH
Appraisal. 24 Jan 1803/ 2 May 1803
Appraisers: William Barrow, Sr., Jacob Louder, S. L. Rogers
(p. 112-113)

KERLIN, JOHN
Appraisal; Acct. current. 2 May 1803
Examiners: John Jolliffe, Francis Stribling
Admr: David Rose
Name noted: Hanah Kerlin (p. 113-115)

BARR, PETER
Will. 25 Feb 1803/ 2 May 1803
Wife: Elizabeth Barr
Children: Frederick Barr, Peter Barr, Mary Barr, Caty Barr, Polly Barr, Sally Barr
To wife, all estate during her natural life, and at her decease to my children equally. All perishable part of estate to be sold immediately upon my decease; if insufficient to pay debts, executors to sell houses and land where I live.
Exrs: Sons Frederick and Peter Barr
Wit: (German script, illegible)
Sec: Christian Freyhorn, Christian Schrach, $1,500(p. 115-116)

LYNN, GEORGE
Appraisal. 22 Mar 1803/ 2 May 1803
Appraisers: Robert Gray, Nathan Anderson, Daniel Longacre, John Ferguson (p. 116-117)

NEILL, JOSEPH
Appraisal & Sale Acct. 16-19 Apr 1796/ 2 May 1803
Appraisers: James Simrall, Stephen Pritchard
Among buyers: Lewis Neill (p. 118-120)

NEILL, JOSEPH
Estate Settlement. July 1796/ 2 May 1803
Exrs: Lewis Neill, John McPherson
Examiners: John Jolliffe, Francis Stribling (p. 121-122)

STALEY, JACOB
Appraisal. 3 May 1803
Appraisers: Vance Bush, William McLeod, William Henning (p. 122-123)

SIMRALL, JAMES
Account current. July 1798/ 3 May 1803
Acting Exr: William F. Simrall
Examiners: W. Davison, I. Caldwell (p. 124-127)

PRATT, WILLIAM
Appraisal. 2 Mar 1803/ 3 May 1803
Appraisers: William Northen, George Dearman, Benjamin Redding (p. 128)

STALEY, JACOB
Account current. 5 Sep 1803
Admx: Barbara Staley
Examiners: Brian M. Stephens, John Henning (p. 128-130)

FARNLEY, WILLIAM
Appraisal. 29 May 1800/ 5 Sep 1803
Memo of articles disposed of.
Appraisers: Joseph Haines, Thomas Fawcett, Jr., John Haines (p. 130-131)

HARRISON, JOHN
Appraisal. 25 July 1801/ 5 Sep 1803
Appraisers: Jasper Ball, T. A. Ware, Jr., Griffin Taylor (p. 131-132)

HENDRY/HENRY, DEBORAH (executrix of George Hendry)
Account current. 1799/ 5 Sep 1803
Admr with will annexed: William Hendry

Legatees: Isaac Hendry - sold right to James Baker; to Isaac Hendry for Jeremiah Dunkin and Rebecca his wife, late Rebecca Hendry, who sold right to Gen. Daniel Morgan, sold by Morgan to Isaac Hendry, then sold to James Baker. To Elizabeth Bourdon (Borden?); to John Worley and Ann his wife, late Ann Hendry; to Jesse Humphries and Mary his wife, late Mary Hendry; to Deborah Hendry (dec'd), legacy.
No accounting of personal estate filed, being willed to Abraham and Isaac Hendry, who disposed of property before issuance of letters of administration.
Examiners: Samuel Kercheval, John Brownley, Francis Gilchrist
(p. 133-134)

CLOPTON, GEORGE
Appraisal. 5 Sep 1803
Appraisers: William Helm, Samuel Bryarly, William Kearfott
(p. 134-136)

CLEVENGER, JOSEPH
Will. -- June 1803/ 5 Sep 1803
Wife: Mary
To wife, all estate
Exrx: Wife Mary
Wit: Thos. Smith, George Neale (p. 137)

BAINS, CHARLES
Will. 4 Aug 1797/ 5 Sep 1803
Children: John, Charles, Joseph, Hannah, Rachel Curlett, Sarah Ruddell, Ann Keene, Brish(?) Whitney, Rebecca Laney
Son-in-law: Ulrich Keenes
Personal property to be sold and equally divided among Charles, Hannah, Joseph and son-in-law Ulrich Keenes; sons Charles and Joseph and daughters to have land, to be sold and divided among them equally. To oldest son John, £ 1.
Exrs: Sons Charles and Joseph and son-in-law Ulrich Keenes
Wit: John Adams, Joseph Bains, Jr., Jean Laney (p. 137-139)

HONTSBERGER/HOTZBERGER, JACOB (Parish of Frederick)
Will. 3 June 1797/ 5 Sep 1803
Children: Henry, Conrad, Mary Davis wife of Michael Davis, Sophia Martin, Margaret Snyder, Catherine Sperry (dec'd), Ann Catherine Smith (dec'd
Gr. ch: Unnamed
To son, Henry, land he lives on bought of John Shipler(?), 211 acres in Frederick Co.; to son Conrad, land bought from George Mercer, Barbara Stiss and Palmer Foulks, 239 acres in Frederick Co., residue of land given to Henry; to daughter Mary Davis wife of Michael Davis, $100 to be paid by son Henry out of property given him, to be paid one year after my decease; to daughter Sophia Martin, $100 to be paid by son Conrad from property left him, one year after my decease; to daughter Margaret Snyder's two children, $5 between them; to deceased daughter Catherine Sperry's two children, $5 between them; to deceased daughter Ann Catherine Smith's children, $5 as a remembrance, their mother having been provided for, to be paid by two sons. All other property to sons Henry and Conrad as joint residuary legatees.
Exrs: Sons Henry and Conrad Hontsberger
Wit: John Smith, Thomas Lewis, John Baily
Sec: Thomas Lewis, $1,000 (p. 140-141)

BUTTERFIELD, THOMAS
Appraisal. 5 Sep 1803
Appraisers: Daniel Magruder, John Baker, Levi Smith
(p. 141-144)

CLARKE, ABNER
Will. 16 May 1803/ 5 Sep 1803
Wife: Hanah Clarke
Children: Abner, George, Hanah Steer, Barbary Rummins(?)
To wife, one third profits of land during life and one third of movable property; to son Abner, 150 acres and all profits and privileges of saw mill; to son George, remainder of land and sawmill privileges; to daughter Hanah Steer, £ 20 to be paid by brother George in four payments; to daughter Barbara Rummins(?), £ 20 paid by brother Abner; to son Abner, large chest, large Bible, bed and bedding. All remaining movables to Abner for support of his mother during her lifetime
Exrs: Son Abner, friend Sampson Babb
Wit: John McCoole, Benjamin Hull, Robert Crocket
Sec: Peter Babb, George Bible, $2,000 (p. 144-146)

GOSS, FREDERICK
Appraisal. 13 Aug 1803/ 5 Sep 1803
Appraisers: John Carter, John Hunford (Hurford?), Isaac Burk, Jacob Haughman (p. 146-148)

WEAVER, LEONARD
Sale Account. Aug 1802/ 6 Sep 1803
Exrx: Ann Weaver
Buyers: Ann Weaver, John Weaver, Jacob Weaver (p. 148-152)

POLLARD, JOSEPH
Will. 27 Nov 1802/ 6 Sep 1803
Wife: Unnamed
Children: Unnamed
Property to be equally divided among wife and children.
Exrs: Oley(?) Taylor, George Williams, William Carnagy
Wit: James Baker, Samuel Dodd, John I. Williams
(Proved by John I. Williams, James Baker, William Carnagy and Mandley Taylor, Admrs.)
[Kitty Pollard nee Taylor m Stephen Davis, 22 Sep 1803; Fdk.Co. Marrs., possibly unnamed widow.] (p. 152)

COLVILL, JOHN
Appraisal. 27 Apr 1803/ 3 Oct 1803
Appraisers: David Neiswander, Charles Bains, Joseph Luckey (p. 153-155)

ROBERTS, THOMAS (of Hampshire Co.)
Carpenter and joiner
Dau: Catharine Roberts
Friend: Louis Barnet
To friend Louis Barnet, chest of joiner and carpenter tools; chest of my clothes and woman's apparel; man's saddle; notes, bonds and book debts to be appraised and sold to pay debts; and any residue to maintaining daughter Catharine Roberts.
Exr: Louis Barnet
Wit: Thomas L. Williamson, Tom Carter Doster, John Schultz (p. 155-156)

ZULL/ZOLL, HENRY
Will. 13 Oct 1798/ 5 Dec 1803
Wife: Catharine
Children: Frederick, Catharine. Barbara
To wife, life estate in all property during widowhood. To son Frederick, to live on plantation and support his mother until wife's death or remarriage; to daughter Catharine wife of Thomas Tombleton, 20 shillings; to daughter Barbara wife of Samuel Gander, 20 shillings.
Exr: Friend Benjamin Fry called Big Ben Frye
Wit: P. Williams, George Coghill (Cogle), William Caldwell

Codicil: 15 Feb 1801 - Revocation of provision for wife. Son Frederick to receive plantation and live with mother and work the plantation. Son and wife to have personal estate.
Wit: P. Williams, Benjamin Frye, Johan (?) (German, illegible)
Sec: John Fry, $2,000 (p. 156-158)

HAYHURST, CUTHBERT
Appraisal & Sale Acct. Apr 1803/ 5 Dec 1803
Appraisers: William Jolliffe, James Bruce, Francis Stribling (p. 158-160)

GARROTT, LUKE
Appraisal. 5 Nov 1803/ 5 Dec 1803
Appraisers: John McAuley, John Self, Daniel Daughty (p. 160-161)

CATLETT, JAMES
Div. of Estate; Sale of Negroes 5 Dec 1803
Submitted by William Headley, J. Allensworth (p. 162-163)

BAINS, CHARLES
Appraisal. Ordered Sep 1803/ 5 Dec 1803
Appraisers: David Newswander, Michal Mock, Robert Mattox (p. 163-164)

COLVILLE, JOHN
Sale Account. 5 Dec 1803
Examiners: John Adams, William Morgan, sister Jane Senseny, co-partners
Among buyers: Jane Colville, John Colville (p. 164-170)

CLEVENGER, SAMUEL
Appraisal. 5 Dec 1803
Appraisers: William Harnot, Robert Whitaker, Moses McKay (p. 170-171)

LITTLER, SAMUEL
Appraisal & Sale Acct. 24-30 Apr 1802/ 6 Dec 1803
Appraisers: Thomas Lloyd, John Jolliffe, David Ridgway
Admrs: Nathan and Elijah Littler
Among buyers: Nathan Littler, Sr., Elijah Littler, Nathan Littler, Jr., John Littler, Sr., Isaiah Littler (p. 171-178)

GIBSON, WILLIAM
Appraisal. 11 Oct 1799/ 6 Dec 1803
Appraisers: Hezekiah Turner, Joseph Pollard, Samuel Turner (p. 179-180)

POLLARD, JOSEPH
Appraisal. 20 Oct 1803/ 7 Dec 1803
Appraisers: Edmund Newman, William Cook, Richard Fawcett, James Baker (p. 180-183)

FROST, WILLIAM
Appraisal & Sale Acct. 14-18 Aug 1801/ 2 Jan 1804
Appraisers: Thomas Stribling, Thomas Hennon, William Castleman, Thomas Neill (p. 183-186)

FROST, WILLIAM
Account current. 2 Jan 1804
Admr: Bushrod Taylor
Examiners: Warner Washington, Thomas Stribling (p. 187)

MILLER, GOTTFRIED (living in Winchester)
Will. 6 July 1803/ 2 Jan 1804
Wife: Anna Maria
Children: John, Abraham, Gottfried, Peter, Rebecca
To wife, life estate during widowhood until children get an education; Lot No. 209. To son John, Lot "C" - pay widow Ł 5 each

year of widowhood; to daughter Rebecca, Lot "D"; to son Gottfried corner Lot "E" when of age; pay widow Ł 5 each year of widowhood. Must work for mother on farm until of age. To Peter, Lot 209 when of age; pay widow Ł 5 each year of widowhood. If widow dies before Peter is of age, sons John and Abraham to execute wishes. One-sixth part of estate to wife, John, Abraham, Rebecca, Gottfried and Peter. To son Abraham, third part of lot bought from Neil Smith.
Exrs: John and Abraham Miller
Wit: Adam Kurtz, Frederick Kurtz
Sec: Frederick and Adam Kurtz, $16,000 (p. 188-190)

CATLETT, ROBERT
Appraisal. 1803
Appraisers: William David, Richard Rout, Lewis Ashby (p. 191-193)

LITTLER, SAMUEL - ORPHANS
Barnet, Rebeccah, Elizabeth, Ann
Guardianship Acct. Settlement. 15 Apr 1802/ 6 Feb 1804
Guardians: Nathan and Elijah Littler
Examiners: David Ridgway, Lee Ray D(?) (Illegible) (p. 193-194)

WILLIAMS, BARNETT
Account with Samuel Littler, dec'd, and Elijah Littler, surviving executor. 27 June 1795/ 6 Feb 1804
Balance due estate by above exrs - Ł 6.16.11; Ł 15 to be paid above executors for adjusting and settling estate.
Examiners: Meredith Helms, David Ridgway (p. 195-196)

KING, THOMAS
Appraisal. 28 Jan 1804/ 6 Feb 1804
Appraisers: James Marquis, Joseph Wood, John Wright (p. 196-197)

LEHEU, SPENCER
Appraisal. 6 Feb 1804
Appraisers: Henry Trent, Daniel Cline(?), T. Allensworth (p. 198-200)

FERGUSON, JOHN
Will. 9 Oct 1803/ 6 Feb 1804
Wife: Martha
To wife, two children's shares of whole estate. After Henry Negley pays to my executor $9.83, executors to provide title to property in his patent made out by Thomas Brown. Executors to sell land I live on whenever necessary.
Exrs: Wife Martha, Collin Carroll
Wit: William Harvey, Collin Carroll, George Bruce (p. 200-201)

ALLENSWORTH, WILLIAM
Appraisal. 4 May 1802/ 6 Feb 1804
Appraisers: John Self, Richard Bayerly, H. G. Martin (p. 202)

HEIRONIMOUS, CHRISTIAN
Appraisement. 6 Feb 1804
Appraisers: Joseph Adams, John Lewis, Jacob(?) (in German) (p. 203-204)

FENTON, SARAH
Will. 21 Dec 1803/ 7 Feb 1804
All property to daughter Judith Fenton
Wit: James Bennet, Titus UnderDonk (p. 204)

CLARKE, ABNER
Appraisal. 2 Jan 1804/ 3 Apr 1804
Appraisers: John McCoole (p. 205-206)

BUCKANNON, THOMAS
Appraisal. 3 Apr 1804
Appraisers: Peter Hurst, John Hammond, William Hurst
(p. 206-207)

LARRICK, CASPER
Adm. Account. 3 Aug 1801-24 Feb 1804/ 3 Apr 1804
Admrs: John Larrick, Jacob Larrick, Henry Larrick
Examiners: Moses Russell, James Singleton, P. Williams
(p. 207-208)

BOND, SAMUEL
Adm. Account. 14 May 1803/ 3 Apr 1804
Admr: Joseph Longacre
Examiners:: Edward McGuire, Jr., William Baylis, James Singleton
(p. 208-209)

DOYLE, EDWARD
Nuncupative will. 15 Feb 1804/ 3 Apr 1804
Affidavit by William Davis says he was sent for to go to home of deceased on morning of 15 Feb 1804, and found there Mr. Peter Bare (Barr?). Decedent announced he was very ill and wanted William Davis to write his will. Deceased asked to be buried beside his wife, to arrange to manumit slave Molly and her child, and to free three young negroes at 21. The affiant was asked to take deceased's bonds, books and papers and appraise his money, and he "knew what to do with them." The condition worsened and will was not written.
Wit: Peter Barr
Proved by oath of Peter Barr, Paul Andrews, William Kercheval, and Mary, his wife, next of kin to deceased. Wife Mary contested the will. William Davis granted letters of administration with will annexed.
Sec: William Cooke, David Timberlake, Stephen Davis, $10,000
William Kercheval appealed to next District Court at Winchester, giving bond. (p. 209-210)

BEEMER, GEORGE
Will. 27 June 1804/ 3 Apr 1804
Wife: Hannah Beemer
Children: John, Frederick, Benjamin (eldest sons), William, George, Samuel (youngest), Catharine Hooper, Susannah Beemer, Margaret Beemer.
To wife, house and lot where I live for three years after decease; then to son John said house and lot, he to build house for wife on two acres between present house and James Gray. At wife's death, house and lot to be sold and money equally divided among sons. Son John to send three youngest sons to school for one year each and pay for schooling, lodging and clothing. To son Benjamin, immediately on my decease, choice of one horse, new saddle and bridle to be purchased out of my personal property when sold. Also, house and lot adjoining James Simrall. To son Frederick, four-acre lot on south side of main road from Kernstown to Winchester joining John Brown. To son William, remainder of tract joining John Brown. To son George, two acres on south side of said road. To son Benjamin, two acres on south side of said road (pasture lot joining George Beemer, Jr.). Remainder on south side for use of wife and executors until youngest son becomes 21, then land to be sold and son Samuel to be paid £ 50 from proceeds. Remainder equally divided among all sons. In one month after my decease, executors to sell personal property exclusive of three beds my wife is to have use of as long as she lives. One-third of proceeds to wife Hannah. To daughter Catharine Hooper $50 paid seven months after my decease; to daughter Susannah Beemer, $50 paid seven months after my decease; to daughter Margaret Beemer, $50

at age 18.
Exrs: Benjamin and John Beemer, sons
Wit: Adam Kern, Thomas Hemons (p. 211-213)

LARRICK, JOHN
Will. 17 Jan 1804/ 3 Apr 1804
Wife: Margaret (Margred)
Children: Abraham, Mary, Jenny, Susana, Elizabeth, Joseph, Nancy.
To wife, her thirds, full possession of plantation unless she remarries, then to have only one equal share with children. After her decease, estate to be equally divided among children except son Abraham, his share to provide for him at discretion of executors. Other children, equal shares. To sons John and Joseph, a horse, saddle and bridle valued at Ł 25 as soon as possible after my decease. Movable estate to be sold and equally divided.
Exrs: Jacob Danner, George Flanencham(?), son Joseph
Wit: George Larrick, Jr., Isaac Larrick, Rebecca Larrick
Sec: Peter Senseny, $5,000. (p. 214-215)

RINKER, CASPER
Will. 22 Apr 1802/ 3 Apr 1804
Wife: Mary
Children: Jacob, Mary wife of John Rogers, Elizabeth wife of Joel Allemon (Allamong?), Catherine
To wife, Ł 100 current money of Virginia for life, plantation and two tracts where I live (147 acres) purchased of William Stuard, 190 acres granted to me by deeds of Thomas Lord Fairfax dated 13 Mar 1775. After wife's decease, plantation and two tracts and appurtenances to son Jacob. Also to Jacob, 219-1/4 acre tract where he now lives, lying on both sides of the Great Road from Winchester to the South Branch conveyed to me by Isaac Lupton and Elizabeth his wife. To daughter Mary now wife of John Rogers, tract of 224-1/2 acres with appurtenances lying on both sides of Back Creek conveyed to me by John Stonebridge and wife Mary; also to Mary, tract on drains of Isaac's Creek (133 acres) all that part of tract I hold of tract conveyed to me by Richard Wood. To daughter Elizabeth wife of Joel Allemon(?), tract of 338 acres with appurtenances on drains of Isaac's Creek granted to me by deed from Thomas Lord Fairfax. Executors to dispose of all land remaining by public sale, and money to be divided into four equal shares and distributed to children: Jacob, Mary, Elizabeth, Catherine. All personal estate to wife during natural life; after her decease to be divided equally among four children.
Exrs: Wife Mary and son Jacob
Wit: John McCoole, Joseph Gordon, John Schultz. Bond $20,000. (p. 215-219)

CHRISMAN, JACOB
Account current. Oct 1778/ 4 Apr 1804
Appraisement returned 4 Nov 1783
Payments to James Scott, husband of daughter Rebecca.
Exr: George Chrisman
Examiners: W. Davison, Jo. Tidball (p. 220-224)

CUNNINGHAM, JOHN
Appraisal. 30 Apr 1804/ 5 Apr 1804
Examiners: William Helm, William Kerfoot, Samuel Bryarly, Joseph Carter (p. 224-226)

KEMIN/KEMERS, CHRISTIAN
Appraisal. 5 Apr 1804/ 30 Apr 1804
Examiners: Joseph Parrell, Jr., Conrad Huntsberg (p. 226-227)

LAREW (LARUE?), PHEBE
Appraisal & Sale Account. 1801/ 30 Apr 1804
Appraisers: John Lindsey, Thomas Lindsey, James Clare, Bartholomew Smith
Sale Account filed by James Larew (p. 227-231)

HAMMACK, RUDOLPH
Account current. Jan 1803/ 1 May 1804
Admr: Daniel Shambaugh
Examiners: John Hickman, Daniel Henry (p. 231)

McCOOLE, JAMES
Will. 2 Sep 1804; pro 30 Apr 1804/ 1 May 1804
Wife: Deborah McCoole
Children: Gabriel, Lewis(?), Thomas, Gracy Babb, Ann Darlington, Charity McCoole
To wife, all estate during widowhood. If she remarries, one-third personal estate and one-third yearly profits from real estate. To son Gabriel, tract on which I live, after decease of his mother, he to pay $100 to each of other children. To son Lewis(?) McCoole, and to son Thomas, $30 each. To daughter Gracy Babb, $20. To daughter Ann Darlington nothing, she having received her share in full. To daughter Charity McCoole $20 and all household furniture remaining at her mother's death. All remainder of estate to Gabriel.
Exrs: Wife Deborah McCoole and friend Thomas Mitchell
Wit: Lewis McCoole, Deborah Mitchell, Asa Hoge. (p. 232-233)

ZULL/ZOLL, HENRY
Appraisal. 7 Dec 1804/ 2 Feb 1804
Appraisers: Michael White, John Cooper, Henry Bull(p. 234-235)

MILLER, RICHARD
Account. 2 Dec 1801/ 2 July 1804
Admr: William Chiply; Admx: Martha Miller
Examiners: J. B. Tilston, Joseph Fawcett, Joseph Lucky, Jacob Leonard (p. 235-237)

MILLER, GODFRIED
Appraisal. 3 Feb 1804/ 2 July 1804
Refers to "store near the bridge"
Appraisers: Charles Brent, Jr., Christopher Witzel, Simon Lauck (p. 237-238)

WASHINGTON, HANNAH "of Fairfield"
Will. 14 May 1802/ 3 Sep 1804
Children: Fairfax, Whiting Washington, Mildred Throckmorton, Hannah Whiting, Catherine Nelson
Gr. ch: Lucinda Nelson, Hannah Throckmorton, Catharine Throckmorton, Louisa Whiting, Hennah Nelson, Hannah Whiting
Nephew: Tom Fairfax
To all legatees, specific slaves. Sons Fairfax and Whiting received a large number of slaves listed by names as residue of estate. Negro Cynthia is to have freedom immediately after decease of testator, she having been given to testator by her husband to dispose of.
Exrs: Nephew Tom Fairfax and sons Fairfax and Whiting Washington.
No witnesses. Handwriting proved by oaths of Nimrod Taylor and Warner Washington
Sec: Warner Washington, $20,000 (p. 238-240)

POWERS, JOHN
Sale Account. 12 Jan 1804/ 3 Sep 1804
Examiners: Wyatt Whitehead, James Powers
Among buyers: James Powers, Widow Powers (p. 240-245)

HIETT, LETTY (LETTIS)
Will. 4 May 1804/ 3 Sep 1804
Sisters; Rebecca Rankin (elder), Mary Smith, Nelly Vanhorn
Bro-in-law: William Vanhorn
To sister Rebecca Rankin, mare, furniture, pewter ware; to sister Mary Smith, mare and colt, furniture, pewter ware; to sister Nelly Vanhorn, furniture and pewter ware; to William Vanhorn, livestock, note executed by John Packet and John Grantham for $20, note of John Hiett for £ 25, noting credits. All residue of estate to William Vanhorn.
Exr: William Vanhorn (husband of Eleanor [Nelly] Vanhorn
Wit: John Lindsey, Charles McCormick, Ab-aham Frost
Sec: John Lindsey, $1,500 (p. 246-247)

PEPPER, JAMES
Will. 14 Jan 1803/ 3 Sep 1804
Wife: Arabella
Children: Nancy, Joseph and William Pepper, Mary Mayers.
All estate to be sold. Pay $1 to each of children, balance to loving wife.
Exrx: Arabella Pepper
Wit: Daniel Thornbrugh
Sec: Daniel Thornbrugh

BEEMER, GEORGE
Appraisal & Sale Acct. 3 Sep 1804
Among buyers: Mrs. Beemer (p. 248-254)

WHITE, ALEXANDER
Will: 26 May 1804/ 3 Dec 1804
Wife: Sarah
Legacies to nephews and nieces; Alexander, Robert, Thomas and John White also John White, son of my nephew Alexander White, Anne, Margaret, Mary, Barbara and Sarah "sisters of my nephew Robert White".
"Land bequeathed to me by Theodrich(?) Lee to be divided between Caroline Lee and his other children after the death of Grandmother." Mentions land bequeathed to him by John Rolfe. Provides freedom for slaves. Bequests to Margaret Beall, Mary White and Sarah Middleton-possibly same people named above.
Exrs: Wife Sarah, or if she is deceased, nephews Alexander and Robert White.
Wit: Charles Magill and Archibald Magill
Sec: Joseph Tidball, Adam Douglas and Lawrance Butler
(P.1-3)

McKAY, ANDREW
Will: 30 Sept 1803/3 Dec 1804
Wife: Jane
Sons: Moses, Jacob and Enos
Daus: Margaret, wife of Oliver Frenston and Patience, wife of Robert Whitaker
Brother: Jacob McKay
"To Jonathan Lupton the elder, William Grubb the elder, John McPherson and Jonathan Wright- money to aid in the emancipation of persons unlawfully held in bondage"
Mentions land purchased from Robert and Thomas Branson and land surveyed by B. Ashby. Legacy to friend Goldsmith Chandlee.
Exrs: Goldsmith Chandlee, Robert Whitaker and sons Moses and Jacob McKay
Wit: William Lupton, John Cooper, Solomon Lupton, John Roper and Thomas Grubs
New executors at court: Thomas Smith and Noah Haines
(P.3-9)

PARKINS, JONATHAN
Will: 19 June 1800/ 3 Dec 1804
Wife: Elizabeth
Sons: John, Jonathan and David
Daus: Phebe Wright, Hanah Smith, Ann Warmed and Mary Shion
To daughter Phebe Wright; land in Hampshire County adjoining lands of John Lewis. To daughter Mary Shion; land adjoining Mercer Babbs. Lands adjoining David Lupton, John Wright, Thomas Evans, James Smith and Isaac Perkins bequeathed to other children
Exrs: James Gawthrop and Goldsmith Chandlee
Wit: Joseph Parker, Lydia Hollingsworth and Mary Bolt
(P.9-10)

CRUM, ANTHONY-also signed Andrew Crum
Will: 11 Sept 1804/ 3 Dec 1804
Wife: not named
Sons: Christian, Henry and Anthony
Daus: Catherine Weaver, Mary Shreet, Anna Dill/Deal and Elizabeth(wife of Daniel Heckindorn).
"To my widow one hundred dollars, to my well beloved children the residue" Legacies to the children of Anna Deal namely George, Caty, Mary, John, Conrad, Barbara, Eve, Elizabeth Anna and Suzanah. Legacies to the children of Mary Shreet by her first husband namely Jacob, Barbara and Caty Weaver. Legacies to "seven children of Catherine Weaver namely

Henry Mack George Weaver Elizabeth Weaver Philip Weaver Lewis Weaver Henry Weaver and Anthony Weaver" (sic)?
Exr: My beloved son Christian
Wit: George Smith, Christian Heckatoin (sic) and Anthony Crum
Sec: George Price and Robert Hodge
(P. 10-12)

MORGAN, JOSEPH
Will: 10 Nov 1804/ 3 Dec 1804
Wife: Martha
Children: John, Isaiah, Polly and Deborah
Exr: Wife Martha
Wit: Thomas Mitchell. J.T. Gristine and Mary Hoge
Sec: Thomas Mitchell and John Griffeth
(P.12-13)

CALMES, BETTY
Will: 23 Sept 1804/ 3 Dec 1804
Sole Legatee: nephew John Harrison Calmes
Exrs: Nathaniel Jackson and Joseph Vincent
Wit: Daniel Pool, Philip Smith and Henry Stiger
(P.13-14)

HUNSICKER, DANIEL
Will: 26 Apr 1804/ 3 Dec 1804
Wife: Christina
Sons: Jacob and Peter
Daus: Christina, Caty, Betsy, Margaret and Susanna
Legacies to daughter Susanna's five children and mentions granddaughter Susannah "who lives with me"
Exrs: Henry Haines and Peter Hunsicker
Wit: Michael Smith and Michael Everhart
Sec: Arthur Carter and Michael Everhart
(P.14-16)

ROSS, DAVID
Will: 3 Nov 1804/ 3 Dec 1804
Wife: Catherine
Sons: Enos, David, Jonathan and Thomas
Daus: Rachel Hunt, Phebe Ross and Lydia Ross
Mentions provisions made for daughters in will of Evan Thomas.
Exrs: Sons Enos and David
Wit: Thomas Williams, Abraham Branson and David Ridgeway
Sec: Thomas Campbell and Jacob Reese
(P.16-17)

HOGE, ASA
Inventory and appraisal: 9 Oct 1804/ 3 Dec 1804
Appraisers: James Curl, Thomas Mitchell and Joseph Myers
(P. 17-19)

McMURRY, JAMES
Will: 12 Sept 1804/ 3 Dec 1804
Sons: "William and John, if ever they come forward"
Niece: Jean McMurry
Exrs: "my three brethren, Peter, Samuel and John"
Wit: John McMurry, Elizabeth McMurry and John Dill
Sec: James Carter and William Brown
(P.19-20)

TAYLOR, MAYLON
Account Current: 4 Dec 1804
Examiners: J. Mittan and Bushrod Taylor
(P. 20-21)

MOORE, ELISHA
Sale of estate: 4 Dec 1804
(P. 21-22)

HELM, MEREDITH
Will: 29 Sept 1804/ 4 Dec 1804
Wife: Frances
Son: Strother
Daus: Roberta; other daughters mentioned but not named
Son Strother to inherit plantation called "Neckline", also plantation purchased of Walker and Jacob Smith
Exrs: Wife Frances and friends Doctor Robert Mackey and Hugh Holmes
Wit: Elijah Littler, Robert Dunbar and Benjamin Harris
Sec: Francis Stribbling, John Jolliffe and Benjamin Harris
(P. 23-24)

NICHLIN, JOSEPH, SR.
Settlement of estate: 6 Dec 1804
Admr: Joseph Nichlin
Examiners: LeRoy Daingerfield and Fra. Stribling
(P. 25-26)

RINKER, CASPER
Inventory and appraisal: 6 Dec 1804
Appraisers: Joseph Gordon and Will Adams
(P. 27-28)

CHRISTMAN, HENRIETTA
Orphan of Henry Christman
Guardian: Isaac Christman
Guardianship account: 4 Feb 1805(?)
John Clark listed as husband of Henrietta
(P. 29)

LUPTON, JOHN
Will: 2 Jan 1803/Cod signed 13 Apr 1804
Wife: Ann
Sons: Joshua, Nathan, John, Joseph and Jonah
Daus: Grace Steer, Mary Raley and Sarah Russell
Mentions land adjoining John Hamilton
Exrs: Jonathan Lupton and "my two sons Joshua and Nathan"
Wit: Joseph Gutherie, James Nutt, Saml. Gilpin, Gideon Ruse, George Lessinger, James Carpenter and Gideon Ross
(P. 29-33)

MERCER, MOSES
Will: 28 Sept 1796/
Wife: Dianna
Sons: John, William, Gideon and Edward
Daus: Dianna, Mary and Ann (dec'd with three children)
Mentions property lines adjoining Thos. Farrell and Peter and Thos. Babb
Exrs: John and William Mercer
Wit: Daniel Thornburg, John White and Eliz. Thornburg

RE-RECORDATION OF WILL OF MOSES MERCER
"It appearing to the court that the record of the will of Moses Mercer has by some person been removed, it is ordered that the clerk's copy of said will be inserted in place of the original"
(P. 34-35)

GREENLEE, ELIZABETH
Estate Settlement: 4 Feb 1805
Legatee: John Greenlee, under age
Executors: Joseph Carter and Jn. Jones
Exam: George G. Norris(?) and Bushrod Taylor
(P. 36)

BROWN, William
Will: 28 Nov 1801/ 4 Feb 1805
"After payment of all my just debts, I give to Mrs. Barbara Siller of Winchester, all my property"
Exrs: " My friends Isaac Siller and Isaac Bush"
Wit: Jacob Kiger, Daniel Siller and Abraham Siller
(P. 37)

BUSH, ANDREW
Will: 12 Jan 1801/ 4 Feb 1805
Wife: Regina
Exrs: "My friends Conrad Gress and Regina Bush"
Wit: Danl. Siller, Jacob Hoffman and Abraham Siller
(P. 38)

MARQUES, JAMES
Inventory and appraisal: 4 Feb 1805
Appraisers: Robt. Glass, Jno. Hotsenpillar and Joseph Lucky
(P. 39-40)

KIMMER, CHRISTIAN
Inventory and appraisal: 5 Feb 1805
Appraiser: Thos. Lewis
(P. 40-42)

McCOOLE, JAMES
Inventory and appraisal: 5 Feb 1805
Appraisers: Gabriel Darlington, Gabriel Davis and Abraham Weaver (P. 42)

CLENDENING, JOHN
Inventory and appraisal: 5 Feb 1805
Appraisers:Thomas Parker, Thomas Stribling and Richard Matthews (P. 43)

McMURRY, JAMES
Inventory and appraisal: 5 Feb 1805
Appraisers: George Hollingsworth, Peter Luke and Mabra Madden (P. 43-47)

CONNER, ANN
Inventory, appraisal and sale: 5 Feb 1805
Subscribers: George Hollingsworth, Peter Luke and Mabra Madden
Principal Buyer: David Greenlee (P. 48-51)

HELM, MEREDITH
Inventory and appraisal: 5 Feb 1805
Appraisors: Elijah Littler, John Milburn and Jas. Bruce
(P. 51-55)

DINSMORE, JOHN
Inventory and appraisal: 5 Feb 1805
Appraisers: Thomas Baldwin, James Curl and Richard Hollis
(P. 56-57)

WICKERSHAM, WILLIAM
Will: 9 Oct 1804/ 5 Feb 1805
Wife: Mary
Sons: Enoch, William and Isaac
Daus: Lydia, Rebecka, Elizabeth, Catherine and Mary
Exrs: wife Mary, son Enoch and James Steer
Wit: Isaac Nevell, Samuel Collins and Sarah Nevell
(P.57-58)

HODGSON, ROBERT, SEN.
Estate account: 1780/ 5 April 1805
Exec: Elizabeth Hodgson
Exam: Goldsmith Chandlee and H. Beatty
(P. 58-59)

MOYERS, JACOB
Inventory and appraisal: 2 April 1805
Appraisers: John Hening, Daniel Mytinger and William McLeod
(P. 59-60)

O'BANION, JOHN
Account current: 2 April 1805
Admr: Thos. Stribling
Examiners: Tarlton Webb, B. Taylor and George Harris
(P.61-62)

McCLUNN, THOMAS
Will: 11 Mar 1804/ 2 Apr 1805
Wife: Hannah
Children: Thomas, John, other children mentioned, not named.
"To my son Thomas, property adjoining Kline's, Nicodemus and William Barrow, this to include land he sold to John Henry and Jacob Philips". Mentions two grandchildren; Rachel and Mary Beall.
Exrs: Hannah McClunn and son John
Wit: Goldsmith Chandlee, Isaac Parkins and Isaac Hollingsworth
(P. 63-64)

KRYSOR/CRYSOR, CHRISTOPHER
Inventory, appraisal and sale: 2 Apr 1805
Admrs: Jacob Danner and Elizabeth Krysor
Appraisers: Charles Barns, John Adams and George Larrick
(P. 64-71)

HOLT/HOTT?, George
Will:14 Sept 1800/ 2 Apr 1805
Wife: Eve
Children: Samuel, Magdalene, George, John, Conrad, Susannah Eve, Barbara, Jacob and Margaret
Granddaughter Elizabeth, daughter of Peter Holt, dec'd
Exrs: Sons George and John Holt
Wit: Thomas and Richard Barrett
(P.71-72)

FENTON, ENOCH
Will: 23 Mar 1789/ 2 Apr 1805
Wife: Unnamed
Sons: John, Joseph, Benjamin and Enoch
Dau: Rebeckah
"To beloved wife, property adjoining Jacob Smith, Able Walker and Joshua Woodrow lines".
Exrs: "beloved wife" and son John
Wit: John Parkins, Joseph Adams and Mary Adams
Codicil dated 21 Jan 1805: provides freedom for slaves
Wit: Thomas and Richard Barrett and Jon Mercer
(P. 73-75)

MERCER, MOSES
Inventory and appraisal: 5 Apr 1805
Appraisers: Richard Barrett, Jacob Rinker and Thomas Babbs
(P. 76-77)

HOLT/HOTT(?), Henry
Inventory and appraisal: 2 Apr 1805
Appraisers: Thomas and Benjamin Barrett and James Curl
(P. 77-78)

SCHRECK/SHRAAK, ANDREW
Estate Sale: 3 Apr 1805 (P. 79-81)

WRIGHT, MATTHEW, SR.
Inventory and appraisal: 2 Apr 1805
Appraisers: John Warmley and G.H. Harris
(P. 81-82)

SHNYDER, JACOB
Inventory and appraisal: 6 May 1805
Appraisers: Jacob Leonard, Brian Stephens and Nicholas Samsel
(P. 82-84)

LISTER, CORNELIUS
Will: 26 Sept 1804/ 6 May 1805
Wife: Sarah
Children: William, John, Cornelius and Polly Ryley
Entire estate to wife Sarah, at her decease to son William
Exr: Wife Sarah
Wit: Danl. Thornbough and Michael Kelley
(P. 84)

CLARK, JOSEPH
Inventory, Appraisal and sale: 6 May 1805
Admr: John Clark
Subscribers: Philip and John Earhart and Philip Smith
(P. 85-88)

RUTHERFORD, BENJAMIN
Will: 14 Feb 1803/ 6 May 1805
Dau: Elizabeth Glass, wife of Samuel Glass, sole legatee
Exr: John Peyton
Wit: Thomas McKewan, Thomas Tidball and Robert Kinnon
Executor deceased; Samuel Glass appointed executor by court
(P. 88)

LIKENS, JONAS
Will: 2 Apr 1805/ 6 May 1805
Wife: Mary
Children mentioned not named
"To my wife Mary, all my estate"
Wit: Thomas Rowland, George Rowland and Robert Milburn
(Jonas Likins married Mary Eckstine 22 Aug 1786- Fdk Co Marrs)
(P. 89)

BARR, PETER
Inventory and appraisal: 5 May 1803/ 1 July 1805
Sale includes buyers Elizabeth and Frederick Barr
(P. 90-92)

BRINKER, CATHERINE
Accounts: Funeral expenses Rec 1 July 1805
Exr: Frederick Haas
(Will of Henry Brinker Rec Aug 1772)
(P. 92)

TAYLOR, JOHN
Will: 26 Jan 1798/ 1 July 1805
Wife: Mary
Children: Septimus, Elizabeth, John and Mary
Exrs: Wife Mary and friend B. Martin Stephens
Wit: Philip Trout, Casper Kline and Daniel Smith
Sec: William McLeod and Simon Carson
(P. 92-93)

PEYTON, JOHN
Inventory, appraisal and sale: 1 July 1805
Sale stopped in consequence of suit in progress in Superior Court of Chancery for Richmond District
Admrs: Jn. Brown, Addison B. Armistead and Henry J. Peyton
Appraisers: W. Davison and E. Smith
(P. 93-101)

EARHART, PHILIP
Inventory, appraisal and sale: 1 July 1805
Appraisers: J. Millar, Wm. Kershival and Bushrod Taylor
Among buyers: Mary, John and Philip Earhart
(P.101-107)

MEADE, RICHARD KIDDER
Will: 4 Nov 1797/ 1 July 1805
Wife: Mary
Children mentioned, not named
To wife, "in whose justice, prudence, good sense and maternal affection I can so fully rely I give to her everything that I enjoy on this earth".
Exr: wife Mary
Wit: Robert Page and Robert Burwill
(P.107-108)

SETTLE, JOHN
Inventory and appraisal: 2 Sept 1805
Appraisers: Jno. Singleton, Jn. Catlett and George Leach
(P.108)

KLINE, ADAM
Account current: 2 Sept 1805
Exr: Andrew Redd
Examiners: B. Wilder, Elisha Phelps and George Lynn
(P.109-112)

ROSS, DAVID
Inventory, appraisal and sale: 2 Sept 1805
Appraisers: Thos. Williams and David Ridgway
Among buyers: Jonathan, David, Enos, Lydia and Catherine Ross
(P.112-115)

PYATT, WILLIAM
Inventory and appraisal:2 Sept 1805
Appraisers by court order dated Dec 1804: Elijah Littler George Bruce and Jas. Bruce
(P.115)

WHITE, ALEXANDER
Inventory and appraisal: 2 Sept 1805
Appraisers: Robert Mackey, Alex Balmain, Isaac Brown and W. Davison
(P.116-122)

SMITH, SAMUEL
Inventory and appraisal: 2 Sept 1805
Appraisers: Jno. Coole, Joseph Gorden and John Roger
(P.123-125)

STONEBRIDGE, JOHN
Will:21 Jun 1805/ 2 Sept 1805
Daus: Rebecka Royse, Mary Crumly and Hannah Dalby
Sons-in law: Joseph Dalby and James Crumly
"To my daughter Rebecka Royse, my still and no more"
Exrs: Mary Crumly and Hannah Dalby
Wit: John Coole, John Rogers and Meredith Darlinton
(FDK. Co. Marrs.- Rebecca Stonebridge married Moses Rice 20 May 1788, Hannah Stonebridge married Joseph Dalby 13 Nov 1788)
(P.125-127)

MAUCK, MATTHEW
Inventory and appraisal: 2 Sept 1805
Appraisers: James McDonald, Nathan Littler and Thomas Lloyd
(P. 127-128)

FENTON, ENOCH
Inventory and appraisal: 16 May 1805
Appraisers: Peter Babb, Martin Friese, David and Thomas Barrett
(P.128-130)

PAINTER, ISAAC
Will: 26 Mar 1805/ 2 Sept 1805
Wife: Sarah
Sons: Isaac, Abraham, Mahlon and John
Daus: Hannah Ramey (wife of Benjamin Ramey)and Abigail
Exrs: Wife Sarah and sons Abraham and Mahlon
Wit: Isaiah Oglesby, John Fawcett and Robert Painter
(P.130-133)

BUSH, ANDREW
Estate Sale: 2 Sept 1805
Subscribers: Peter Hain, Jacob Kiger, Nathan Anderson and Jacob Sperry
Principal buyer: William Bush (P.133-134)

BROWN, JOHN
Will: 5 Aug 1805/ 3 Sept 1805
Sisters: Mary Pusey and Margaret Fawcett
Brother: Joel Brown
Property to be sold and money divided among children of my sisters Mary Pusey and Margaret Fawcett. To beloved niece Margaret Pusey, my silver watch. To nephews Joshua, David and Nathan, wearing apparel. To nephew Elijah Fawcett, mare.
Exrs: John and Elijah Fawcett
Wit: Peter Coole, Hannah McClunn and Margaret Fawcett
(P.135-136)

CRUM, ANTHONY
Estate Sale: 22 Dec 1804/ 30 Sept 1805
Exr: Christian Crum
Among buyers: Anthony Crum and Christian Crum
(P.137-139)

KING, JOSEPH
Will: 20 Oct 1804/ 30 Sept 1805
Daus: Amelia Kiger and Alley Catlett
To Nancy Ramey, widow of William Ramey, bed and furniture
To John Catlett, son of Joseph Catlett, fifty pounds
To my daughter Amelia Kiger, 200 pounds
Remainder of estate to be divided among grandchildren,to wit, Nancy Lehue, Elijah Catlett, Henrietta Allensworth, Louisa Catlett, Polly Catlett, Patsy Catlett, Matilda Catlett and John Catlett, children of my daughter Alley Catlett, dec'd, also the children of my daughter Amelia Kiger-Patsy, Susan, Joseph, Mariah, Louisa and Thomas Kiger
Exrs: Benjamin O'Rear and John Catlett
Wit: Melinda O'Rear, John O'Rear and Jesse O'Rear
(P.139-141)

MADDEN, MABRA
Will: 27 May 1805/ 2 Sept 1805
Wife: Jane
Sons: William, Mabra, John and Jacob
Daus: Nancy, Elizabeth, Susan, Mary and Jane
Exrs: Wife Jane and sons Mabra and Jacob
Wit: Tarlton Webb, Samuel Bonham and Peter Luke
(P.142-144)

BROUNLEY, ARCHIBALD
Will: 17 May 1805/ 2 Sep 1805
Wife: Elizabeth
Sons: William and John
Daus: Sally, Emelia, Fanny, Nancy and Elizabeth
To son William, 150 pounds, to son John, 400 pounds. Remainder of estate divided among daughters. "To my beloved wife, my silver watch".
Exrs: Wife Elizabeth, William Cook and Mandley Taylor
Wit: Samuel Kerchival, Mason Pilcher and Benj, Tilden

Further Notation:
"At open court held 4 Feb 1806, Elizabeth Brounley came into court and declaimed that she would not take or accept the provisions made for her by this will or any part thereof and unowned all benefit which she might claim by the said will, which is ordered to be certified by the court."
(P.145-148)

ROGERS, EVAN
Will: 12 Aug 1805/ 2 Dec 1805
Sons: John, Josiah, James and Evan
Daus: Mary Campbell and Sarah Williams
"To daughter-in-law Rhody Rogers, 40 pounds; to grandson Elisha Ellis, 40 pounds; to grandsons Evan and Isaac Pickering, each 20 pounds; to five grandchildren by Evan Rogers- Thomas, Evan, Gabriel, Ann Rogers and Jane Kile, each 2 pounds; to daughter Mary Campbell, bed and bedding; remainder to be divided between sons John and Josiah Rogers, daughter Sarah Williams and the children of James Rogers".
Exrs: Son John Rogers
Wit: Jno. Coole, Jonathan Pickering and Benjamin Pickering
(Frederick Co. Marriages- Mary Rogers m James Campbell 27 Jan 1790)
(P.148-150)

WHITE, JACOB
Estate Settlement: 30 Sept 1805
Exrs: John Frye and I. Mapp
Examiners: James Singleton and Moses Russell
(P.150-152)

RUTHERFORD, BENJAMIN
Inventory and appraisal: 2 Dec 1805
Appraisers: William Maruis and Joseph Luckey
(P.152-153)

CATLETT, JAMES
Inventory and appraisal: 26 Sep 1797/ 2 Dec 1805
Appraisers: Edmund Newman, John Latham and Joseph Haines
(P.153-155)

MASTIN, CHARLOTTE
Will: 20 July 1805/ 2 Dec 1805
"All my estate to be divided equally amongst all my children-Francis, John, Sally, Polly, Betsy and Nancy".
Exrs: Sons John and Francis
Wit: Jacob Danner and Reed Wright
(P.156-157)

PARKER, JOHN
Inventory and appraisal: 2 Dec 1805
Appraisers: Nathaniel Jackson, Philip Smith and Joseph Vincent
(P.157-158)

STONEBRIDGE, JOHN
Inventory and appraisal: 2 Dec 1805
Appraisers: John McCoole, John Rogers and Joseph Gordon
(P.159-161)

MARQUES, MARY
Sale account: 2 Dec 1805
(P.162-166)

VANCE, SAMUEL
Estate settlement: 2 Dec 1805
Admr: Samuel Vance
Examiners: H. Beatty, D. Carlisle and J.G. Hening
(P.166-168)

MADDEN, MABRA
Inventory and appraisal:30 Sept 1805
Appraisers: Adam Aldridge, Meridith Helm and Frederick Dobyns
(P.168-171)

BROUNLEY, JOHN
Estate settlement: 2 Dec 1805
Admr: Betsy Brounley
Examiners: John Woodcock, Fran. Gildard and Philip Nelson
(p.171-180)

ROGERS, EVAN
Inventory and appraisal: 6 Jan 1806
Appraisers: Joseph Gordon, Joseph Adams and David Darlington
(P.180-182)

ANDERSON, ABRAHAM
Will: 16 Nov 1805/ 6 Jan 1806
Wife: Sarah
Sons: Abraham, Richard and Eliamin(?)
Daus: Frances, Rhodia, Sarah, Herbia(?) and Abigail
"money due me from Elic(?) Sweringer's estate to be divided"
Exrs: Wife Sarah and son-in-law Henry Coe
Sec: Cornelius Anderson and James Stuart
(Frederick Co Marriages- Henry Coe m Sarah Anderson 27 Dec 1787; Abigail Anderson m Henry French 11 May 1790; Rhody Anderson m George Black 31 Aug 1786) (P.182-183)

TURNER, SAMUEL
Inventory and appraisal: 6 Jan 1806
Appraisers; William Monroe and William Headly (P.183-184)

LIKENS, JONAS
Inventory and appraisal: 7 Jan 1806
Appraisers: Nathan Littler, Peter McMurray and Thomas Lloyd
(P185-186)

STEPHENS, GEORGE WILLIAM
Will: 22 Dec 1784/recording info below
Formerly of Lincoln County, Virginia
"To my mother, Mary Stephens, tract of land adjoining Stephensburg. my land in Kentucky to be sold and monies divided among my brothers-Jacob, Isaac, Lawerence and Bryan Martin Stephens". Legacies to half brothers-John and Peter Stephens and to sisters Mary Earnest and Sarah Bowman.
Exrs: Mother Mary Stephens and brothers Joseph and Lawerence
Wit: Watson Henry, P. Hite. Abm. Bowman and Robert Craig
This will was recorded at Harrodsburg, Mercer County, Kentucky 28 Apr 1789 and rerecorded at Frederick County, Virginia 3 Feb 1806. (P.186-187)

ROGERS, CATHERINE
Inventory and appraisal: 3 Feb 1806
Appraisers: Robert Vance, Wm. Kerfoot and Thomas Relph
(P.188)

CATLETT, ROBERT
Estate sale: 3 Feb 1806
Includes inventory of property taken by Mrs. Mary Catlett at time of appraisal.
Listed among buyers: George, Robert, Mary, David, Jesse and Henry Catlett (P.189-191)

BROUNLEY, JOHN
Account current: 3 Feb 1806
Admr: Betsy Brounley
Examiners: John Woodcock, Philip Nelson and Francis Gildard
(P.191-192)

CONRAD, JOHN
Account current: 3 Feb 1806
Admr: John Peyton
Examiners: Joseph Tidball and Joseph Caldwell
(P.192-196)

CARTER, WILLIAM
Inventory and appraisal: 3 Feb 1806
Appraisers: Francis Berry, James Oliver and Stephen Grubs (p.196)

GRUBS, HUMPHREY
Estate Sale: 4 Feb 1806
Listed among buyers: Stephen, Darvis, Betsy and Jesse Grubs (P.196-198)

STEPHENS, LEWIS, SR
Will: 10 Feb 1797/ 4 Feb 1806
Wife: unnamed
Son: Lewis Stephens
Dau: Mary Emmett
To wife, life estate in tract of land purchased of Mary Wolfe and Christian Niswanger, also land adjoining Capt. James Bush. To son Lewis, land patented by my father and by him conveyed to me, said tract commonly known as "the muster ground".
(Lewis Stephens, Sr. was a trustee when Winchester was established, witnessed possessions of Jost Hite's second wife in 1741, founded the City of Stephensburg, arrived with Jost Hite's settlers, son of immigrant Peter Stephens)
Exr: Lewis Stephens
Wit: R.W. Peacock, Edward Howe and Eliza Peacock (P.198-199)

CARTER, JAMES
Estate account: 5 Feb 1806
Exrs: Joseph and James Carter (P.200-202)

DINSMORE, JOHN
Estate Sale: 1 Apr 1806
Buyer: Mary Dinsmore (P.202-203)

KING, JOSEPH
Inventory and appraisal: 2 Apr 1806
Appraisers: Josiah Craig, Thornly Berry and Charles Graves (P.203-204)

HOLT/HOTT(?), HENRY
Additions to appraisement: 2 Apr 1806
Appraisers: Thos. Barrett, James Curl and Benjamin Barrett (P.204)

BELL, JAMES
Inventory, appraisal and sale: 2 Apr 1806
Appraisers: Abner Babb, John Housman, Jesse Britton
Admr: Thomas Bell
Listed as buyers: Eliner, Thomas and Stephen Bell (P.204-206)

EARHART, PHILIP
Sale account: 2 Apr 1806
Sale of two slaves (P.206)

CONNER, Ann
Settlement of estate: 5 May 1806
Exrs: David Greenlee and William McIntire
Legatees: Israel Jones, Ann Conner, Abraham Nelson, Wm. McIntire and David Greenlee (P.207)

TAYLOR, JOHN
Inventory and appraisal: 5 May 1806
Appraisers: William McDonald, Lewis Stephens and Jared Williams (P.207-210)

BRACKNEY, JOSEPH
Inventory and appraisal: 6 May 1806
Appraisers: L. Catlett, Joseph Hainey, David Brown
(p. 211-212)

MYERS, STEPHEN
Estate Account. 6 May 1806
Exr: Jacob Myers
Examiners: Samuel Kerchival, John Hening, Lewis Stephens
(p. 213-214)

CARTMELL, EDWARD
Will. 5 Nov 1803/ 6 May 1806
Wife: Unnamed
Children: George, Regina, Elizabeth, Jane, Parthenia, Rachel
Children by former wife: Harrison, Martin, Hannah Bevins, Rebecca Weaver
"To loving wife, land leased to Ezekiel Carter"
Exrx: Wife
Wit: Thomas McClunn Jr., Abraham Larrick, Samuel Clark
(p. 215-216)

ZOLL/ZOOL, HENRY
Estate Account. 6 May 1806
Examiners: Henry Frye, Elias Kackley, Moses Russell
(p. 216)

KIMMER, BARBARA
Sale Account. 30 June 1806 (p. 217)

DICK, PETER
Inventory & Appraisal. 30 June 1806
Appraisers: Robert Luttrell(?), Benjamin Jolly, James Laing
(p. 218-219)

HOLT (HOTT?), GEORGE
Inventory & Appraisal. 30 June 1806
Appraisers: James Curl, Benjamin Barrett, David Barrett
(p. 220-221)

WICKERSHAM, WILLIAM
Inventory & Appraisal. 30 June 1806
Appraisers: John Cowgill, Moses Coats, Isaac Nevill
(p. 222)

ZANE, GENERAL ISAAC
Estate Sale. 30 June 1806
Admr: Joseph Longacre
Examiners: James Singleton, Martin Cartmell, Robert Glass
Principal buyers: Joseph Longacre, Jr., Joseph Longacre, Sr., Andrew Longacre (p. 223-226)

BELL, MARY
Inventory & Appraisal. 30 June 1806
"Her death which was July 9, 1805"
Appraisers: Joseph Gordon, Walter Denny, William Adams
(p. 226-227)

HAAS, FREDERICK, SR.
Inventory & Appraisal; Sale Account. 30 June 1806
Appraisers: Jacob Poe, Thomas Kernnan
Principal buyers: Elizabeth Haas, John Haas, Polly Haas
(p. 227-230)

MARQUIS, JOHN
Estate Account. 1 Sep 1806
Exrs: Francis Hutchings, William Wiley
Accounts settled by Matthew Wright and Thomas Stribling
"in obedience to a court order of 30 Aug 1798" (p. 230-232)

FRYE, JOSEPH
Inventory & Appraisal. 1 Sep 1806
(No appraisers listed) (p. 232-234)

VOWELL, THOMAS
Will: 30 Oct 1800/ 1 Sept 1806
Wife: Sarah
Sons: John, Samuel, Ebenezer, Benjamin and Thomas
Grandson: John, son of Thomas
Dau: Harriett Beatty, wife of Coe Beatty of Kentucky
Legacies to following dear friends; Rev. William Marshall of Philadelphia, Rev. John Anderson of Pittsburg and George Fulton, in my employe. Mentions land patented in Cumberland Co., Penn. in names of daughter Harriett and son Benjamin.
Exrs: Wife Sarah and friend Archibald Magill
Wit: H.W. Baker and Robert Dunbar
CODICIL: Should sons John and Thomas create dispute over settlement of this will they are to be disinherited.
2nd CODICIL: Because of present unkind and unfriendly conduct of sons John Creps Vowell and Thomas Vowell, they to receive $120 dollars each and no more. To grandson John Vowell, son of Thomas, five acres purchased of John Lantz. Further legacies to friends; William Hill and Robert Dunbar. Wit. to 2nd codicil; Adam Kiger and Alex Lanham.
(P.235-239)

WOLFE, GEORGE
Inventory and appraisal: 4 Apr 1804/ 1 Sept 1806
Admr: Benjamin Williams
Appraisers: Henry Richards, Philip Boucher and Elias Kackley
Listed among buyers: Agneys Wolfe (P.239-251)

ASHBY, LEWIS
Will: 20 May 1806/ 1 Sept 1806
Wife: Leanah
Children: Judy, Alfred, Mildred, Jenny, John, Buckner, Sidney, Lewis, Lucy Lewis Catlett and Kitty Morehead
Mentions land in Kentucky bequeathed "to me by my father"
Also requests that tract of land where I now live be sold and land purchased in Kentucky or some other part of western Country.
Exrs: Wife Leanah and son Alfred
Wit: Lewis Smith (P.251-252)

MUMMA, JACOB
Inventory and appraisal: 1 Sept 1806
Appraisers: Robert Ewing and Christopher Ellis
(P.252-254)

HOLMES, REBECCA
Will: 10 Sept 1806/ 6 Oct 1806
Daus: Elizabeth McGuire, Rebecca Conrad and Gertrude Holmes
Son: Andrew Hunter Holmes and Joseph Holmes
Exrs: Archibald Magill and Thomas Fawcett
Wit: Ann Kean and Jane Watkins
Exrs. refused executorship; new admrs. appointed by court, James Singleton, Martin Cartmell and David Holmes.
(P.254-255)

McILWIE, DAVID
Inventory and appraisal: 1 Dec 1806
Admr: Bennett Hale
Appraisers: John Kackley, Jacob Fry and Henry Clouser
(P.255)

LONGACRE, JOSEPH
Will: 13 Oct 1804/ 1 Dec 1806
Wife: Elizabeth
Sons: John, Andrew, Israel, Isaac, Ireson and Joseph
Daus: Mary, Elizabeth, Sarah, Hannah, Rebecca, Abigail and

Margaret.
Legacy of a horse to sons Joseph, Andrew, John and Ireson. Israel to learn a trade "in lieu of an horse". Money legacies to Mary, Sarah, Hannah, Rebecca, Abigail, Isaac and Margaret "in lieu of an horse"
Exrs: Sons Joseph amd Ireson Longacre
Wit: Jno. Fawcett, Thomas Fawcett Jr., Isaac Fawcett, Elijah Fawcett and John Fawcett Sr.
CODICIL: "I am in possession of a tract of land in Shenandoah County, which General Isaac Zane purchased of Benjamin Wilson. This land conveyed to me by Elizabeth McFarland, mother of Isaac Zane 3rd. Said land to be divided among my seven daughters" (P.256-261)

FARMER, WILLIAM
Will: 22 Feb 1801/ 1 Dec 1806
Wife: Susa
Children: William, Sarah and Nancy (only ones named)
Testator refers to six daughters and four sons.
Exrs: Wife Susa and friend Jacob Rinker
Wit: John Rogers, Frederick Light and Joseph Fisher
(P.261-262)

LUKE, PETER
Inventory and appraisal: 1 Dec 1806
Appraisers: Peter McMurray, William Taylor and Thomas Jackson (P.262-263)

LITTLER, ISAAC
Will: 20 Jun 1806/ 2 Dec 1806
Wife: Barbara
Sons: Daniel, Joseph, James and Isaac
Daus: Betsy McMunn and Maria Littler
Grandson: William R. Littler
Plantation called "Barley's Place" to wife. To son Daniel, property on Abraham Creek. To son James, coppersmith tools.
Exrs: Wife Barbara and sons Daniel and James
Wit: Thomas Heist and Lemuel Bent
(Frederick Co. Marriages; George McMunn m Elizabeth Litler 12 Dec 1793) (P.264-265)

HAAS, FREDERICK
Administrator's account: 2 Dec 1806
Admr: John Haas
Examiners: Abraham Miller ans James Littler
(P.266)

CLEAVER, EZEKIEL
"of Montgomery County, Pennsylvania"
Will: 7 Apr 1785/ see recording information below
Children: Ezekiel, Ellis, Sarah, Mary, Elizabeth, Peter and Martha
Exrs: Dau Sarah and sons Ezekiel and Ellis
Wit: John Cleaver, John Evans Jr. and Nathan Cleaver
This will recorded in Montgomery Co., Pa, 25 May 1785
Re-recorded in Frederick Co., Va, 2 Dec 1806
(P.267-268)

RINKER, CASPER
Administration Bond: 3 Dec 1806
Admr: Jacob Rinker
Bondsmen: Edward Talbott, Jesse Pugh, William Farmer, Daniel Abbott, Jacob Weaver and Hugh Holmes
(P.268-270)

McGUIRE, EDWARD, SR.
Will: 19 July 1806/ 1 Dec 1806
Sons: John, William, Edward, and Samuel
Daus: Elizabeth, Ann, Susannah and Mary McDonald
Grandchildren:Angus William, Milicent Susannah and Edward Charles McDonald, children of daughter Mary.
"IT is my will that the lot upon which the Catholic Chapel now stands shall be forever appropriated for that use and no other".
Wit: Goldsmith Chandlee and Benj. Chandlee
(Frederick Co. marriages; Milicent Doby m Edward McGuire 27 July 1774) (P.270-273)

HOLMES, REBECCA
Account current: 5 Jan 1807
Division of the dower slaves of Rebecca Holmes to the heirs of Joseph Holmes, to wit; Judge Holmes, Rebecca Conrad, Gertrude Holmes, Nancy Boyd, David Holmes, Edward McGuire, J. Tidball, James Singleton and Richard Barton (P.273-274)

FARMER, WILLIAM
Inventory and appraisal: 5 Jan 1807
No signatures (P.274-275)

HOLMES, REBECCA
Inventory and appraisal: 5 Jan 1807
Appraisers: Martin Cartmell, Thomas Cartmell and Richard Barton (P.275-277)

MAUCK, MATHIAS
Account current: 5 Jan 1807
Exr: Anthony Mauck
Examiners: Tarlton Webb and George Blakeman (P.277-278)

PARKINS, JOSEPH
Account current: 5 Jan 1807
Exr: Joseph Steer
Examiners: W. Davison and J. Tidball (P.278-280)

TURNER, SAMUEL
Estate Sale: 5 Jan 1807
Adm: Zeph. Turner (P.281)

GAWTHROP, JOHN
Inventory and appraisal: 6 Jan 1807
Appraisers: Peter Babb, Richard Barrett and David Barrett (P.282)

MURRAY, GEORGE
Orphan's accounts: 2 Feb 1807
Guardian: John Woodcock
Orphans: George Murray, Jane Bryarly wife of David Bryarly, Polly Murray and Cyrus Murray
Examiners: Sam Bryarly, George Catlett and Oliver Frenston (P.282-283)

LUKE, PETER
Will: 20 Nov 1803/1 Sept 1806
Wife: Elizabeth
Sons: Jacob, Peter and John
Other sons and daughters mentioned not named.
Exrs: My friends Jacob Luke and Amos Clayton
Wit: John Madden and George Blakeman (Recording of this will delayed pending deposition of John Madden, residing in Bourbon Co., Kentucky) (P.283-284)

WOOD, ROBERT
Inventory and appraisal: 2 Feb 1807
Appraisers: J. Tidball, Robert Mackey and H. Holmes (P.284-287)

MILLER, RICHARD
Account Current: 2 Feb 1807
Examiners: Joseph Luckey and Jacob Lenard (P.287-288)

MARKER, JACOB
"agreeably to an order of court directed to John B. Tilden, Elisha Phelps and George Linn for the settlement of the estate of Jacob Marker,dec'd, with his execs. George Linn and John B. Tilden met at the house of James Henning, the surviving exec and Andrew Redd, exec of Adam Kline,dec'd, Jan 13, 1807, when the following document was produced -----"? (P.288)

ANDERSON, ABRAHAM
Inventory and appraisal: 2 Feb 1807
Appraisers: Thos. Littleton, Jasper Bale and John Scarff (P.289)

ASHBY, LEWIS
Inventory and appraisal: 3 Feb 1807
Appraisers: John Wiatt, Andrew Turner and James Oliver (P.289-292)

RISLER, JOHN
Inventory and appraisal: 3 Feb 1807
Appraisers: Nathan Littler and Peter McMurray (P.292-293)

SNAPP, ADAM
Will: 8 Aug 1803/ 3 Feb 1807
Wife: Elizabeth
Son: John
Dau: Mary Fry
Grandchildren: Adam and Elizabeth Fry
"Estate to be sold and money used to support son John"
Exr: George Swihar
Wit: William Panaker and William Baily (P.293)

FURLONG, PATRICK
Inventory and appraisal: 3 Feb 1807
Appraisers: Nathan Littler, William Bond and Peter McMurray (P.294)

YOUNG, LEWIS
Inventory and appraisal: 7 Apr 1807
Appraisers: William Shaw and Ambrose Barnett (P.294)

SHNYDER, JACOB
Esatate sale: 8 Apr 1807
Admr: Jacob Snider and D. Snyder
Examiners: M. Tilden and James Singleton (P.294-298)

LEWIS, HENRY
Inventory and appraisal: 9 Apr 1807
Appraisers: Joseph Gordon, John Rogers and William Ames (P.298)

SNAPP, ADAM
Inventory and appraisal: 4 May 1807
Appraisers: Thomas Barrett and George Deal (P.299)

RITTER, ADAM
Will: 16 Mar 1807/ 4 May 1807
Wife: Hannah
Dau: Susannah Haymaker
"Entire estate to wife during her lifetime, at her decease everything to daughter Susanna" (P.299-300)

IRELAND, JAMES
Estate sale: 6 July 1807
Listed among buyers: Francis, James and Lucinda Ireland
Examiners: Thos. Castleman for Sheriff Isaac Hite
(P.300-303)

DRAKE, JOSEPH
Inventory and appraisal: 6 July 1807
Appraisers: William Kershival, John Sowers and Peter Lauck
(p.304)

ORNDORFF, JOHN
Estate sale: 6 July 1807
Among buyers: Hannah, John, Jonathan, Philip and Saml. Orndorff (P.305-309)

SIDWELL, SAMUEL
Account current: 7July 1807
Guardians for orphans of Samuel Sidwell-Nathaniel White and Sarah Sidwell, orphans not named.
Examiners: W. Davison and Obed Waite (P.310-312)

McDONALD, ANGUS
Account current: 7 July 1807
Exr: Ann McDonald
Accounts beginning with funeral expenses 1778
Examiners: John Smith and J. Caldwell (P.312-315)

JOHN, FREE NEGRO
Will: 25 Apr 1807/ 31 Aug 1807
"Last will and testament of Mr. free John (negro)"
Wife mentioned, not named
Children: "my three sons and one daughter by my first wife, Benjamin, Atram, Henry and Jane". "To my Nancy and daughter Minta, all the rest of my estate".
Daughter Minta's children; Henry and Daniel
Exr: David Lupton
Wit: Dan Magruder, Jonathan Wright and Midas Scarff
(P.315)

RITTER, ADAM
Inventory and appraisal: 31 Aug 1807
Michael Copenhouer, Andrew Kiger, William Helpherstine; Appraisers (P.316)

HOUSMAN/HORSMAN, DAVID (miller)
Will: 13 June 1806/ 31 Aug 1807
Wife: Ruth
"To wife Ruth, land on Sleepy Creek in Berkeley County"
Exr: Wife Ruth
Wit: Joshua Lupton, James Carpenter and Jonah Lupton
(P.316-317)

JENKINS, WILLIAM
Account current: 31 Aug 1807
Admr: Edward Jenkins
Exam: W. Davison and J. Tidball (P.317)

ALBERT, ADAM
Will: 5 May 1807/ 31 Aug 1807
Wife: Flora
Children: George, Adam, Betsy, Polly, Sally, Susannah and Catherine
"Should any property fall to me from the estate of Henry Shipler, dec'd, of from his surviving widow, said property to go to my daughter Betsy". Executors to negotiate with James Chambers of the state of Kentucky, for a certain tract of land in that state.
Exrs:Son George and my trusty friends Daniel Lynn and John

Fry
Wit: William Bond, Joseph Wood and John Wright
Sec: John Parrell and Joseph Parrell (P.317-318)

DINSMORE, JOHN
Estate settlement: 31 Aug 1807
Admr: Mary Dinsmore
Examiners: LeRoy Daingerfield and Fras. Stribling (P.319-321)

DILLON, JAMES
Will: 19 Apr 1807/ 31 Aug 1807
Property to be sold and monies divided among my nine children; Ann, wife of John Banks, John, Rachel, Rebecca, Nathan, James, Moses, Levi and Joel. To my oldest son William, one dollar.
Exrs: "my beloved son William and my trusty friend Thomas Barrett"
Wit: Benjamin Barrett, John Antram and John Wright (P.321-322)

HANCHER, SARAH
Will: 30 Nov 1802/ 31 Aug 1807
Widow of John Hancher
Sons: William and David
Daus: Layda and Susanna
Granddaughter: Sarah Moncer(?)
"To Layda Hancher,a single woman, horse and furniture" To son David, land purchased of Cornelius Garde and Robert Cooper.
Exr: David Hancher
Wit: John Lynn, Thomas Baldwin and John Chapman (P.322-323)

CAMPBELL, JOHN
Will: 30 May 1807/ 31 Aug 1807
Wife: Elizabeth
Children: Son Ever only one named
"All the property I now possess in America to my beloved wife Elizabeth; all the property I possess in the Kingdom of Great Britain to be equally divided among my children".
Exrs: Wife Elizabeth and son Ever
Wit: R. Holliday, Edward Slater and Angus McDonald (P.323-324)

WOLFE, GEORGE
Account current: 31 Aug 1807
Admr: Benjamin Williams
Examiners: Philip Bucker and Moses Russell (P.324)

GRIFFETH, THOMAS
Inventory and appraisal: 1 Sept 1807
Appraisers: James Steer, John Cowgill and William McIntire (P.324-325)

KING, JOSEPH
Sale account: 1 Dec 1807 (P.325-330)

KEMP, JOHN
Will: 3 Sept 1807/ 5 Oct 1807
Wife: Nancy
Children: William Kemp, Elizabeth Doughty, John Kemp, Jane Harriett(?) and Jesse Kemp
"it shall be discretional in my wife, at her death, to bestow to any one of my heirs or posterity, my silver watch".
Exrs: Wife Nancy and son William
Wit: Moses Payne, Thomas Watson and Minty Northern
Sec: John Kemp and George Cooper (P.330-331)

PARKINS, ELIZABETH
Will: 14 May 1806/ 30 Nov 1807
Sons: John, David and Jonathan
Daus: Phebe Wright, Mary Shion, Hannah Smith and Ann Harned
To son John, 5 shillings and a book "No Crop-No Crown". To daus. Phebe Wright and Mary Shion and son David, each 5 shillings. To daughter Hannah Smith, Bible and a book. To Ann Harned, looking glass, warming pan and two books. Remainder of estate to be sold and monies to be divided between son Jonathan and daughter Ann.
Exr: Goldsmith Chandlee
Wit: Pamela Way, Hannah Miles and Jonathan Wright
(P.331-332)

GAWTHROP, JAMES
Will: 11 Jun 1807/ 30 Nov 1807
Wife: Patience
Sons: James and Thomas
Daus: Edith Taylor, Hannah Jenkins and Rachel Gawthrop
To wife, "two thirds of profits from plantation during her life and chaste widowhood". To son James, land known as Plummer's Survey, deeded to me by Henry Lee, Esq., Govenor dated 1 July 1793. To son Thomas, my watch. Monies divided among daughters.
Exrs: David Lupton and David Barrett, son of Benjamin Barrett dec'd
Wit: Jacob Jenkins and George Dawson
Sec: Thomas Barrett, Jacob Rinker, Benjamin Barrett, Thomas Gawthrop, David Barrett, Daniel Wade, Jacob Taylor and James Gawthrop (P.332-333)

ALBERT, ADAM
Inventory and appraisal:30 Nov. 1807
Appraisers: Conrad Huntsberger, William Tyler and Joseph Parrill, Sr. (P.333)

LUKE, PETER
Sale account dated 21 Apr 1807 (P.333-336)

MARTIN, ALBINA
Estate account: 1 Dec 1807
Admr: Isaac Hite
Isaac Hite ordered to pay William Davison for the use of Thomas Singer (P.336)

CRUM, ANTHONY
Inventory and appraisal: 1Dec 1807
Appraisers: Henry Seviers, Joshua Cooper and Bartholomew Smith (P.336-337)

IRELAND, JAMES
Accounting: 1 Dec 1807
"Bonds taken by Thomas Castleman and Isaac Hite for property belonging to the deceased". (P.337-338)

MARQUES, JAMES
Account current: 30 Nov 1807
Admr: Mary Marques
Legatees: George Taylor, William Marques, John Marques, William Morrison(his wife's legacy), Abner Reeder and Moses Bonham. (A. Reeder married Elizabeth Marques 10 Nov 1798- Mary Marques security) (P.338-339)

WILSON, JOHN
Inventory and appraisal: 4 Jan 1808
Appraisers: John Hamilton and Nicholas Kern (P.340-341)

FAWCETT, JOHN
Estate Account: 1786
Examined and recorded 4 Jan 1808 (P.341-342)

POWERS, JOHN
Estate settlement: 4 Jan 1808
Acting Admr: Wyatt Whitehead
Examiners: James Baker, William Cook and Samuel Kercheval (P.342-343)

MADDEN, JACOB
Inventory and appraisal: 1 Feb 1808
Appraisers: William Taylor, Peter McMurray and Meredith Helm
Sales account; listed among buyers; Charles Madden, Mabra Madden and Jane Madden (P.344-345)

STRIBLING, JOHN-Orphans
Account current: July 1802/ 1 Feb 1808
Guardian: Alexander Milton
Examiners: Wm. Castleman and Thos. Kinnon (P.345-349)

MOFFETT, JOHN
Accounts current: 1 Jan 1801/ 1 Feb 1808
Examiners: John Tilden and William McLeod (P.349-351)

HENDRON, JANE
Appraisal: 1 Feb 1808
Exr: Samuel Hendron
Appraisers: Samuel Richardson, John Catlett and William Hand
"Her estate pending upon the settlement of her father's (Rev. James Ireland) estate". (P.351)

WHITMAN, HENRY, SR.
Will: May 1804/ 1 Feb 1808
Sons: Edward, Jacob, Daniel, Henry, Amos and Ezekiel
Dau: Mary Jones
"To son Henry Whitman, part of plantation adjoining lines of William Barrett and Nathaniel Carter; to son Amos, land adjoining Martin Frieze and Edward Whitman". Son Henry to pay 8 pounds each to Ezekiel and Richard Whitman and Mary Jones.
Exr: Son Jacob
Wit: John Hollandhead, Martin Frieze and Michael Fries (P.351-353)

DILLON, JAMES
Inventory and Appraisal: 2 Feb 1808
Appraisers: Thomas Barrett, James Curl and John Griffeth (P.353-354)

CAMPBELL, JOHN
Inventory and appraisal: 2 Feb 1808
Admr: Elizabeth Campbell (P.354-355)

KEMP, JOHN
Appraisal and Sale account: 2 Feb 1808
Appraisers: James Sinclair, Wm. Northern and John Haddox (P.355-356)

BRANSON, MARTHA
Will: 12 Feb 1805/ 2 Feb 1808
Daus: Martha Fawcett, wife of Thomas Fawcett; Eunice Painter, Elizabeth Branson, Sarah Baily and Amelia Larrick(?)
Grandchildren: Hannah Farnby and Abraham Branson

"mother's share to surviving children of my daughter Elizabeth Branson"
Exr: Son-in law Thomas Fawcett
Wit: Goldsmith Chandlee and Joseph Wood
Sec: Isaac Baker and Goldsmith Chandlee (P.356-357)

MYERS, JACOB
Inventory and appraisal: 2 Feb 1808
Appraisers: John Snider, Jacob Hammack, Jacob Shambaugh and Jacob Snider. Estate sale lists buyer Henry Myers (P.357-358)

CORDER, JOSEPH, SR.
Will: 12 Oct 1807/ 4 Apr 1808
Wife: Martha- only child named daughter Lucy
"At the death of my wife, estate to be equally divided among all my children, except my youngest daughter Lucy, she to have negro girl Hannah"
Wit: Zachariah Selmon, John McDonald, George Farrow and Benjamin Corder (P.358-359)

FISHER, JOSEPH
Will: 12 Dec 1804/ 4 Apr 1808
Wife: Elizabeth
Children: Lewis, Lydia, Hannah, Mary, Eleanor and Elizabeth
Stepchildren: Charity and Levi Lewis
"Wife to have all profits and priviliges of land during her lifetime, after her decease all to son Lewis Fisher"
Exrs: Wife Elizabeth and Lewis McCoole
Wit: John McCoole, Darlington and John Fisher
(Frederick Co. Marriages- Joseph Fisher m wid Elizabeth Lewis 11 Mar 1790) (P.359-360)

MYERS, STEPHEN
Orphans Account: 4 Apr 1808
Report of commissioners on orphans account (P.360)

ROSS, DAVID
Account current: 5 Apr 1808
Exr: Enos Ross
Examiners: David Ridgeway and John Jolliffe (P.360-361)

PLUM, CASSIMER
Will: 8 Jan 1808/ 5 Apr 1808
Sons: Vance and Ab.
Daus: Elizabeth Bradford, Polly Campbell and Rebecca Peters
Grandchildren: John, Peggy and Polly Bradford, Sally Peters and John and Ab. Tipple
Exrs: Vance Plum and son-in-law William Campbell
Wit: Lewis Stephens and George Lynn (P.361-362)

SETTLE, STROTHER
Inventory and appraisal: 5 Apr 1808
Appraisers: B. Farrow, Valentine Leach and John Singleton (P.362-363)

MORRISON, MARY (alias Mary Spinder)
Will: 18 Jan 1808/ 5 Apr 1808
"House purchased of John Taylor, deeded to William Spinder, I give to my brother William McLeod"
Exrs: William McLeod and George Lynn
Wit: George Lynn and M. Baker
(Frederick Co. Mar. Mary Spinder m James Morrison 19 Aug 1800) (P.363-364)

HOLLINGSWORTH, ROBERT
Inventory and appraisal: 20 Jan 1800/ 2 May 1808
Appraisers: Bartholomew Smith, William McCormack and John Lindsey (P.364)

BROWN'S ORPHANS
Guardian account: 2 May 1808
Guardian: Elisha Phelps
Orphan: Eleanor Scholfield, nee Brown
Examiners: William McLeod and Jacob Lenard (P.364-365)

CONRAD, DANIEL, (Doctor)
Inventory and appraisal: 2 May 1808
Appraisers: Jn. Tidball, John Bell and Ab. Miller (P.365-371)

GORDEN, JOSEPH
Will: 26 Apr 1808/ 2 May 1808
Wife: Rachel
Mother: Mary
Son: John
Sisters: Hannah Sellars, Rachel Yarnell and Ann Smart
"Estate to wife, at her decease, to son John. If he dies without heirs, to my sisters. Wife to pay Mother 10 dollars".
Exrs: Wife Rachel and Meredith Darlington
Wit: Wm. Holliday, John Rogers, B.Fisher and James Holliday
(Frederick Co. Mar. Joseph Gordon m Rachel Follis 18 Dec 1792) (P.371)

KEELER/KULER, JOHN
Inventory and appraisal: 2 May 1808
Admr: Jacob Huddle, Jr.
Appraisers: Jacob Danner, John Lindsey and Lewis Rode (P.372-374)

FAWCETT, REBECCA
Statement of Deputy Sheriff Charles McCormick that said Rebecca Fawcett died with no apparent personal estate.
Recorded 2 May 1808 (P.374)

BALL, JASPER
Inventory and appraisal: 4 July 1808
Appraisers: William Taylor, Jas. Ware and Thos. Kernan
Among buyers: Edward Ball (P.374-376)

FISHER, JOSEPH
Inventory and appraisal: 4 July 1808
Appraisers: Joseph Gorden and M. Darlington (P.376)

CORREL, CHARLES
Inventory and appraisal: 4 July 1808
Appraisers: Jacob Danner, John Lindsey and Abraham Nisewander (P.377)

SPERRY, JACOB
Will, inventory, appraisal and sale: Recorded 4 July 1808
Will dated 5 Nov 1807
Wife: Elizabeth
Children mentioned-not named
Exrs: Abraham Lauck and Frederick Kurtz
Wit: George McCard(?), Samuel Kuran and John Brown
Appraisers: John Schultz, Adam Kirtz and Peter Ham (P.377-382)

GLENN, WILLIAM
Account current: 5 Sept 1808
Acting Admr: John Wright
Examiners: John Kearsley and Dan Morgan (P.383)

SEABERT, JACOB
Inventory, appraisal and sale: 5 Sept 1808
Admrs: Mordecai and James Bean
Appraisers: Michael White and Jacob Frye
Among buyers: Adam and Jacob Seabert (P.383-386)

POOL, DANIEL
Inventory and appraisal: 5 Sept 1808
Court order of Jan 1805
Appraisers: Ja. Mitchell, Jas. B. Rice and Meredith Helm (P.386)

DOWDE, WILLIAM
Inventory and appraisal: 5 Sept 1808
Appraisers: James Davidson and John Larrick (P.386-387)

HENRY, DANIEL
Inventory and appraisal: 5 Sept 1808
Appraisers: James Moore, John Newman and John Jacobs (P.387-395)

CRYZER, JACOB
Inventory and appraisal: 5 Sept 1808
Appraisers: James Moore, Wm. Headley (P.395)

COOPER, JEREMIAH
Account current: 8 Sept 1802/ 3 Oct 1808
Admrs: Rotecia(?) and Jacob Cooper
Examiners: B.Tilden and Isaac Hite (P.396)

McMURRAY, JAMES
Account current: 3 Oct 1808
Admr: Peter McMurray
Examiners: Bushrod Taylor and G.H.Harris (P.397)

BALL, JASPER
Division of slaves: 5 Dec 1808
Legatees: Edward Ball, Samuel Conner, William Foley and Jasper Ball
Subscribers: Jas. Ware, Thos. Kennon and William Taylor
(Frederick Co. Mar.-Catherine Ball m William Foley 10 Mar 1798; Samuel Conner m Sally Ball 12 Jan 1789) (P.397)

CAMPBELL, COLLIN
Will: 27 Oct 1808/ 5 Dec 1808
Dau: Nancy Baker
"I bequeath my entire estate to my daughter, Nancy Baker".
Exr: "my good friend and son-in-law James Baker"
Wit: John Bragg, Jacob Berlin and John Steele (P.398)

McILWIE, DAVID
Account current: 6 Dec 1808
Admr: Capt. Bennett Hale
Examiners: Jas. Singleton and Moses Russell (P.398-399)

KLINE, ADAM
Account current: 6 Dec 1808
Exr: Andrew Redd
Examiners: B.Tilden and Elisha Phelps (P.399-400)

ALLAMONG, JACOB
Inventory and appraisal: 2 Jan 1809
Admr: John Allamong and Elizabeth Allamong (P.400-401)

COOPER, ROBERT
Inventory and appraisal: 2 Jan 1809
Appraisers: LeRoy Daingerfield, Thomas Baldwin,Jr. and Joseph Flair (P.401-402)

COCKRELL, JOHN
Inventory and appraisal 2 Jan 1809 (P.403-404)

McCLEARY, JANE
Will: 31 Jan 1804/ 6 Feb 1809
Sister: Isabella
Nephew: James Gordon Hening
Exr: Archibald Magill
Wit: Ann Magill, J.H. Gordon and Thomas Lyles (P.404)

HAYNIE, PRESLY
Inventory and appraisal: 6 Feb 1809
Appraisers: Solomon Van Meter and James Moore (P.405-407)

PETERS, HENRY
Inventory and appraisal: 7 Dec 1804/ 6 Feb 1809
Appraisers: Joseph Lucky, Nicholas Kern, John Hotsapiller
Account current: Recorded 6 Feb 1809 (P.408-409)

ANDERS, EARNEST
Orphan's guardianship account:6 Feb 1809
Orphans: Milly, Jacob, Henry, Isaac, Earnest and Molly
Guardian: William Tyler
Examiners: W. Davison and Jno. Tidball (P.409-410)

SETTLE, STROTHER G.
Sale Account: 6 Feb 1809
Exr: Larkin Settle
Listed among buyers: Larkin and Wilford Settle (P.410-412)

COOPER, ROBERT
Sale Account: 6 Feb 1809
Exr: Thomas Cooper
Among buyers: Thomas and Elen Cooper (P.412-414)

McKAY, ANDREW
Inventory and appraisal: 7 Feb 1809
Court order of Dec 1804
Appraisers: Sam. Kerchival, Wm. Hand and Thomas Grubb (P.414-415)

HOGE, ASA
Accounts current: 7 Feb 1809
Examiners: Jn. McCoole and John Wright (P.415)

JONES, STEPHEN
Inventory and appraisal: 7 Feb 1809
Appraisers: Peter McMurray, Thomas Jackson and Michael Earhart (P.415-417)

CARTER, MARY
Sale account: 8 Feb 1809
Ordered by Dec 1807 court
Subscribers: Thos. Castleman and Cornelius Baldwin (P.417-418)

CLEVENGER, ASA
Inventory and appraisal: 6 Mar 1809
Appraisers: G. Catlett, Henry Catlett, Esaias Earle and Wyall Whitehead (P.418-420)

LOWRY, ROBERT
Will: 11 Jan 1805/ 8 Mar 1809
Wife: Agneys
Sons: Moses and John
Daus: Jane Todd, widow of James Todd; Margaret McMurran, wife of Joseph McMurran; Hannah and Agneys Lowry
"Son Moses to provide my widow firewood, wheat, Indian corn and twenty dollars; also son John to provide my widow firewood, wheat, Indian corn and twenty dollars"
Exrs: Wife Agneys, son John and Nathan Lupton
Wit: John Darlington, Joshua Lupton and Hannaniah Pugh
All three designated executors refused to act; New Exrs: Joseph Baker and his security Jacob Weaver
(Fdk. Co. Mar. James Todd m Jane Lowry 17 Jun 1794)
(P.420-422)

GEORGE MURRAY'S ORPHANS
Orphans: Cyrus, George, Polly Murray and Jane Bryarly
Guardianship account: Jan 1807/ 4 Apr 1809
Guardian: John Shearman Woodcock
Examiners: W. Davison, J. Tidball and E.Smith (P.422-425)

MOCK, CHRISTOPHER
Will: 10 Jan 1809/ 4 Apr 1809
Wife: Rozena
Brothers and sisters: Daniel Mock, Geo. Mock, Catherine Everly, Christina Harmon and Susanna Mock
"To wife, that property of which she was in possession previous to my intermarriage with her; to my brothers and sisters, estate left to me by my father together with my own".
Exr: Abraham Nisewander
Wit: Lewis Amiss, John Snyder and F. Martin
(Fdk Co Mar; Christina Mock m Jacob Harmon 29 Oct 1797)
(P.425-426)

JONES, STEPHEN
Sale account: 4 Apr 1809
Among buyers: Catherine Jones
(Fdk co Mar; Steven Jones m Catherine Bonham 23 Mar 1783)
(P.427-432)

WRIGHT, WILLIAM
Inventory and appraisal: 1 May 1809
Appraisers: Luis Roads, Joseph Heck and Joseph Stump
(P.432-433)

HAMMOND, CHARLES
Account current: 1 May 1809
Admr: Samuel Mengies
Examiners: Sam. Baker and Joseph Miller (P.433)

DEMOSS, THROCKMORTON
Inventory, appraisal and sale: 1 May 1809
Appraisers: Micajah Crupper, Geo. Lane and Edward Jones
Among buyers: Nancy Demoss (P.434-435)

BROWN, JOHN
Account current: 1 May 1809
Exr: Elijah Fawcett
Examiners: Jno. Ball and Wm. Bayles (P.436)

JACKSON, SARAH
Will: 3 Feb 1809/ 1May 1809
Widow of Edward Jackson. Formerly resident of Maryland
Sons: Nathan N. Jackson and Henry Jackson
Daus: Elizabeth, wife of Joseph Longacre
"To son Nathan, money derived from proprty sold in Maryland in estate of Edw. and Sarah Jackson"

Exr: Son Henry Jackson
Wit: B. Tilden, Daniel Mytinger and Simon Carson (P.436-437)

SCARFF, JOHN
Inventory and appraisal: 1 May 1809
Appraisers: Philip Porter, W. Touchstone and John Hoover (P.437-438)

HENRY, DANIEL
Account current: 2 May 1809
Admrs: William Van Meter and Rebecca Henry
Examiners: J. Marshall and Thomas Mullan (P.439-441)

PAYNE, MOSES
Inventory and appraisal: 5 Jun 1809
Appraisers: John Jacobs, James Moore and Thomas Mullan (P.441-442)

HAMMOND, CHARLES
Inventory and appraisal: 20 Feb 1804/5 Jun 1809
Appraisers: C. Beall, Sam. Baker and A.G. Barrett (P.442-444)

LARRICK, JOHN
Inventory, appraisal and sale:5 Jun 1809
Appraisers: Michael Mauck and John Adams
Among buyers: Margaret, Joseph, Elizabeth, Jane, Susanna and John Larrick (P.445-450)

HAYNIE, MATTY
Inventory, appraisal and sale: 6 Jun 1809
Appraisers: Solomon Van Meter, John Jacobs and James Moore
Among buyers: Griffen, Presly, Molly and Catherine Haynie (P.450-451)

DRAKE, JOSEPH
Estate settlement: 6 Jun 1809
Admr: Saml. Drake (P.452-454)

JONES, CATHERINE
Inventory and appraisal: 6 Jun 1809
Appraisers: Peter McMurray, John Helm, Sr, and Joseph Hedges (P.454-455)

MURRAY ORPHANS
Guardianship account: 6 Jun 1809
Guardian: Geo Catlett
Orphans: Cyrus and George
Examiners: Sam. Kerchival and Esas Earle (P.455-456)

DOWELL, WILLIAM
Account current: 3 July 1809
Exrs: Charles Johnston and Mary, his wife, "late Mary Dowell"
Examiners: Robert Gray and J. Tidball (P.456)

ROUT, PETER
Sale Account: 3 July 1809 (P.457-458)

HOLT/HOTT(?), Henry
Account current: 31 July 1809
Admr: Adam Holt
Examiners: W. Davison and J. Tidball (P.458-459)

McKEARN, HUGH HENRY
Inventory and appraisal: 31 July 1809
Appraisers: W. Davison and J. Tidball (P.459-461)

WHITE, ALEXANDER
Account current: Beginning account 27 Dec 1804
Exr: Sarah White
Slaves delivered to Robert, John, Margaret, Alexander and Polly White
Examiners: E. Smith and W. Davison (P.461-464)

SITTLER, ISAAC
Inventory and appraisal: 31 July 1809
Appraisers: Jos. Gamble, Robert Gray and Isaac Burk (P.464-465)

WOLFE, CHRISTOPHER
Will: 5 Feb 1809/ 31 July 1809
"Everything to my wife (not named) as long as she remains single. At her death, everything to Phebe, Caty and Susan except 200 acres of land in Hampshire County, to be divided by Isaac and Jacob Gwen". relationships not defined.
Wit: George Tresler and Peter Cooley (P.465)

SITTLER, ISAAC
Account current: 31 July 1809
Admr: Barbara Sittler
Examiners: E. Smith and J. Tidball (P.466-467)

LEWIS, HENRY
Inventory, appraisal and sale: 31 July 1809 (P.468-471)

GAWTHROP, JAMES
Inventory and appraisal: 31 July 1809
Appraisers: Peter Babb, David Lupton, James Curl and Joseph Lupton (P.471-472)

FOLK, ROBERT
Inventory, appraisal and sale: 1 Aug 1809
Appraisers: Lewis Amiss, John Snyder and T. Mastin (P.472-473)

PRICE, GEORGE
Estate settlement:18 Dec 1797/ 4 Sept 1809
Examiners: Elijah Littler and Joseph Wood (P.474-475)

McCABE, JOHN
Inventory and appraisal: 4 Sept 1809
Appraisers: John Ferguson, Jesse O'Rear and David Anderson (P.475)

BOND, RICHARD
Sale account: 4 Sept 1809
Signed by Fredwell Smith
Among buyers: William Bond (P.475-476)

HAYNIE, MATTI
Account current: 4 Sept 1809
Adm. accounts of Daniel Henry, dec'd. New admr. appointed George Reynolds
Examiners: Wm. Headley and James Moore (P.476-477)

HAYNIE, PRESLEY
Account current: 4 Sept 1809
Adm. accounts of Daniel Henry, dec'd.
Surviving admr: Elizabeth Haynie
Examiners: Wm. Headley, James Moore and Thomas Mullan (P.477)

BALDWIN, THOMAS
Will: 12 July 1809/ 4 Sept 1809
Wife: Elizabeth
Sons: William and Thomas
Daus: Rebecca Martin, Lidia Mooney, Jane Cox and Elizabeth Dunn
To wife, one third part of estate; daughter Rebecca Martin to have cabin and small lot during her widowhood and no longer; sons to pay money legacy to children of deceased daughter Lidia Mooney.
Exrs: Wife Elizabeth and sons William and Thomas
Wit: LeRoy Daingerfield (P.478-480)

JACKSON, SARAH
Inventory and appraisal: 4 Sept 1809
Appraisers: Simon Carson, Daniel Medinger and Richard Galloway (P.480-484)

WHITTINGTON, WILLIAM
Inventory and appraisal: 4 Sept 1809
Appraisers: Thomas Jackson, Peter McMurray and Carter Chandler (P.484-485)

SETTLE, STROTHER G.
Distribution of slaves: 4 Sept 1809
Distributed to Wilford Settle, George Berry, John Hennston(?), Larkin Settle and Mansfield Settle
Subscribers: William Monroe, Wm. Headley and Jn. Catlett (P.485-486)

BRANSON, MARTHA
Inventory and appraisal: 5 Sept 1809
Appraisers: Jno. Fawcett, Jos. Longacre and Jos. Snapp (P.486-489)

MYERS, JACOB
Account current: 5 Sept 1809
Admr: E. Carter
Examiners: John Frederick and Daniel Mock (P.489-490)

GAINS, BENJAMIN
Will: 5 Nov 1808/ 2 Oct 1809
"I give unto Christopher Crigler all my property, he to pay to each of my brothers and sisters one hundred dollars after my decease". (brothers and sisters not named)
Wit: Jacob Crigler and Nathaniel Jackson (P.490)

CARTMILL, EDWARD
Inventory and appraisal: 20 Oct 1809
Appraisers: Charles Barns, Michael Mock and Jacob Danner (P.490-493)

BUSH, ANDREW
Account current: 2 Oct 1809
Exr: Conrad Grebs
Examiners: Charles Brent and John Bell (P.493)

CLEVENGER, ASA
Sale account: 2 Oct 1809
Admr: Jacob Cleavenger
Among Buyers: David, Jacob, Hannah and Asa Cleavenger (P.494-496)

MASTIN, CHARLOTTE
Inventory and appraisal: 2 Oct 1809
Appraisers: Abraham Nisewander, Thos. Bush, Jr and Lain Baker (P.496-498)

McWHORTER, ROBERT
Will: 15 Aug 1809/ 5 Nov 1809
Sons: Alexander, John, Robert and Hugh
Daus: Elizabeth Furr, Jane Dick, Mary and Agneys McWhorter
Exr: George Smith of Back Creek
Wit: Andrew Smith, Jonathan Lovett, Margaret Boyd and
Ebenezer Williams (P.498-499)

CAMPBELL, JOHN
Sale account: 4 Dec 1809
Among buyers: Thomas, John and Ever Campbell (P.499-500)

CAMPBELL, ELIZABETH
Inventory and appraisal: 4 Dec 1809
Appraisers: Charles Lee, Geo. Bruce and Casper Seever
(P.500)

PERRY, IGNATIUS
Inventory and appraisal: 4 Dec 1809
Appraisers: Elijah Littler, Fran. Stribling and LeRoy
Daingerfield (P.501-504)

LARUE, JAMES
Will: 7 July 1804/ 5 Dec 1809
Wife: Clary/Clara
Sons: Samuel and John
Daus: Phebe and Clarissy
To son John, plantation I purchased of Jacob Larue. Daughters
to have lands in Kentucky and land purchased of Edmond
Taylor. Slaves to be freed at age 30.
Exr: Clara Larue
Wit: Robert Page and John McPherson (P.505-507)

MERCER, DINAH
Will: 10 Apr 1810/ 7 Jun 1810
Sons: Edward, Gideon and David
Daus: Mary Dawson and Dinah McVicker
Grandchildren: Diana Fair and Moses Dawson
Exr: Abraham Lewis
Wit: John Barnard, Aaron Mercer and John Mercer
(Fdk. Co. Mar.; Edward Mercer m Mary Dinah Steers 29 Apr 1783;
Dinah Mercer m William McVicker Sept 1797, Moses Mercer
surety) (P.507-508)

BUCKANON, JOHN
Will: 24 Jan 1789/ 1 Jan 1810
Wife: Elizabeth
Brother: Henry Buckanon
Sisters: Mary Cavenagh and Elizabeth Kern
Half-brother: William Chambers
Exrs: Wife Elizabeth and trusty friend Samuel Neal
Wit: Alexander Brown, Lewis Neal and James Stewart
Introduced at court 9 Apr 1789 with oath of Alexander Brown;
Recorded on oath of James Stewart 1 Jan 1810 (P.509-510)

POWERS, JOHN-ORPHANS
Guardianship account: 1 Jan 1810
Orphan Sally Powers now Sally Payne
Guardian James Powers
Examiners: James Baker and Saml. Kerchival (P.510-511)

SNYDER, JACOB
Inventory and appraisal: 5 Feb 1810
Appraisers: William Barrow, Michael Mock and George Larrick
(P.511-513)

CARTMILL, EDWARD
Estate settlement: 5 Mar 1810
Admr: John Snider (P.513-514)

HOTZENPILLAR, JOHN
Account settlement: 5 Mar 1810
Admr: John Pitman (P.514-515)

SYDNOR, WILLIAM
Sale account: 17 Aug 1798/ 5 Mar 1810
Among buyers: Ann and Sam. Sydnor (P.516-521)

HOGE, ASA
Orphans Jesse, Israel and Asa Hoge guardianship account by Guardian Mary Hoge (P.521-522)

MASTIN, CHARLOTTE
Account current: 6 Mar 1810
Admr: F.T. Mastin (P.522-523)

LAUBINGER, BARBARA
Will: 19 Feb 1808/ 7 Mar 1810
Children: Michael, Catherine(wife of Henry Brinker), Rosana (widow of William Campbell) and Susanna (wife of John Bartlett)
Granddaughter Barbara, daughter of John Laubinger.
Exr: "the person in whose hands this will may be deposited at the time of my death"
Wit: James Reily, George Harrison (P.523-524)

WARMLY, JOHN
Sale account: 8 Mar 1810
Admr: Bushrod Taylor (P.524-525)

FRYE, JACOB
Inventory, appraisal and sale: 2 Apr 1810
Exrs: John Frye and Joseph Snapp (P.525-529)

MOUNT, Samuel
Will: 22 Jan 1810/ 4 Jun 1810
"To my three grandsons, Samuel, John and Richard Armstrong, one dollar each; also unto the sons of James Dillon, one dollar each; unto my grandson Jeremiah Armstrong, the residue of my property"
Exr: Jeremiah Armstrong
Wit: Ann and Wm. McCauly and Mary Shrew (P.529-530)

ROMINE,JOHN
Inventory and appraisal : 4 Jun 1810 (P.530-531)

LARUE, JAMES
Inventory and appraisal: 4 Jun 1810 (P.531-533)

ROUT, PETER
Account current: 4 Jun 1810
Exr: Peter Timmons (P.533-534)

SMITH, JAMES
Will: 17 Apr 1810/ 5 Jun 1810
Wife: Hannah
Sons: Jonathan and Edmund
Exrs: Beatty Carson and John Windle (P.535)

WALTERS, THOMAS B.
Children: Suzannah, Sarah, Thomas, Alexander and Mary
Exrs: My father Lawerence Walters and Thos. Smith (P.536-537)

WILL BOOK NO. 9, 1810-1816

CAMPBELL, THOMAS
Will. 18 June 1810/ 6 Aug 1810
Wife: Elizabeth
Children: Thomas, John
Gr. ch: Elizabeth Campbell
To son Thomas, lands known as Crossroad Farms purchased from Mathias Hoover and William Bailis. To granddaughter Elizabeth Campbell, land in Jefferson County. To sons, land in Harrison County purchased from William Campbell; land in Green County, Ohio. Mentions land purchased from James McRea in 1798; land purchased from Edward Dodd and Thomas Finch; lands adjoining George Bruce and David Ridgeway; lands purchased from Joseph Morgan and William Harvey; lands purchased of Pendergast in 1788; lands purchased from Daniel Hoigh(?), Isaac Larue and Joseph Abiel Thomas
Exrs: Sons John and Thomas, and David Ridgeway
Wit: Geo. Bruce, C. Baldwin
Oath of Cornelius Baldwin and Robert Montgomery
Sec: Nathaniel Cartmell, Robert Rogers, Joel Ward, Morris Rees
(p. 1-4)

ROMINE, JOHN
Will. 3 Sep 1809/ 10 Aug 1810
Wife: Joanne
Children: James, Cornelius, Rebecca, Esther, Joanne, Myriam; Mary Jay
"To my son James by a former wife, daughter Mary Jay, and children of son Cornelius, $1 each
Exrs: Esais Earle, Mandly Taylor
Wit: Saml. Kerchival, Benjamin Ramey
Presented at Court 6 Nov 1809. (p. 4-5)

COLVILLE/COLVIL, JOHN
Account current. 1804/ Aug 1810
Exrs: William Marquis, John Adams
Examiners: R. Vance, Joseph Lucky (p. 6-9)

LOUTHAN, GEORGE
Inventory & Appraisal. 13 Dec 1809/ 3 Sep 1810
Appraisers: Daniel Sowers, William Kerfoot, Jas. Sowers
(p. 9-12)

BEALOR/BEELER, JOSEPH (ORPHANS)
Account current. Feb 1808/ 3 Sep 1810
Guardian: Thomas Neill for orphans Geo., Polly, Lucretia
Examiners: Griffin Taylor, Wm. Castleman (p. 12-17)

BELL, MARY
Estate Settlement. July 1805/ 1 Oct 1810
Admr: John McCool
Examiners: Jonathan Levett, Jonathan Pickering (p. 17-18)

LYONS, MICHAEL
Account current. Feb 1808/ 5 Nov 1810
By Richard Lyon, James Casidy
Examiners: Geo. Smith, Jesse Manly (p. 18-19)

McWHORTER, ROBERT
Inventory & Appraisal. 16 Nov 1809/ 5 Nov 1810
Appraisers: Jonathan Levett, Calib Seal (p. 19-20)

CAMPBELL, ELIZABETH
Estate Account. Feb 1809/ 6 Nov 1810
Admr: Jno Campbell
Examiners: Jno. Bell, Jno. Baker (p. 20)

GAWTHROP, JAMES
Account current. 8 Nov 1810
Admr: Thomas Barnett (p. 21-22)

BUTTERFIELD, THOMAS
Account current. 1803/ 9 Nov 1810
Admrs: Ann Butterfield, Francis Baker
Presented to Examiner Lemuel Bent by Jas Butterfield and David Barrett (p. 22-23)

SELLERS, PHILIP
Will. 28 Mar 1810/ 3 Dec 1810
Wife: Hannah
Children: Unnamed
"In first place I leave to my wife Hannah all my estate, real and personal, and after her decease all my children shall have equal shares."
Exr: Wife, Hannah Sellers
Wit: Robert Lockart, William Kile, Richard Davison, James Butler (p. 24)

FARMER/BOWER, JOHN
"John Farmer alias John Bower, late of Lancaster County, Pa."
Children: Daniel Bower alias Farmer, Mary Grice
"To my son Daniel Bower, otherwise Daniel Farmer, land in Powell's Valley, Pa. (formerly in Lancaster Co.) conveyed to me by Benjamin Carpenter deed bearing the date 20 Aug 1780." "To my daughter Mary lately intermarried with George Grice, land in Lancaster, Pa., conveyed to me by Alexander Porter, deed bearing date 17 Aug 1780."
Exrs: Son Daniel, George Grice
Wit: S. Kercheval, Thomas Castleman (p. 24-25)

WHITINGTON, WILLIAM
Account. 1808/ 4 Feb 1811
By Joseph Whitington
Examiners: Geo. Blackmore, Thomas Jackson (p. 25-26)

FERGUSON, JOHN
Inventory, Appraisal & Sale; Account current. 4 Feb 1811
Admrs: Martha Ferguson, Collin Carroll
Appraisers: James Bruce, Wm. Jolliffe, John Campbell
Examiners: Elijah Littler, John Jolliffe (p. 26-29)

MYTINGER, ISAAC
Will. 27 Dec 1810/ 4 Feb 1811
Wife: Elizabeth
Father: Daniel Mytinger
Exr: Father, Daniel Mytinger
Wit: Richard Wells, William Denny, J. B. Tilden
Sec: Andrew Pitman (p. 29)

TAYLOR, JOHN
Sale Account. 15 Nov 1805/ 4 Feb 1811
Exr: Mary Taylor
2nd Sale Account. 23 May 1809/ 4 Feb 1811
Surviving Exr: Bryan M. Stephens (p. 29-33)

DONALDSON, HANNAH
Will. 16 Jan 1811/ 4 Feb 1811
Widow of John Donaldson, formerly widow of John Rice
Children: John, George, Edmund and James Rice, Mary (Rice) McDonald, Sarah (Rice) Cowan
Mentions sale of seven half-acre lots, four having houses on

them, in Martinsburg, Berkeley Co.
Exrs: Son John Rice, William Abbott
Wit: Wm. Kerr, William Bailey, James Scott
Sec: James Scott, George Rice (p. 34-35)

JONES CATHERINE
Estate sale. 22 May 1809 & 31 Oct 1809/ 4 Feb 1811
No signatures (p. 35-38)

KERFOOT, WILLIAM
Will. 9 Apr 1805/ 7 Mar 1811
Wife: Nancy
Son: William
Gr. ch: Alfred Howard
Sister: Mary Carter, wife of Arthur Carter
Brother: Samuel Kerfoot
To wife, one-third during life; at her decease, all to son William
Appraisal by L. Butler, Ferguson Bell
Exrs: Son William, wife Nancy, brother Samuel Kerfoot
Wit: Robert Page, John Kerfoot
Sec: John Kerfoot, William G. Kerfoot (p. 38-41)

BRANSON, LIONEL
Inventory & Appraisal. 6 Mar 1811
Appraisers: William Headley, James Moore (p. 41-42)

ASH, URIAH
Account current. July 1798/ 2 Apr 1811
Submitted by William Ash
"We the subscribers do find William Ash indebted to the estate aforesaid two hundred and thirty one pounds, fifteen shillings, Va. currency, as follows: to Littleton Ash, 83 pounds 3 shillings, to Peggy Ash, 33 Pounds 3 shillings, to Uriah Ash, 38 pounds 3 shillings - all legatees of the late Uriah Ash, and to Pamely Ash (widow of the late Uriah Ash), 9 pounds 1 shilling; also Dolly Ash, 38 pounds 3 shillings."
Examiners: J. Wyatt, John Singleton, Jno. Newman (p. 42-43)

BUTLER, LAURENCE
Will. 4 May 1811/ 3 June 1811
Relationship of legatees not given.
"My farm on which I now reside to Richard M. Beckwith, son of Jennings Beckwith." "To Jonathan W. B. Beckwith the house in Winchester in which he now resides." "To Edmund Beckwith, son of Jennings Beckwith, £ 100." "To Jonathan Beckwith, Sr., and Richard Beckwith, Sr., £ 100." "To Barns Beckwith, brother of Richard and Jonathan, £ 100." "To Rebecca Beckwith, wife of Brokenbrough Beckwith, £ 90." "To the heirs of John Ashton, Sr., dec'd, £ 100." "To Lawrence Ashton, Sr., brother to John, and to Major Burdett Ashton, Sr., £ 100." Bridge over Mattocks Creek in Westmoreland Co., Va., to be sold; lands in Kentucky to be sold; land in dispute in Ohio to be sold if regained.
Exrs: Joseph Fauntleroy, Sr., Col. Thomas Parker, LeRoy Daingerfield, Sr.
Wit: Robert Stribling, Samuel Kerfoot, Wm. M. Fauntleroy
Executors refused burden; new exr: Robert Page
Sec: Thomas Parker, James Singleton
[According to Norris's History of Lower Shenandoah Valley, Gen. Laurence Butler came from South Carolina, was an officer in the Revolutionary War, and is buried in Boyce, now Clark Co., Va.] (p. 44-45)

VANCE, WILLIAM (ORPHANS)
Account. 1793/ 4 June 1811
Exr: James D. Vance
Boarding fees paid for James, William, Elizabeth, Polly and Betsey Vance
Examiners: Jos. Longacre, Thos. Kramer (p. 45-47)

DAVIS, JAMES
Account current. Feb 1801/ 4 June 1811
By Hannah Cape
Examiners: David Ridgeway, Aaron Hackney, John Jolliffe
[Hannah Davis m Joseph Cape 27 Oct 1803; Fdk.Co.Marrs.]
(p. 47)

CHIPLEY, WILLIAM
Will. 18 Aug 1808/ 4 June 1811
Children: James, Jonathan, George Washington, William, Elizabeth Kerfoot, Polly (Mary) Hardesty, Hannah Buckels, Sally Hoge
Dau-in-law: Abigail, widow of son Jonathan, now Abigail Morrison, mother of gr dau Priscilla Chipley & other children
Son George Washington not to have his share until he is cured of unsound mind
Exrs: Sons James and William
Wit: Obed Waite, Nicholas Kern, Adam Kern, William Price, John Beamer
"It is to be understood that James Chipley nor Preslah(?) Chipley is to have no part of my estate."
Sec: Daniel McCauley, David Carlisle, Adam Kern, Thomas Mullan (p. 48-52)

TAYLOR, ABRAHAM
Will. 24 Apr 1811/ 6 June 1811
Wife: Mary
Children: Hiram (youngest), James (eldest), possibly other sons, Nancy Green, Catherine Smith, Sarah Donley, Lidia Craig, Mary Taylor (youngest dau)
To wife, all my personal estate. To Hiram, that part of plantation where James Smith lives; to James plantation where I live.
Codicil: To daughters Nancy Green, Catherine Smith, Sarah Donley, Lidia Craig, $1 each; youngest daughter Mary Taylor to have as much as any of the rest of my daughters have had.
Exrs: Son James, Robert Russell
Wit: David Davis, James Smith, Sr.
Sec: Arthur Carter, James Carter
[Lidia Taylor m Samuel Craig 10 June 1804; Fdk.Co.Marrs.)
(p. 53-54)

DESPONET/DISPONET, ABRAHAM
Sale Account. 20 Sep 1798/ 7 June 1811
Examiners: Moses Russell, Henry Richards (p. 54-56)

TAYLOR, ABRAHAM
Inventory & Appraisal. 5 Aug 1811
Appraisers: Nathan Littler, Henry Seevers (p. 56-58)

SMITH, JAMES
Inventory & Appraisal. 6 Aug 1811
Appraisers: James Vance, Isaac Hollingsworth, William Cochran (p. 58-59)

ALLAMONG, JACOB
Account current. May 1809/ 6 Aug 1811
Admrs: Elizabeth Allamong, John Allamong
Examiners: John McCool, Joshua Gordon (p. 60)

COOPER, ROBERT
Account current. 8 Aug 1811
By Thomas Cooper
Examiners: David Ridgeway, John Jolliffe (p. 61-62)

ALTRITH, MICHAEL
Will. 18 Mar 1807/ 8 Apr 1811
Wife: Margaret
Children: Frederick, John Michael, Margaret Grotz, Mary Riley, Susannah and Catherine Altrith
Exrs: Wife Margaret, son Frederick
Wit: John Irwin, Anthony Kurtz, Samuel Windle (p. 62-63)

MERCER, MOSES
Account current. 2 Sep 1811
Exr: William Mercer
Examiners: Peter Babb, David Barrett (p. 63-64)

FAWCETT, JOHN
Will. 6 July 1811/ 2 Sep 1811
Wife Margaret
Children: Isaac, Elijah, Nathan, David, Jesse, Alban, Sally, Betty, Susa
To wife, all my wearing apparel
Exrs: James Singleton, son Elijah, wife Margaret
Wit: Jos. Longacre, Wm. Fawcett, Elisha Fawcett (p. 64-66)

SMITH, ANDREW
Inventory & Appraisal. 2 Sep 1811
Includes inventory of the "property which said Smith got with his last wife, which belonged to the estate of Anthony Moore, dec'd."
Appraisers: John McCool, James Crumley, John Rogers
[Andrew Smith m Margaret Moore 13 Feb 1810; Fdk.Co.Marrs.]
(p. 66-68)

POWERS, THOMAS
Deceased orphan of John Powers, dec'd
Inventory, Settlement & Division. 2 Sep 1811
"This settlement and division of the estates of John Powers, Thomas Powers, and dower estate of Frances Powers, late Frances Paine."
Admr: James Powers
[Frances Powers m William Pain (sic) 30 Aug 1804; Fdk.Co.Marrs.]
(p. 68-69]

LEACH, GEORGE
Inventory & Appraisal. 2 Sep 1811
Appraisers: John Singleton, Jno Newman, William Momar (Mumma?)
(p. 70)

LAUBINGER, GEORGE MICHAEL
Inventory & Appraisal. 4 Sep 1811
No estate found. Mention of one of daughters of deceased, Rosanna Campbell, and widow of deceased, Barbara
Exr: Lewis Hoff
Examiners: Jos. Gamble, Robert Gray, Pendleton Heironimus
(p. 71)

TEAWALT/TEWALT, JOHN
Will. 17 Sep 1811/ 4 Nov 1811
Wife: Christina
Children: John, Abraham, Joseph, Leah, Eleanor
To son John the plantation he now lives on lately purchased of John Kackly. To son Abraham the plantation I bought of Jacob Teawalt. To son Joseph the plantation where I now live, after my wife's decease. To daughters Leah and Eleanor, each £ 50.

Exrs: Wife Christina, John Richards, Henry Richards
Wit: Moses Russell, Jacob Wolfe, Henry Richards (p. 71-72)

BECKWITH, RICHARD (ORPHAN)
Guardianship Acct. 4 Nov 1811
Guardian: Thomas Parker
Receipt from Richard Beckwith approved by guardian for gun purchased at estate sale of Major Butler. (p. 72)

CONRAD, JOHN (ORPHANS OF)
Guardianship Account. 1805/ 4 Nov 1811
Guardian: Lawerence A. Washington
Examiners: W. Davison, Edw. McGuire, John Bell (p. 73-78)

WOODS, ROBERT
Account current. Dec 1806/ 4 Nov 1811
Admr: Lawrence A. Washington
Examiners: W. Davison, Edw. McGuire, John Bell (p. 78-84)

PURVIS, JAMES
Will. 16 Oct 1811/ 2 Dec 1811
Wife: Cassandra
To James Purvis Riley, son of James and Cassandra Riley, $400
To my brother William Purvis, 1/3 part of remainder. To Susan Purvis, sister of said William, 1/3 part. To John Purvis, son of John Purvis, dec'd, 1/3 part.
Exr: Wife Cassandra and James Riley
Wit: James Riley, Thomas Dent, George D. Harrison(p. 84-85)

DENNY, WALTER
Will. 8 May 1810/ 2 Dec 1811
Wife: Jane
Brothers: William, John, Robert, Samuel (living in Ky.)
Cousin: Samuel Lockart
Legatees: Daniel and Ann Dillon of Miami; John Jay and wife Betty of Miami; Michael Jinkins and wife Rachel nee Pugh; surviving children of Evan Rogers, Jr., and wife Sally nee Pugh, both deceased.
All personal property to be sold and monies to my four brothers living in Kentucky. "Respecting lands which my wife Jane and I sold to William Adams ..." Virginia land bounded by F. Fisher, Thomas Fisher, Jasper Cather, William Chenowith, John McCool, 49 acres, to be sold and monies divided between brothers John and William. Lands of wife Jane sold to William Adams, Sr., bound by Job Pugh, John McCool, William Adams, Samuel Boyd, formerly property of Thomas Pugh - one parcel of 51 acres bequeathed by will of Thomas Pugh to daughter Lydia Pugh who, in turn, bequeathed land to wife Jane as payment for care of Lydia in latter years, will witnessed by Martha Hackney but not recorded, Charity Sidwell, her daughter, now deceased. If my right in land is good, Adams to pay $800 as set forth, distribution as follows: To Daniel and Ann Dillon of Miami, $100; second year, $100 to brothers John and William Denny of Ky.; third year $100 income divided into thirds and paid to John Jay and wife Betty of Miami, Michael Jinkins and wife Rachel nee Pugh, and to surviving children of Evan Rogers, Jr., and wife Sally nee Pugh, both dec'd. Next year, $100 to be equally divided between brothers John and William Denny of Ky. Remaining $400 to be paid to Daniel and Ann Dillon.
Exrs: Joseph Baker, Cousin Samuel Lockart
Wit: Thomas Cather, John Rogers, Saml. Lockart, Thomas Mitchell
Samuel Lockart and Thomas Mitchell declined administration
New admr: Jonathan Pickering
Sec: William Adams, John Rogers (p. 85-88)

DERMAN, PETER
Will. 5 June 1811/ 2 Dec 1811
Legatees' relationship not given.
"I give to John Derman, Mary Derman, Ann Derman and Betsy Derman all my property. It is my desire these four persons should live together as long as each of them should live."
Exr: John Derman
Wit: John D. Ferguson, James Strother, Michael Dearmont
(p. 88)

JONES, STEPHEN
Account current. 2 Dec 1811
Admr: Samuel Bonham
Examiners: Griffin Taylor, G. H. Harris (p. 88-90)

MACKY, HANNAH (late Hannah Smith)
Assignment of Dower. 2 Dec 1811
Dower in lands of her former husband, James Smith, deceased.
[Hannah Smith m John Macky 26 Feb 1811; Fdk.Co.Marrs.]
(p. 91-92)

RIDGEWAY, RICHARD (of Berkeley Co.)
Will. 24 Mar 1806/ 6 Jan 1812
Children: David, Hannah Wright, Sally Rees, Patience Beeson, Becky/Beely(?) Cleavinger
Gr. ch: Jane Beeson, daughter of Patience
Son-in-law: Jonathan Wright
To son David, land where he now lives. To daughters Hannah Wright and Sally Rees, the plantation where I live. To daughters Patience Beeson and Becky(?) Cleavinger, the tract of land formerly the property of Minto and Samuel Hanley, Patience to have that part on which Jonathan Roberts lately resided: Becky to have that part on which Jesse Johnston lately resided. Jane Beeson, daughter of Patience. To son-in-law Jonathan Wright, land in Ohio
Exrs: Son David Ridgeway, Jonathan Wright
Wit: J. Stephenson, Joel Ward, Robert Wilson
Sec: Jonathan Wright (p. 91-92)

MORGAN, JOSEPH
Account current. 6 Jan 1812
Admr: Martha Morgan
Examiners: S. McCoole, Wm. M. Holliday (p. 92-93)

CARTER, BENJAMIN
Account current. Mar 1805/ 7 Jan 1812
Admr: Joseph and Rachel Carter
Examiners: Bushrod Taylor, Peter McMurry (p. 94)

THROCKMORTON, WILLIAM
Will. No date/ 6 Jan 1812
Wife: Not named
Children: Unnamed; references to unmarried daughters
"I give to my beloved wife all my property, both real and personal, to do with as she pleases during her natural life and to maintain her single daughters. After her decease and daughters' marriage, all my land to be divided amongst surviving children."
Wit: Ariana Wormley; proven on oaths of George H. Norris and William J. Throckmorton
Mary Throckmorton refused burden of execution (identified as widow of deceased, page 97 of Will Book No. 9)
New Exr: William J. Throckmorton
Sec: John Carter (p. 94-95)

FAWCETT, JOHN
Inventory & Appraisal. 3 Feb 1812
Examiners: John Russell, John Richards, Jacob Woolfe
(p. 95-96)

BRILL, HARMAN
Inventory & Appraisal. 3 Feb 1812
Appraisers: Charles Brent, John Richards, Michael White
(p. 96-97)

THROCKMORTON, MARY
Relinquishment of executorship. 3 Feb 1812
Widow of William Throckmorton filed statement relinquishing executorship of his will and nominates "my son, William Throckmorton" (p. 97)

LOUTHAN, HENRY
Inventory & Appraisal; Sales Account. 3 Feb 1812
Appraisers: William Kerfoot, John Sowers, Samuel Kerfoot
Among buyers: Polly Louthan (p. 97-100)

RIDGEWAY, RICHARD
Inventory & Appraisal. 3 Feb 1812
Appraisers: David Lupton, Samuel Lupton, Levi Smith
(p. 100-101)

LOUTHAN, GEORGE
Sale Account. 3 Feb 1812
No signatures (p. 101-102)

EDMONDSON, THOMAS
Will. 9 Nov 1811/ 2 Mar 1812
Mother: Nancy Edmondson
Aunt: Elenor Talbott
Brothers and sisters: Not named
To my beloved mother, Nancy Edmondson, that parcel of land willed to me by my Aunt Elenor Talbott. Rest of my estate to be divided amongst my brothers and sisters
Exr: Mother Nancy Edmondson
Wit: Alexander Miller, Zadok (Zedick) Rogers, Josiah Harding
(p. 102-103)

PURVIS, JAMES
Inventory & Appraisal; Sales Acct. 23 Dec 1811/ 2 Mar 1812
Exrs: Cassandra Purvis, James Riley
Only buyer: Cassandra Purvis (p. 103-104)

McWHORTER, ROBERT
Account current. 2 Mar 1812
Admr: George Smith
Examiners: Jonathan Lovett, John McCool (p. 104-105)

READ, JOHN
Will. 12 Nov 1809/ 2 Mar 1812
Wife: Agnes
Son: Samuel Read
Brother: James Read of Loudoun County
Legatee: Lewis Strawden
"Fifty pounds of money to Lewis Strawden(?) whom I sent to the State of Ohio to be raised by William Campbell" (No relationship given).
Widow Agnes disclaimer included
Wit: George Leach, Valentine Leach, Jesse Kemp (p. 105-106)

PEYTON, JOHN
Account current. 1805/ 2 Mar 1812
Admr: John Brown
Examiners: E. Smith, W. Davison (p. 106-107)

RICE, PATRICK
Account current. 1799/ 2 Mar 1812
Exr: George Hollingsworth
Examiners: Marquis Blakemore, R. S. Redman (p. 107-108)

PICKENS, DAVID
Inventory & Appraisal. 3 Mar 1812
Appraisers: James Davis, Henry Larrick, John Larrick (p. 108)

CARTMELL, EDWARD - ORPHANS
Guardianship Account. Nov 1810/ 5 Mar 1812
Guardian: Thomas McClunn
Examiners: F. Martin, E. Barrett, Michael Mauck (p. 109-110)

BERRY, ENOCH
Inventory & Appraisal of slaves. 3 Feb 1812
Distribution to Lettita N. Hogan, Edwin Berry, Matilda Berry, Winny Berry
Appraisers: Daniel Sowers, Sr., Wm. Alexander, and Joseph Whittington (p. 110-111)

McPHERSON, NATHANIEL
Inventory & Appraisal. 6 Apr 1812
Appraisers: John Singleton, Valentine Leach (p. 111-113)

REED, JOHN
Inventory & Appraisal. 6 Apr 1812
Appraisers: Valentine Leach, John Singleton, Jesse Kemp (p. 113-115)

MARTIN, JOHN
Inventory & Appraisal. 5 Apr 1812
Appraisers: Lewis Hoff, Geo. Reed, John Davenport (p. 115-116)

FRIEDLY/FRIETLY, ANDREW
Inventory & Appraisal. 6 Apr 1812
Appraisers: Lewis Hoff, Joshua Newbrough, Jacob Kiger (p. 116-117)

LITTLE, ADAM
Will. 28 Feb 1812/ 6 Apr 1812
Wife: Martha
Children: John, Jacob, Sarah Patton, David, Martin, Phillip, Catherine, William, Elizabeth (refers to 10, names only 9)
Children of wife: James, Nancy(probably surnamed Patton as Adam Little m Martha Patton, 1 Sep 1808; Fdk.Co.Marrs)
To his 10 children (9 named), money to be divided among them; to wife's two children, James and Nancy, $24 to be divided equally.
Wit: Joseph Thomas, Thomas Relph, William Relph
Exr: appointed by Court - John Little
Sec: Michael Ridenour (p. 117-118)

KLINE, ADAM
Account current. Aug 1805/ 5 May 1812
Examiners: W. Davison, Jo. Tidball (p. 118-119)

SYDNOR, SAMUEL B., ORPHAN OF WILLIAM F. SYDNOR
Guardianship Account. 1799/ 5 May 1812
Guardian: John S. Ball
Examiners: Saml. Baker, W. Vance (p. 120-128)

SIMPSON, ROBERT
Inventory & Appraisal. May 1811/ 1 June 1812
Appraisers: Alfred Ashby, Christian Hope, Ezekiel White (128-129)

CRUM, ANTHONY
Account current. 1 June 1812
Exr: Christian Crum
Examiners: John Davenport, Jr., Geo. Reed (p. 129-131)

TOLIVER/TOLOVER, NANCY
Will. 17 Feb 1812/ 1 June 1812
Husband: Moses Tolover
Legatee: Jesse Henderson (no relationship given)
"I give to Jesse Henderson my servant Moses. I give all my goods of every description to my loving husband Moses Tolover"
Wit: Mary Ann Timberlake, Fanny Timberlake, Easter Timberlake, Martin Timberlake
Will proven by oaths of Martin Timberlake and William Timberlake (p. 131-132)

FAWCETT, JOHN
Inventory & Appraisal. 1 June 1812
Appraisers: Charles Brent, Jr., Thos. Sexton, Jos. Longacre (p. 132-138)

DAWSON, WILLIAM
Inventory & Appraisal. 5 June 1812
Appraisers: Meredith Darlinton, William Adams, David Adams (p. 138-139)

WOOD, MARY
Will. 20 Sep 1790/See recording info below
Husband: Col. James Wood, dec'd
Sons: James, Robert
Gr. ch: Mary Dorcas Wood; Mary Ann, Elizabeth and Mary Harrison; James and Robert Welsh Wood
"A lot or parcel of ground lately purchased of Charles Magill and one square of lots in the addition made by my late husband, Col. James Wood" to son Robert and his sons James Wood and Robert Welsh Wood. To granddaughter Mary Dorcas Wood, featherbed, furniture and silver spoons. To granddaughters Mary Ann, Elizabeth and Mary Harrison, lots in Town of Winchester. To son James, three slaves. All slaves to be freed as they reach age 36.
Exrs: Sons James and Robert
Wit: Alex White, Thos. White
This will first proved 2 July 1798 on oath of Alexander White. On 5 Feb 1811, Negro Sarah claimed her freedom under the will, refused by the Court on motion of Peter Lauck. Counsel for negro Sarah filed for exceptions to Superior Court. This will finally recorded 4 June 1812. [Col. James Wood died 6 Nov 1759, aged 52; founded Winchester, was first Clerk of Frederick County. He and Mary (Rutherford) Wood had five children: Elizabeth wife of Hon. Alexander White; James, Rev. War General, m Jean Moncure, named Governor of Virginia in 1798; Mary wife of Col. Matthew Harrison, officer in Rev. War; John, M. D., m Susannah Baker; Robert, m Comfort Welsh. Cartmell's history gives family genealogy.] (p. 139-141)

BABB, SAMPSON
Sale Account. 6 July 1812
Among buyers: Abner Babb, Nancy Babb, Peter Babb (p. 141-145)

CLEVENGER, ASA
Account current. 1809/ 6 July 1812
Admr: Jacob Clevenger
Examiners: Geo. Catlett, James Freland, Edmund Pagett (p. 145-146)

BRANSON, REBECKAH
Will. 2 Nov 1811/ 3 Aug 1812
Daus: Hannah Leheu, Mary Branson
"To daughter Hannah, my husband's wearing apparel, remainder of estate to daughter Mary."
Exrx: Mary Branson
Wit: James Mitchell, Ellender Dean (p. 147)

FURR, ABRAHAM
Inventory & Appraisement; Sale Account. 3 Aug 1812
Appraisers: Henry Janes, George Armstrong, Elijah Glasscock
Among buyers: Ephrim Furr, Sarah Furr, John Fur (p. 147-149)

BUTLER, LAURENCE
Inventory & Appraisement; Sale Account. 3 Aug 1812
Appraisers: Ferguson Bell, William Kerfoot, James Bell

CLARKE, JOSEPH
Estate Account. 4 Aug 1812
Admrs: John H. Clarke, J. Reynolds
Examiners: Jos. Gamble, Robt. Gray (p. 156-158)

RICE, GEORGE
Account current. 1801/ 5 Aug 1812
Admr: William McCormick
Legatees: George Rice, George Kiger, Lehugh Rice(?), Ruth Roatch (Roach?), Joshua Wilson, and "my children on behalf of my late wife" - unnamed
Examiners: Griffin Taylor, Wm. Castleman, Eben Taylor (p. 158-159)

BECKWITH, RICHARD M.
Guardianship Account. 31 Aug 1812
Guardian: Thomas Parker
Examiners: Edw. McGuire, Robt. Gray, William Morris (p. 160-161)

CATHER, JASPER
Will. 13 Apr 1812/ 4 Aug 1812
Children: Thomas, John, David, James, William, Robert, Jane, Mary, Sarah, Hannah
"Sons Thomas and John and daughters Jane and Mary having already received such assistance as my circumstances will permit I give them no more." "My sons William and Robert and my daughter Hannah, children of my second marriage, left me in time of distress; I give 5 shillings each." To sons David and James, plantation where I live. To daughters Sarah and Mary, $50 each.
Exrs: Sons David and James
Wit: Jacob Rinker, Michael Brill (p. 161-163)

RODES, JACOB
Will. 29 Mar 1812/ 31 Aug 1812
Wife: Unnamed
Children: Abraham, Jacob, Jr., Esther, Christina
To beloved wife, bed and bedding. To son Abraham, plantation. To son Jacob Road(sic), Junior, 140 pounds. To daughter Esther, 100 pounds. To daughter Christina, two lots in town.
Exrs: My son Jacob and son-in-law Peter Geeting(?)
Wit: Abraham Nisewander, John Senseney, John Grim (p. 164-165)

POOL, DANIEL
Sale Account. 3 Mar 1808; Account current. 31 Aug 1812
Admrs: George Brown, Burgess Berly, Daniel Pool
Legatees: Joseph Vincent, Robert Page (agent for Richard Hodge), George Brown, Berges Beckley
Examiners: LeRoy Daingerfield, Rom. Abbott (p. 165-170)

CATHER, JASPER
Inventory & Appraisement. 31 Aug 1812
Appraisers: Jno. White, John Hedges (p. 170-172)

BABB, SAMPSON
Inventory & Appraisal. 31 Aug 1812
Appraisers: Alex Miller, Benjamin Fenton, David Barnett (p. 172-173)

DERMAN, PETER
Inventory & Appraisal. 5 Oct 1812
Appraisers: Jesse O'Rear, James Marshall, William Franks (p. 174)

WALTER, THOMAS B.
Account current. 5 Oct 1812
Admr: Lawrence Walter
Examiners: Abraham Nisewander, F. Mastin, John W. Burgess (p. 174-175)

ROMINE, JOHN
Account current. 5 Oct 1812
Exr: Esais Earle
Examiners: George Catlett, John Rust, Wm. Mitchell (p. 175-176)

McPHERSON, NATHANIEL
Sale Account. 3 Nov 1812
Admr: Edward Turner, Peter C. McPherson
Among buyers: Peter McPherson, Nancy McPherson (p. 176-177)

JONES, JOHN
Inventory & Appraisal. 30 Nov 1812
Appraisers: Wm. Green, Peter Murry, Samuel Bonham(p. 177-179)

LOWTHER, GEORGE
Account current. 30 Nov 1812
Examiners: Ferguson Beell, Samuel Bryarly (p. 179)

McMICKIN, FRANCIS
Estate Settlement. 30 Nov 1812
Admr: Thomas Steel
Examiners: S. Kercheval, William McLoud (McLeod?), George Lyn (p. 179-180)

MADEN/MADDEN, JACOB
Account current. 30 Nov 1812
Examiners: Thomas Jackson, Peter McMurry (p. 181-182)

MUSE, JOHN (of the Manor of Leeds)
Will. 25 Aug 1810/ 3 Nov 1812
Wife: Unnamed (See WB 9, p. 218, widow's name Susannah)
Children: Warren Johnson, Randall Muse Johnson
Nephews: Edward Muse, John Armstrong
Brother: Rober (sic) Muse
Sister's husband: George Armstrong
To nephew Edward, son of brother Rober(sic) Muse, mill and land; to nephew John Armstrong, son of George Armstrong, sister's husband, negro girl Hannah. Residue of estate to "my two natural children born of Suckey Johnson...Warren Johnson and John Randall Muse Johnson."
Exrs: Capt. John Beavers, Richard Turner, Thomas Hamilton, James Steward
Wit: John Courtney, James Stuart, Jonathan Pullen
[John Muse m Susannah Johnson, 1 Oct 1811; Fdk.Co.Marrs.] (p. 182-183)

HOFFMAN, JACOB
Will. 13 Oct 1812/ 30 Nov 1812
Wife: Mary Ann
Children: Katherine Amick wife of Philip Amick; Barbara Dick

wife of John Dick; Jacob Hoffman; Rebecca McKindley wife of Nicholas McKindley; Elizabeth Correll wife of Joseph Correll; William Hoffman; Henry Hoffman
Gr.ch: Augustus McKindley son of Rebecca; Jacob Correll son of Elizabeth
To wife, furniture and only one bed. Lots in Winchester purchased of Jonathan Perkins, Conrad Crebs, joining lots of James Vance, Simon Lauck and Lewis Wolfe, to be sold and monies divided among seven children. Daughter Rebecca's share to be held in trust by John Dick after her decease to be paid to her son Augustus McKindley. Daughter Elizabeth's share to be held in trust by John Dick and at her death paid to her son Jacob Correll.
Exrs: John Dick and Philip Amick, sons-in-law
Wit: Lem'l Bent, John Windle, Conrad Crebs
Sec: Isaac Hollingsworth, Samuel Glass, William Marques.
"Mary Ann Hoffman, widow of said Jacob Hoffman, dec'd, in open court, refused taking the provisions made for her in said will in lieu of her dower." (p. 183-184)

JACOBS, JOHN
Inventory & Appraisal. 30 Nov 1812
Examiners: James Moore, Jacob Cline, Henry Trout (p. 185)

FAWCETT, THOMAS
Will. 25 June 1812/ 4 Jan 1813
Wife: Sarah
Children: William, John, Elisha, Josiah, Ely, Simon, Levi, Jehu, Lydia, Elizabeth
To sons William, John, Elisha, Josiah, Ely, Simon, land in Columbiana County, Ohio. To son Levi, land in Fawcett's Town, Ohio, purchased of Thomas Fawcett. To daughter Lydia bed and bedding; to daughter Elizabeth and son Jehu, land where I now live adjoining property of Jn. Baylis and Thomas Fawcett, Sr., to be rented. (Ohio County referred to as Columbia in one place, Columbiana County in another.)
Exrs: Joshua Lupton and sons William, John and Elisha
Wit: William Baylis, Thomas Fawcett, Jos. Fawcett, Jos. Longacre. (p. 186-189)

BUSH, PHILIP
Will. 4 Sep 1810/ 4 Jan 1813
Children: Philip (dec'd), Mathias, John, Henry, Polly Bush, Elizabeth Smith wife of Edward Smith, Catherine Ambler
Gr. ch: Norbourn Norton, son of daughter Catherine Ambler
To daughter Polly Bush, house and lot in Winchester. Legacies to daughter Elizabeth Smith, son Henry Bush, grandson Norbourn Norton, son John Bush, children of deceased son Philip, son Mathias. "I earnestly request my executors to use their best endeavors to receive from the United States the claim which I have against the said states."
Exrs: Sons-in-law John Ambler, Edward Smith, Henry St. George
Wit: D. Lee, Christian Streit, Edw. Slater
Codicil: Reiterates legacy to daughter Polly. Devises legacy of son Mathias to be held in trust by executors. Second Codicil dated 5 Oct 1812: Gives further consideration to daughter Polly.
[Catherine Bush m John Hatley Norton 27 Mar 1790; Catherine Norton, widow, m John Ambler 21 Nov 1799; Fdk.Co.Marrs.]
(p. 189-193)

TAYLOR, JOHN
Account current. 4 Jan 1813
Surviving exr: Bryan Stephens
Examiners: Sam. Kerchival, Jared Williams (p. 193-195)

PARKINS, ALFRED
"Alfred Parkins, infant son of Joseph Parkins"
Account. 1 Feb 1813
Guardian: Joseph Steer (p. 196)

LITTLER, SAMUEL - ORPHANS BARNET, REBECCA, BETSY
Account with estate of Nathan Littler, dec'd, who was one of the guardians. 1804/ 4 Oct 1813
Surviving guardian: Isaiah Littler (p. 197-204)

PARKINS, JOSEPH
Account current. 1803/ 5 Feb 1813
Admr: Joseph Steer (p. 206-206)

BUSH, PHILIP
Inventory & Appraisal. 1 Feb 1813
Appraisers: Edw. McGuire, W. Davison, Lem'l Bent (p. 207-209)

ZANE, ISAAC, 3rd
Inventory & Appraisal. 1799/ 1 Mar 1813
Large library inventory included, 18 May 1799
Appraisers: Jn. Fawcett, Thomas Fawcett, Joseph Snapp
Estate Sale 31 May 1799
Account current 1799/ 1 Mar 1813
Examiners: James Singleton, Robert Glass, Martin Cartmell (p. 210-214)

SMITH, MARTIN
Inventory & Appraisal. 2 Mar 1813
Appraisers: Butler Allensworth, John Self, John Ramey (p. 214-217)

MUSE, JOHN
Widow: Susannah Muse
Relinquishment of will provisions in favor of those made by law. 2 Mar 1813
Testators: Dolphin Drew, Thomas Hamilton (p. 218)

CHAPMAN, THOMAS
Will. 23 Nov 1812/ 4 Jan 1813
Wife: Rachel
Children: Son Thomas Chapman; others unnamed
At decease of wife, all estate to be sold and monies divided equally amongst "all my children."
Probate granted 2 Mar 1813 on bond of Thomas Chapman, Joshua Chapman, Daniel Thornburg (p. 218-219)

BONHAM, ANN
Will. 13 Nov 1812/ 1 Mar 1813
Children: Unnamed, except Humphrey Francis Christian
Legatee: Ann Christian
Estate to be sold and money given to son Humphrey Francis Christian, now "in service of United States." If deceased, money to be divided amongst "all my children." "It is my desire that Ann Christian, daughter of Edward Christian, have equal shares with my children."
Exr: Henry Catlett
Wit: William Timberlake, Calmes Catlett
[See will of Francis Christian, 15 Dec 1785/Apr 1788, Fdk. Co., naming wife Ann Christian as excx, with sons Humphrey, Edward (wife Martha Shannon) and daughter Betsy (Murray?). Geo. Murray, exr., son-in-law, m Mary Christian 21 Mar 1786; Ann Christian m Hezekiah Boneham, 15 Jul 1792; Fdk.Co.Marrs. ... Edward Christian admitted to practice law in Jefferson Co., 1801 (Norris's history).] (p. 219)

TROUT, PHILIP
Will. 21 Aug 1812/ 2 Mar 1813
Wife: Molly
Mother and children: mentioned but not named in will
To wife, house and lot on main street of Stephensburg; support mother out of estate. After death of wife and mother, estate equally divided among children.
Exrs: Henry Trout, Jacob Boyers
Wit: Wm. Van Meter, George Reynolds, Thomas Thatcher
[Mother, Barbara Trout, in will of Jacob Trout 1 Feb 1790/ 8 Apr 1790.] (p. 220)

MILBURN, JOHN
Will. 25 Aug 1812/ 3 May 1813
Wife: Elizabeth
Wife's sister: Bathsheba
Brothers: David, Robert
Nephew: Robert, son of David
Legatees, relationships not shown: Andrew Summers and wife Leah; the Methodist Episcopal Church; John Milburn, Jr., of Tenn., son of William Milburn; Elizabeth Milburn; Elizabeth Milburn, daughter of John Milburn, Jr., of Tenn.; Joseph Milburn, son of John and Eleanor Milburn.
To wife, plantation where we live. After her decease, to be sold and monies divided amongst John Milburn, Jr., of Tenn. and sons of brother Robert Milburn. To brother David Milburn, land in Hampshire Co.; after his death to his son Robert. Also to brother David note executed to me by John Harmon of Kanawha Co. To Andrew Summers and his wife Leah, tract of land in Hampshire Co. To Methodist Episcopal Church, one acre of land. To my wife's sister Bathsheba, note executed to me by David Milburn, son of William Milburn, both of Tenn. To John Milburn, Jr., of Tenn., note executed to me by his father William Milburn. To Elizabeth Milburn, daughter of John Milburn, Jr., of Tenn., $500. To Joseph Milburn, son of John and Eleanor Milburn, $500.
Exrs: William Tyler, John Wright, Lewis Smith
Wit: Abraham Merchant, James Smith, Jr., David Stip (Stipp), Robert Milburn. (p. 220-221)

McCLELAN, DAVID
Sale Account. 5 Apr 1813
No signatures (p. 222-224)

FRYE, JACOB
Account current. 1808/ 5 Apr 1813
Admr: John Frye
Examiners: Chas. Brent, Jr., Ja. Singleton, Wm. Baylis (p. 224-226)

McCLUNN, THOMAS
Inventory & Appraisal. 3 May 1813
Appraisers: Stephen Pritchard, Nich. Kern, Philip Hoover (p. 226)

COCHRAN, JOHN
"At his father's house in Winchester, Va."
Will. 23 Apr 1813
Mother: Unnamed
Brothers: Robert, Harry Bell(?)
To mother, bay gelding bought of Edmund Smith; to brother Robert, my waggon; to brother Harry Bell(?) equal share.
Exr: Robert Cockran, Jr.
Wit: Richard Lemon, Wm. Cochran
Sec: Robert Cochran, Robert Cochran, Jr. (p. 227)

WIGGINTON, SARAH
Will. 31 Aug 1811/ 31 May 1813
Children: Benjamin, James, Nancy Mitchell, Mary Thornburg wife of Samuel Thornburg
Gr. ch: Children (unnamed) of daughter Nancy Mitchell, Betsy Settle wife of Edward Settle, William Pendleton Wigginton, James Bott Wigginton.
To daughter Nancy Mitchell, slaves and household goods from my plantation in Culpeper Co. After her death, all to her children except her son, William Mitchell. To son Benjamin Wigginton, land in Stafford Co. To son James Wigginton, slaves and furniture. To grandchildren Betsy Settle, William Pendleton Wigginton, and James Bott Wigginton, negroes.
Exrs: Sons Benjamin and James Wigginton
Wit: Willis Butler, Darnall Wood, John Wigginton, William Colston. (p. 227-229)

CURLET, RACHEL
Will. 1 Sep 1807/ 31 May 1813
Children: Jane Curlet, Rachel Cochran, Elizabeth Brown, Rebeckah McKartney (McCarty?)
To daughter Jane Curlett, all estate except feather bed with calico counterpin(sic); to daughter Rebeckah McKartney(sic), "feather bed and counterpin(sic). "My share of my father's estate to be divided among my four daughters, Jane Curlet, Rachel Cochran, Elizabeth Brown and Rebeckah McKartney."
Exr: William Cochran
Wit: Thos. Curlet, Jonathan Harry
[Joseph McCarty m Rebecca Curlett, 10 Dec 1795; Fdk.Co.Marrs.] (p. 229-230)

HOTZENPILLER, STEPHEN
Inventory & Appraisal. 3 May 1813
Appraisers: Spencer Leheu, Philip Allensworth, Jacob Vannort (p. 230-231)

MILBURN, JOHN
Sale Account. 31 May 1813
Admr: William Tyler, John Wright (p. 232)

PICKENS, DAVID
Account current. 31 May 1813
Admr: Levi Pickens
Examiners: Timothy Kern, Jacob Luck(?), Jacob Larick (p. 233)

BRANSON, REBECCA
Inventory & Appraisal. 31 May 1813
Appraisers: J. Allensworth, Joseph Haines, Hez B. Leach (p. 234)

STEWART, JAMES
Inventory & Appraisal. 31 May 1813
Appraisers: Isaac Phillips, Robert Muse, Henry Franks (p. 234)

LOUTHAN, GEORGE
Account current. 1809/ 2 Aug 1813
Admr: Lucy Monroe
[Widow Lucy Louthan m John Monroe, 21 Apr 1812; Fdk.Co.Marrs.] (p. 235-236)

REGAL, GEORGE
Will. 1 Feb 1807/ 2 Aug 1813
Wife: Catherine
"To my beloved wife, Catherine Regal, my entire estate."
Exr: Catherine Regal
Wit: Robert Vane, Samuel Tap (p. 236)

WIGGINTON, SARAH
Inventory & Appraisal, Culpeper Co.-
Appraisers: Thos. Jefferies, Richard Jefferies, Francis Jones
Inventory & Appraisal, Frederick Co. 2 Aug 1813
Appraisers: Henry Seevers, Peter McMurry, Samuel Baker, Jr.
(p. 236-238)

WEAVER, LEWIS
Account current. Sep 1811/ 3 Aug 1813
Admr: Henry Mark
Examiners: Lewis Hoff, William Vanhorn (p. 238-239)

HELM, MARGARET
Will. 5 Nov 1806/ 6 Sep 1813
Daughter: Margaret Barnett, wife of Ambrose Barnett
"My entire estate to my beloved daughter Margaret Barnett."
Exr: Son-in-law Ambrose Barnett, Thomas Neill
Wit: Thomas Neill, Jane Better, Elizabeth Barnett, Augustine Smith, Thomas Blakeman (p. 239-240)

CARPER, WILLIAM
Will. 17 Aug 1813/ 6 Sep 1813
Wife: Margaret
Brother: Frederick
Entire estate to wife for care and maintenance of her and small children. If she remarries she must be cut off with her thirds.
Exr: Wife Margaret and brother Frederick
Wit: Samuel Drake, Michael Pierce
Sec: Jacob Anderson, Philip Carper
[William Carper m Margaret Ritter, 28 Mar 1786; Fdk.Co.Marrs.]
(p. 240)

SIDWELL, SAMUEL - ORPHANS
Guardianship Account. 3 May 1813
Guardians: Nathaniel White, Sarah Sidwell, Jacob Rees
Examiners: J. Tidball, Edw. McGuire (p. 241-243)

McCOWAN, MARGARET
Sale Account. 16 July 1810/ 6 Sep 1813 (p. 243)

LITTLE, ADAM
Inventory & Appraisal. 6 Sep 1813
Admr: John Little
Appraisers: Thomas Relph, Henry George, William Relph
(p. 243-245)

THROCKMORTON, HANNAH - ORPHANS
Orphans Hannah and Kitty Throckmorton
Guardianship Account. 1805/ 6 Sep 1813
Guardians: Kitty Throckmorton and Mordecai Throckmorton
Guardianship of Kitty assumed by John Throckmorton
Examiners: Griffen Taylor, J. Ware, D. H. Allen (p. 246-248)

LAWRENCE, MARY
Inventory & Appraisal. 6 Sep 1813
Appraisers: James Oliver, Joseph Smith (p. 248)

LOUTHAN, GEORGE
Dower distribution. 7 Sep 1813
Widow receives dower slaves from Admr. (p. 248-249)

MILBURN, JOHN
Inventory & Appraisal. Aug 1813/ 6 Sep 1813
Appraisers: John Littler, Joseph Wood, Conrad Huntsberry
"We certify that Nathan Littler, who was one of the appraisers, was present and concurring during this appraisal but died before business was fully completed." (p. 249-251)

MEADE, MARY
Will. Undated/ 7 Sep 1813
Children: Richard Kidder, William, David, Susan, Mary, Lucy
To son Richard Kidder, half the Frederick land, choice of 1,000 acres of the Ohio land. To sons William and David, other half of Frederick land and remaining 5,000 acres of the Ohio land; also Dismal Swamp property. Slaves to be sold, added to money in the hands of Matthew, Robert Carter Burwell and Samuel Bryarly, to be equally shared by daughters. Daughter Mary has received her portion.
Exrs: Robert Page, Philip Burwell, and my two eldest sons
Wit: Ann R. Page, Susan Mead (p. 251-252)

BONHAM/BONEHAM, ANN
Inventory & Appraisal. 1 Oct 1813
Appraisers: Geo. Catlett, John Rust, Jacob Cleavinger (p. 252)

CHAPMAN, THOMAS
Inventory & Appraisal. 1 Oct 1813
Appraisers: Peter McMurry, James Carter, Arthur Carter (p. 253)

LITTLER, SAMUEL
Appraisal. 1 Nov 1813
Appraisers: Robt. McCandless, Francis Stribling, David Ridgeway (p. 254-256)

POWERS, JOHN - ORPHANS
James, Martin, Elizabeth and Marti(?) Powers
Guardianship Account. 1 Nov 1813
Guardian: James Powers
Examiners: J. B. Tilden, R. Vance, Elisha Phelps (p. 256-259)

CURLET, RACHEL
Sale Account; dated 26 June 1813;
Inventory & Appraisement. 1 Nov 1813
Appraisers & Examiners: James Cochran, Jacob Anderson, Simon Lauck (p. 259-262)

BURWELL, ROBERT CARTER
Will. 12 May 1806/ 1 Nov 1813
Sisters: Frances Housden Burwell, Anna Burwell, Sarah Nelson wife of Philip Nelson
Cousins: Mrs. Sarah Burwell Nelson, Mrs. Alice Smith, Mrs. Frances Nelson (later Beckley), Nathaniel Burwell
Nephew: Thomas Nelson
Friend: Robert Nelson, Jr.
Servant: Bob Cook
To sisters Frances Housden Burwell and Anna Burwell, tract commonly called Rattlesnake Plantation, surveyed by George Bell, adjoining property lines of Benjamin Gains, Henry Bartlett and my cousin Nathaniel Burwell. To sister Sarah Nelson and her husband Philip Nelson, estate known as Long Branch Farm. Legacies to "my three cousins, Mrs. Sarah Burwell Nelson, Mrs. Alice Smith and Mrs. Frances Nelson of York Town, Va." Legacy to "my friend Robert Nelson, Jr., of York Town." To my nephew Thomas Nelson, land in Prince William County. To servant Bob, calling himself Bob Cook, immediate freedom and piece of land.
Codicil: Cousin, Mrs. F. N. Nelson is now Mrs. Beckley; their legacy to go to their oldest daughters.
Exrs: My two friends and relations, Philip Nelson and Robert Nelson, Jr., of York.
Wit: "At court, there being no subscribing witnesses, this will proved on oaths of Philip Burwell and William Byars Page." (p. 262-264)

CRAMPTON, JOHN (of Hampshire County)
Will. 19 Aug 1813/ 1 Nov 1813
Wife: Ann
Daughter: Jane
Everything to be sold after wife marries. Monies to go to daughter Jane.
Exrs: Jacob Daughner, Francis Martin
Wit: John Hammack, Elijah Dalby, Edward Perrill(?)
Executors both declined to act.
New exr appointed by court 31 Jan 1814: John Snyder
Sec: Daniel Shambough (p. 264)

CLARK, JOHN
Will. 13 Oct 1813/ 1 Dec 1813
Wife: Mary
Children: Mentioned, unnamed
Mentions patent he holds on machinery.
Exrs: John Davenport, Jr., James Curl.
Wit: John Davenport, Sr., Isaac McCormick, John Curl.
(p. 265-266)

REGAL, GEORGE
Inventory & Appraisal. 1 Nov 1813
Appraisers: James Roberts, John Lefevre, John Butler
(p. 266-267)

SMITH, ANDREW
Account current. May 1811/ 6 Dec 1813
Examiners: Jn. White, Jon. Lovett, Wm. Gore
Admr: George Smith (p. 267-268)

BALDWIN, WILLIAM
Inventory & Appraisal. 6 Dec 1813
Appraisers: LeRoy Daingerfield, William Daingerfield, William Hancher (p. 269-270)

MESMER, NICHOLAS
Will. 5 Oct 1813/ 3 Jan 1814
Wife: Anna Maria
Children: John, Jacob, Margaret, Katherine wife of John Crockwell
Gr. ch: Clementina Mesmer
To sons John and Jacob "all my blacksmith tools and use of blacksmith shop."
Exrs: Wife Anna Maria and son-in-law John Crockwell
Wit: Daniel Overaker, Allen Tidball, John Frye
[John Crockwell m Catherine Messmere, 18 Oct 1795; Fdk.Co.Marrs.]
(p. 270-271)

CLARK, JOHN
Inventory & Appraisal. 3 Jan 1814
Appraisers: William Tyler, Danl. Magruder, Robt. McCandliss
(p. 272-274)

LITTLER, SAMUEL - ORPHANS
Barnett, Rebecca, Betsy, Orphans of Samuel Littler
Account with estate of Elijah Littler, Dec'd, who was one of the guardians. 1802/ 4 Oct 1813
Admrs: Nathan Littler and Elijah Littler, dec'd. (p. 274-276)

RICE, GEORGE (Tavern keeper)
Will. 21 Jan 1814/ No recording date shown
Wife: Elizabeth
After payment of debts, "All that remains of my estate, real and personal, to be the property of my beloved wife Elizabeth forever."
Exrx: Wife Elizabeth
Wit: John Hoff, Daniel Overaker, Jno. Coe (p. 277)

BARNETT, MILLY
Will. 6 Apr 1813/ 31 Jan 1814
Dau: Milly
To daughter Milly, entire estate. George Blakeman to be Counselor.
Wit: Hazelwood Ship (p. 277-278)

BURWELL, ROBERT C.
Inventory & Appraisal. 9 Dec 1813/ 28 Feb 1814
Inventory includes extensive library.
Appraisers: Lewis Burwell, Rich. B. Meade, John Kerfoot, Daniel Sowers, Jr. (p. 278-281)

CARPER, WILLIAM
Inventory & Appraisal. 26 Oct 1813/ 23 Feb 1814
Appraisers: Saml. Drake, William Kerfoot, Michael Peirce (p. 281-283)

BECKWITH, RICHARD B. - ORPHAN
Guardianship Account. 1812/ 28 Feb 1814
Guardian: James Roberts
Examiners: Rich. Galloway, F. Bell (p. 283-284)

LITTLER, NATHAN
Will. 16 May 1807/ 6 Sep 1813
Wife: Rebekah
Children: Nathan, John, David, Thomas, Isaiah, Samuel, Catherine Wood, Rachel Talbott
To son Nathan Littler, land in Hampshire County purchased of Owen Rogers and Stacy Besen (Beeson?). Land in Loudoun County purchased of Stephen Rozzel and house in Georgetown purchased of Ely Bealle to be sold; lands in Berkeley County to be sold. Son Samuel and daughter Rachel Talbott have received their full shares. To son Samuel's children (unnamed), $1 each.
Exrs: Sons John, Thomas and Isaiah
Wit: Robert Cobourn, William Hinlin, Barnabus Courtney (p. 284-285)

MOORE, HENRY
Account current; Inventory & Appraisal. 2 May 1814
Admr: Catherine Moore
Examiners: Jos. Gamble, Edw. McGuire
Appraisers: John Miller, B. Carson (p. 285-291)

CHURCHILL, SARAH
Will. 26 May 1814/ 8 June 1814
Son: Richard
"I bequeath unto my son Richard, in consideration that he is lame and infirm, all of the estate of which I may die possessed."
Exr: Son Richard
Wit: Alexander Balmain, Cornelius Baldwin, Leml. Bent

MUSE, JOHN
Inventory & Appraisal. 15 Jan 1813/ 6 June 1814
Appraisers: Thomas Littleton, George Bell, Eli Swearingen (p. 293)

HELM, MARGARET
Inventory & Appraisal. 6 June 1814
Appraisers: John Ship, Augustine Smith, Samuel Taylor (p. 294)

LOVETT, JONATHAN
Will. 27 Apr 1814/ 1 Aug 1814
Wife: Ann
Children: Nancy, Sarah, Jonathan, Joshua, Mahlon, Mary Ann, Caroline
Legatees: Jane, Mary and Margaret, three eldest children of Jesse Pugh.

First, payment in full of debt I owe John Janney of Alexander (sic). To wife Ann, one-third part of estate which comes from estate of Joseph Clowes of Loudoun County; and that which falls to me or my daughter Nancy in consequence of the deaths of Elizabeth, Hannah or Phebe Clowes.
Exrs: Joshua Gore, Sr., of Loudoun Co. and George Smith of Frederick Co.
Wit: William Griffin, Jr., Joseph McKee, William Gore
Codicil dated 24 May 1814: I give to the three eldest children of Jesse Pugh, late deputy surveyor, dec'd., namely, Jane, Mary and Margaret, tract of land joining Wharton's land, Thomas Anderson's land, Frederick Larrick's land and others.
Sec: Samuel Lockheart(sic), David Lovett
[See Joseph Clews' will, 15 Aug 1792/ Oct Court 1792, Loudoun Co. Will Book, p. 271, mentioning daughters Mary, Elizabeth, Anna, Nancy, Ruth, Phebe, and granddaughter Nancy Lovett, daughter of Jonathan Lovett.] (p. 295-296)

HOFFMAN, JACOB
Inventory & Appraisal; Sales Account. 2 Aug 1814
Appraisers: Michael White, John Russell, Philip Bucher (p. 297-301)

CHURCHILL, SARAH
Inventory & Appraisal. 17 June 1814/ 3 Aug 1814
Appraisers: Peter Lauck, B. Carson, Leml. Bent (p. 301-302)

POLLARD, JAMES
Will. 14 June 1813/ 1 Aug 1814
Wife: Milly
Mother: Nancy Pollard
To my mother Nancy Pollard, land and negroes now in her possession from my father's estate; also 30 acres adjoining Saml. Shackleford. Rest of my estate to my wife Milly.
Exr: Mandly Taylor
Wit: Benjamin Elliott, William Mitchell, Rithy (Richard?) Taylor (p. 302-303)

DILLON, JAMES
Sale Account. 4 Nov 1807; Account current. 5 Sep 1814
Admr: William Dillon
Examiners: Wm. Abbott, Alex Miller
Among buyers: William Dillon, Sr., William Dillon, Jr., John Dillon, Jr., James Dillon, Jr., Nathan, Rebekah, Rachel and John Dillon. (p. 303-308)

BATCHELOR, JOHN
Account. Nov 1787/ 5 Sep 1814
Payment to Catherine Bachelor "other" (now) Catherine Mathers; legacy to Mary Batchelor; to John Townsend the legacy of Elizabeth Batchelor; the assignees of Margaret Batchelor (say) Murry, and Ann; allowance for John Bachelor, Sr.
Admr: Moses Russell
Examiners: Joseph Longacre, James Singleton, 17 Mar 1801 (p. 309)

WHITACRE, JOSHUA
Will. 14 Aug 1814/ 5 Sep 1814
Wife: Rachel
Children: Sarah Kerns, George, Nancy, Jonas, Wilson, Rachel, Ruth, Joshua and Washington Whitacre
To daughter Sarah Kerns, wife of Nathan Kerns, cow which I purchased of Nathan.
Codicil: 16 Aug 1814 - After decease or remarriage of wife, my estate to be equally divided amongst my nine children

Exrs: My son George, and George Smith
Wit: Wm. Gore, John Strickling
Sec: John Lewis (p. 309-312)

WALTERS, THOMAS B. - ORPHANS
Alexander, Mary, Sarah, Thomas, Susan
Guardianship Accounts. Aug 1810/ 5 Sep 1814
Guardian: Lawrence Walter
Examiners: John Burgess, Abraham Niswander (p. 312)

WHITE, EDWARD
Account current. 3 Oct 1814
Exr: Joseph White
Examiners: J. B. Tilden, R. Vance (p. 313)

ALBIN, ROBERT (deceased 21 May 1814)
Inventory & Appraisal. 3 Oct 1814
Examiners: George Smith, James Crumly, John Rogers
(p. 314-315)

KING, AQUILA
Will. 8 Sep 1814/ 31 Oct 1814
Wife: Mary
Children: Lucy, Elenor, Mary Allen, and son Reason
First wife's children: Not named.
To wife Mary, best bed, furniture, two mares, three cows, one yearling and ten sheep. To my daughter Lusia (Lucy) King, next bed, furniture and looking glass. To Mary Allen, wife of Joseph Allen, feather bed, furniture and a horse. To John Allen who married my daughter Elenor, one spice mortor (sic) and pessel (sic). To my daughter Lucy (Lucy) Whom married Ransom Kendall, one turkey oil whetstone. To my son Reason King one Fammerly (sic) Bible. After just debts are paid, remainder of estate to be divided between my first wife's children (not identified).
Wit: Cha. Churchwill (Churchill?), John McDonal, George McGruder
[Lucy King m Ranson Kendall 16 Mar 1804; Fdk.Co.Marrs.]
(p. 315-316)

HURST, WILLIAM
Sale Account. 10 Dec 1812; Account current. 31 Oct 1814
Admr: James Hurst
Examiners: Matthew Ransom, Will Fate (Tate?) (p. 316-322)

BRILL, HENRY
Will. 27 May 1814/ 31 Oct 1814
Children: Michael, Henry; Other children mentioned, unnamed.
Gr. ch: Betsy Ann White, Joseph White
To son Michael ten pounds; to son Henry, wagonmaker tools; to granddaughter Betsy Ann White, spinning wheel; to grandson Joseph White, $6.
Exrs: Michael and Henry Brill
Wit: Moses Russell, Philip Bucher
[Elizabeth Brill m Joseph White, 26 Aug 1806; Fdk.Co.Marrs.]
(p. 323)

HAAS, FREDERICK
Account current. Apr 1806/ 1 Nov 1814
Admr: John Haas (p. 324-328)

HALLER, JACOB (Manor of Leeds)
Will. 10 Oct 1809/ 5 Dec 1814
After payment of debts and funeral expenses, "I bequeath to my present housekeeper Shippe(?) Hopewell all property I shall die possessed of."
Exrs: Shipp Hopewell and Edward Marsh

Wit: John Reed, John Frye, William Vanhorn
Edward Marsh declined executorship; New exr: Leppy(?) Hopewell
Sec: Henry Franks (p. 328-329)

HAMPTON, FRANCIS
Will. 14 Nov 1814/ 5 Dec 1814
Children: Ann Ireland widow and relict of (Rev) James Ireland, Thomas Colston Hampton, Sarah Vance wife of Samuel Vance, Peggy McCormick wife of Samuel McCormick
Property to be equally divided among children named
Exr: Son-in-law Samuel McCormick and son Thomas Colston Hampton
Wit: Saml. Bryarly, John Alexander, John Parscale(p. 329-331)

BEAN, MORDICAI
Will. 19 Aug 1814/ 5 Dec 1814
Wife: Juda
Children: Isaac, James, Betsey Frye, Peggy Richards, Sally Cartmill
Gr. ch: Mordicai Bean, son of James
Property bequeathed to grandson Mordecai Bean to be rented until he is 21 and proceeds given to daughters. When Mordecai is 21, property becomes his.
Exrs: Wife Juda and son James
Wit: Jno. White, Robert Tilden, Robert White, James Newbanks
[Betsy Bean m Jacob Frye, 13 Nov 1792; Mary Bean m John Richards 5 June 1798; Sarah Bean m Nathaniel Cartmill, 23 Apr 1807; Fdk.Co.Marrs.] (p. 331-334)

BROWN, JONATHAN
Will. 11 Apr 1803/ 5 Dec 1814
Wife: Deborah
Son: Daniel Brown
Gr. ch: Samuel Brown, Joseph Brown, Elizabeth Brown, Rachel Brown, Ruth Brown, Jona. Brown
Brothers: Isaac and Thomas Brown
After decease of wife, five pounds to my son Daniel; remainder of estate to be divided among named grandchildren.
Exrs: Brothers Isaac and Thomas Brown
Wit: Robert Hodgson, Abner Hodgson, Elizabeth Hodgson (p. 334-335)

DENEALE, GEORGE
Inventory & Appraisal. 2 Feb 1815
"An inventory of the property shewn to us by James C. Deneale on the premises of George Deneale contained in a deed of trust to William Deneale late of Fairfax County from George Deneale, Jr., Dec'd.
Appraisers: George L. Lane, George H. Norris, Carter Chandler (p. 335-336)

GRUBBS, THOMAS
Will. 2 Jan 1815/ 6 Feb 1815
Wife: Elizabeth
Brother: Derias (Darius) Grubbs
Cousin: Stephen Grubb
To wife, one third of estate; "balance between Smith Grubbs Thomas Grubbs his brother Polly Trinary daughter of Nancy Ann Trinary daughter of Nancy Trinary and Hezekiah Trinary son of Nancy Trinary and Sally Trinary daughter of Samuel Trinary. Thomas Grubbs to have two shares and all the others above named one equal share." (Complete statement, unpunctuated as in will)
To brother Derias (Darius) Grubbs, my wearing apparel.
Exr: My cousin Stephen Grubb
Wit: Alex Compton, Stephen Grubbs, Joshua Antram
[Thomas Grubbs m Elizabeth Scott, 21 Jan 1793; Polly Trenary m David Cleavinger, 17 Sep 1807; Samuel Trenary m Sarah Grimes,

5 Sep 1786; Hezekiah Trenery m Elizabeth Handle, 14 July 1823; Darius Grubbs proved his Revolutionary War service, Minutes of Frederick Co. Court between 1834-1838.] (p. 336-337)

SOWERS, JOHN
Will. 16 Jan 1815/ 6 Feb 1815
Children: James, Polly Haskell/Heiskill wife of Isaac Hyskell, Jane Bowen wife of Phemas Bowen
Son-in-law: James Little
Gr. ch: Knight Bowen
To son James Sowers, land on north side of road leading to John Hamilton's; to son-in-law Phemas Bowen, land on south of said road; to daughter Polly Haskell(sic), servants; to son-in-law James Little, riding horse; to grandson Knight Bowen, colt; to daughter Jane Bowen, bed and furniture; to her husband, Phemas Bowen, a saddle. Money due me by bonds, notes or book account, I give to my son-in-law Isaac Hyskell(sic) for payment of my debts.
Exr: Isaac Heiskell
Wit: Saml. Drake, William Knight, Jr., Alexander Frazier. (p. 337-338)

McCOOLE, JOHN
Will. 11 July 1807/ 6 Mar 1815
Wife: Eleanor
Children: Lewis, John, Eleanor McWhorter, Ann Lewis, Olivia McCoole, Martha McCoole
Gr. ch: Eleanor Darlington
To son Lewis, tract of land I purchased of John Rogers, executor of Evan Rogers, dec'd; to son John McCoole, plantation where I now live; to daughters Eleanor McWhorter, Ann Lewis, Olivia McCoole and Martha McCoole, each a feather bed. Legacy to granddaughter Eleanor Darlington.
Exrs: Wife Eleanor and sons Lewis and John
Wit: William Doster, William Farmer, Jo. McKee
[Lewis McCoole m Nancy Weaver, 22 Sep 1808; John McCoole m Sarah Burke, 19 Jan 1821 and Cassandra Dent 3 Oct 1822; Olivia McCoole m Jacob Weaver, 17 Jan 1811; Catherine McCoole m Meredith Darlington 6 May 1802, Catherine deceased before 1809. Fdk.Co. Marrs.] (p. 338-340)

PARRIL/PARRELL, JOSEPH
Will. 12 Jan 1814/ 6 May 1815
Children: Hugh, John, Joseph, Mary, Sarah Sexton, Ann, Elizabeth Grimes, Rebecah Cooper, Ruth Hodge
"To son Hugh Parril the plantation on which I now live provided he and my three daughters who now live with me, namely, Mary Parril, Sarah Sexton and Ann Parril, live together."
Exr: Daniel Thornburgh
Wit: Daniel Thornburgh, Jacob Huntsberry, Ebenezer Parkins, William Ashenhurst (p. 340-341)

MILTON, ALEXANDER
Inventory & Appraisal. 8 Dec 1814/ 6 Mar 1815
Appraisers: William Castleman, Jr., Jacob Kineley, LeRoy Williams (p. 342-343)

SOWERS, JOHN
Inventory & Appraisal. 9 Feb 1815/ 6 Mar 1815
Appraisers: Jas. Glass, John Lafevre, Samuel McCormick (p. 343-344)

RELPH, THOMAS
Will. 22 Dec 1815/ 6 Mar 1815
Wife: Unnamed

Children: Joseph, Sarah, John, Catherine, Rosie, Mary Shell
Mentions having three sons and four daughters
Wit: Saml. Shell, George Shell, Joseph Relph (p. 344)

HOLLAR/HALLER, JACOB
Appraisal. 6 Mar 1815
Appraisers: Elam Carter, Geo. Bell, David Tressler
(p. 345)

PARADISE, JOHN
Appraisal. 7 Mar 1815
Admr: John Hopkins
Appraisers: Lemuel Bent, Charles Magill (p. 345-346)

NEGRO JOHN, FREE JOHN
Account current. Nov 1807/ 3 Apr 1815
Exr: David Lupton
Examiner: Lemuel Bent (p. 346-347)

HOOVER, HENRY
Will. 19 Jan 1813/ 3 Apr 1815
Wife: Charity
Sons: John, Philip; Dau: Catherine Heilsel
Brother: Philip
Dau-in-law: Mary Hoover
To wife, entire estate during her natural life. After decease of wife, to son John, land I purchased of Benjamin Sedwick and land purchased of Geo. Beamer. To son Philip, plantation where I now live. To daughter Catherine Heilsel, note of hand given to me from Chas. Heilsel dated 7 Jan 1793; also land purchased of James Russell, and a tract of land in Shenandoah County.
Exrs: Wife Charity, my brother Philip Hoover, Daniel Hartman
Wit: Nicholas Kern
Codicil dated 16 Mar 1813: "As it has pleased the Almighty to take my son Jno. Hoover out of this world and my son has omitted in his will to provide his wife a home, it is my will that Mary Hoover, wife of my son John, shall have three acres and a house out of my estate." (p. 347-349)

MULLAN, THOMAS
Will. 3 Mar 1815/ 3 Apr 1815
Wife: Arthila
Property in town of Front Royal and perishable property to be sold to pay my debts and funeral expenses. My wife Arthila to have the whole of the remainder to be enjoyed by her forever.
Exrs: Friends Arthila Mullan, George Reynolds, Gabriel ---(?)
Wit: Spence Calmes, William Van Meter, Robert Allen
(p. 349-350)

MARTIN, JAMES LEE (of Berrisville)
Will. 20 Feb 1815/ 3 Apr 1815
Wife: Polly (Mary)
Children: Wilford, Sally, Harriet; (Other children not named)
To son Wilford, $100 at age 21; to daughters Sally and Harriet, $100 each when 21 or married
Exr: George M. Frye
Wit: Thomas Coe, John Clothier
George Frye refused burden of execution; certificate for obtaining letters of administration granted to Mary Martin, her securities Jacob Cooper, Joseph Frye
[James Lee Martin m Mary Frye, 21 May 1793; Fdk.Co.Marrs.]

FRYE, JACOB
Will. 25 Feb 1805/ 4 Apr 1815
Wife: Molly
Children: Joseph, John (dec'd), William, Jacob, Elizabeth wife

of John Keller, Christina wife of Abraham Jamison, Polly wife of Abraham Chrisman, Catherine wife of Isaac Frye
Gr. ch: John and Leah Frye, children of son John, dec'd
To son Joseph Fry, tract of land conveyed to me by Abraham Fry, tract of land conveyed to me by Issaac Zane, and tract granted to me by patent.
To daughter Elizabeth Keller and to son William, each $200. To daughter Christina Jamison wife of Abraham Jamison. To Polly Chrisman wife of Abraham Chrisman, to daughter Catherine wife of Isaac Frye, to son Jacob, to grandchildren John and Leah Frye children of my son John Frye, dec'd., each $100.
Exrs: John Frye, Joseph Snapp
Wit: Proven 1 Feb 1808, oath of Joseph Watson; further oath of Philip Williams
Sec: Thomas Fawcett (p. 351-353)

BRILL, HENRY
Inventory & Appraisal; Sale Account. 21 Nov 1814/ 4 Apr 1815
Sale by Michael Brill, Exr.
Appraisers: Michael White, John Russell (p. 353-359)

JONES, CATHERINE
Account current. Jan 1809/ 4 Apr 1815
Filed by Samuel Bonham (p. 359-360)

BUSH, PHILIP
Account current. Jan 1803/ 4 Apr 1815
Exr: Edward Smith
Examiners: Danl. Lee and Leml. Bent (p. 360-362)

HOOVER, JOHN
Will. 1 Mar 1815/ April 1815
Wife: Unnamed
Children: Unnamed except daughter Sarah
Estate to be divided amongst my wife and all my children except my daughter Sarah. "It is to be understood that when I mention my children that my daughter Sarah is excluded and to have no part whatever."
Exrs: William Cochran, John Wall
Wit: John Hoff, Abraham Miller
William Cochran refused executorship (p. 362-363)

CRAMPTON, JOHN
Inventory & Appraisal; Sale Account. 12 Feb 1814/ 4 Apr 1815
Appraisers: Abraham Niswander, William Barrow
Among buyers: Nancy Crampton (p. 364-365)

ROUT, JOHN "at Shenandoah River"
Inventory. 16 Jan 1815
Subscribers: Benjamin Kendrick, Moses McKay (p. 365-368)

DUNBAR, ROBERT (Doctor)
Will. 3 Mar 1815/ 1 May 1815
Children: John Richard, Robert L. (possibly others), Mary
Wife: Unnamed
"Inventory and appraisal made of everything excepting my medical shop and the things therein which I bequeath to any one of my sons who may choose the profession of a physician. The encyclopedia to my son John Richard as being a present from his friend John Woodcock and his father who ordered it." To son Robert L., property purchased of John Lupton; to daughter Mary, property on which Miss Molly Rust lived "as my beloved wife promised to Miss Molly Rust that this property would be so devised." Property devised to me and my wife by John S. Woodcock to be

equally divided among my children, deducting what Mrs. Francis Woodcock owes to my wife and children as residuary legatees of her deceased husband.
Exrs: Goldsmith Chandlee, Sr., Lewis Hoff, Samuel Briarley; also my two sons if they have arrived at age 21.
Codicil: If my wife is pregnant at time of my decease, child to inherit equal share.
Wit: Archibald Magill, John Hoff (p. 368-372)

DUNBAR, ROBERT
Widow's renunciation. 1 May 1815
"I, Hannah Dunbar, widow of Doctor Robert Dunbar ..."
Wit: Archibald Magill, Danl. Gold, Chas. Magill (p. 372-373)

WILLIAMS, JOHN S.
Will. 26 Aug 1814/ 1 May 1815
Wife: Unnamed
Dau: Matilda
Mother-in-law: Barbary Littler
Property to be equally divided between my wife and child, Matilda. Should my wife have a child nine months after my decease, said child to have equal share. Clock to my mother-in-law Barbary Littler
Exrs: David Castleman, Jr., Charles McCormack, Lemuel Bent of Frederick, and Isaac and James Littler of Tennessee.
Wit: Isaac Littler, Barbara Littler
[Will first proved 5 Dec 1814] (p. 373)

RODD/RODES, JACOB
Will. 7 Jan 1815/ 1 May 1815
Wife: Catherine
Children: David, Henry, Jacob, Elizabeth
To son David, $50
Exrs: Sons Jacob and David
Wit: John Senseney, Peter Senseney, Jacob Danner (p. 374-376)

SCARFF, JAMES
Will. 16 Mar 1815 / No recording date, poss. 1 May 1815
Wife: Mary
Children: William, John, Elizabeth Thompson wife of Abel Thompson, Mary Hollingshead wife of James Hollingshead, Jane and Nancy Scarff, Sarah Scarff (three youngest: Jane, Sarah, Nancy)
"Weakly state of health."
Son John has already received his share.
Exr: Son William Scarff
Wit: Benjamin Barrett, John Dowell (p. 376-377)

CARTMELL, SARAH (widow of Nathaniel)
Will. 20 Mar 1815/ 1 May 1815
Children: Martin, Elijah, Jacob, Elizabeth Larue, Sarah Cochran, Rachel Crist, Mary Willis
Son Jacob to hold in trust shares of Rachel Crist and Mary Willis.
Exrs: Capt. Thomas Cramer
Wit: Nathaniel Cartmell, James Singleton (p. 377-379)

SNYDER, CHARLES
Will. 31 Dec 1814/ 1 May 1815
"I give and devise my whole estate to my dearly beloved wife Mary, and I nominate my said wife Mary executor of this will."
Wit: Saml. Kercheval, Thomas Dann, Robert Ewing (p. 379-380)

CHURCHILL, JOHN
Division of Dower - Slaves. 1 May 1815
To: Philip Clayton, John R. Hodges, Richard & Mary Churchill (p. 380-381)

CLARK, JOHN
Sale Account. 12 Jan 1814/ 1 May 1815
Exrs: John Davenport, James Curl (p. 381-387)

BRADY, CALEB
Inventory & Appraisal. 1 May 1815
Appraisers: Stephen Pritchard, Jr., Benjamin Beemer, Philip Hoover (p. 388)

WOOD, JOSEPH
Will. 27 Nov 1813/ 1 May 1815
Wife: Ann
Children: Joseph, Isaiah, David, Isaac, Joshua, Jesse, Rachel, Margaret, Mary Vass, Esther
Gr. ch: Joseph Ambrose Vass, Elizabeth and Thiaza(?) daughters of Isaac
Brother: Thomas Wood
To wife, tract of land purchased of Jacob Poe adjoining lands of John Milburn, dec'd, and tract purchased of Christian Shreck adjoining lands of John Sperry. Son Isaiah to furnish firewood to mother. To son David, tract of land in Allegany Mountains. He has been so amply provided for by his grandfather. To daughter Rachell, 2000 acres in Ohio. To daughter Margaret, land I purchased of Gen. John Smith. To daughter Mary Vass, two shares of Snickers Gap Turnpike stock - her son Joseph Ambrose Vass. To my son Isaac,my two young daughters Elizabeth and Thiaza(?), my sons Joshua and Jesse and my daughter Esther, legacies. To brother Thomas Wood, my wearing apparel.
Wit: Isaac Parkins, Joseph Parrill, Goldsmith Chandlee (p. 389-393)

GILHAM, DAVID C.
Nuncupative Will. 1 May 1815
Wife: Martha
Children: Unnamed
To wife Martha entire estate, she to raise children, and at her death children to share equally.
Attested by: Ezekiel Gilham, Thomas Gilham (p. 393-394)

CARTMELL, SARAH
Inventory & Appraisal. 5 June 1815
Appraisers: Robert Glass, John Lupton, John Bell (p. 394)

LOWRY, ROBERT
Inventory & Appraisal. 5 June 1815
Appraisers: George Bruce, Christian Crum, Henry Crum (p. 394-395)

LOVETT, JONATHAN
Inventory & Appraisal. 29 Sep 1814/ 5 June 1815
Appraisers: Bennett Hale, Joseph McKee (p. 395-398)

WHITACRE, JOSHUA
Inventory & Appraisal. 5 June 1815
Appraisers: Wm. Gore, George Smith, John Stricklin(p. 398-400)

MARPOLE, EZEKIEL
Inventory & Appraisal. 5 June 1815
Appraisers: Wm. Gore, George Smith, Joseph McKee (p. 400-402)

WALTER, THOMAS - ORPHANS
Thomas Walter, orphan of Thomas B. Walter
Guardianship Account. 1810/ 5 June 1810
Guardian: Lewis Walter
Mary, Alexander, Susannah and Sarah Walter
Guardian: Lawrence Walter (p. 402-406)

BROWNLEY, BETSY (Widow of John Brounley)
Will. 26 Feb 1815/ 5 June 1815
"I bequeath to William Brounley, whom I have raised from a child, the son of Archibald Brounley, dec'd., and grandson of my dec'd. husband, all my estate of every description."
Exr: William Brounley
Wit: Betsey Brounley, William Cornegy, Sally Earle (Bell?)
(p. 406)

SAVAGE, JOSEPH (Doctor)
Inventory & Appraisal; Sale Account. 5 Apr 1815/ 6 June 1815
Appraisers: Henry Catlett, Wm. Carnegy
Among buyers: Jane Savage, John Savage (p. 406-418)

TRACEWELL, GEORGE
Inventory & Appraisal; Sale Acct. 3 Dec 1814/ 6 June 1815
Appraisers: Joseph Smith, John Triplett, John Haddox
Among buyers: George Tracewell, John Tracewell
Exr: Charles Utterback (p. 418-420)

MARTIN, JAMES L.
Inventory & Appraisal; Sale Acct. 6 June 1815
Admr: Mary Martin
Appraisers: John Thompson, Thomas Coe, George M. Frye
(p. 421-425)

PARKINS, JOHN
Will. 14 May 1815/ 3 July 1815
"That spot of ground known by the name burying ground, where my parents and others of our family have been entered(sic) be reserved for the Society of Friends." Sole bequest. "Signed at Hannah Hollingworth's"
Exrs: Isaac Parkins, Sr., Isaac Hollingsworth, Jesse Hollingsworth son of Jonah, dec'd., and Hannah Hollingsworth, and any others nominated by Society of Friends.
Codicil dated 17 May 1815: "Just debts paid."
Wit: Hannah Hollingsworth, Sarah Hollingsworth, Isaac Hollingsworth, William Helphenstine (p. 425-426)

DAVIS, WILLIAM
Nuncupative Will. Presented 6 June 1815/ 31 July 1815
Wife: Margaret Davis
Children: Elizabeth Bartlett only one named
Exrs: Baalis Davis, John Gilkison, David Timberlake, James Davis
Wit: James Davis, Elizabeth Davis
Presented 6 June 1815 and following people ordered to appear to contest said will if they so chose: Margaret Davis, widow of said William Davis, Stephen Davis, James Davis, Henry Bartlett and his wife Elizabeth, John Gilkison and his wife Lucy, David Timberlake and his wife Polly, William Davis and wife Peggy, and Sarah Sowers, legal heirs of William Davis. Heirs failed to appear, so will was recorded 31 July 1815.
[Elizabeth Davis m Henry Bartlett, 2 Jan 1799; Fdk.Co.Marrs.]
(p. 426-428)

NEGRO HARRY, FREE NEGRO
Inventory & Appraisal. 31 July 1815
Appraisers: Danl. Magruder, George Kiger, Jonathan Wright
(p. 428-429)

MOSELEY, JESSE
Inventory & Appraisal. 17 June 1815/ 31 July 1815
Appraisers: Robt. Hodge, James Curl, William Kees(p. 429-432)

MERCER, JOSHUA
Inventory & Appraisal. 31 July 1815
Appraisers: Jonathan Pickering, Benjamin Fenton (p. 432-433)

TAYLOR, BENNETT
Will. 25 Apr 1815/ 31 July 1815
Wife: Susan
Son: John Charles
Sister: Charlotte Taylor
"I bequeath to my son John Charles Taylor all my estate, real and personal, except what my beloved wife Susan Taylor may be entitled to legally."
Exrs: Charles Cock, Susannah Beverly Taylor
Wit: George H. Norris, Daniel Amiss, Samuel Cramer(p. 433-434)

BURWILL, FRANCIS(sic) HOUSDEN
Will. 24 Mar 1815/ 2 Aug 1815
Sisters: Annie Burwill; Sarah Nelson; Jane Burwill
Brothers: Robert Carter Burwill, dec'd., Philip Nelson (in-law)
Nephew: Thomas Nelson
To "my dearest sister Annie Burwill, everything left to me by my dearest brother Robert Carter Burwill, but should she marry this property is not to go to her husband." After her death to my nephew Thomas Nelson; also to him, a watch. "I give to my dear sister Nelson half the money which was my part of our sister Jane Burwill's fortune, the other half to my brother Philip Nelson." "My wardrobe to dear Sarah Jane Nelson after dear papa's death." Legacies to daughter of brother Philip Nelson - Lucy Nelson, Sarah Jane Nelson and Susan Burwill Nelson; to Robert Carter Burwell child of Mrs. Carter Beverly; to Mary, daughter of Robt. C. Burwill. Rest divided amongst nieces and nephews: Philip Nelson, Elizabeth Nelson, Evelyn Taylor, Jamison Nelson and William Nelson. Horse to child of Mrs. Carter Page called after dearest brother Robert Carter Burwill. Legacies to nephews Thomas and William Nelson; to Nelly Jackson (relationship not stated); to Sarah Jane Nelson
Exrs: Wm. Nelson and Annie Burwill, cousin Susan Beverly Wormley
Wit: Susan Whiting, Elizabeth Burwill, Nathaniel Burwill (p. 433-434)

PARKINS, JOHN
Inventory & Appraisal; Sale Account. 4 Sep 1816
Admr: Jonathan Smith
Appraisers: William Cochran, William Helphinstine, Peter Koontz (p. 435-442)

HOOVER, PHILIP
Will. 1 Jan 1815/ 4 Sep 1815
Wife: Elizabeth
Children: Sarah, Polly, Caty, Philip
Exrs: Wife Elizabeth, Danl. Hartman, Jno. Hoff
Wit: Lewis Hoff, Robert Dunbar, John Reed (p. 443-444)

HOOVER, HENRY
Inventory & Appraisal. 13 Apr 1815/ 4 Sep 1815
Appraisers: Nicholas Kern, Stephen Pritchard, Jr., Benjamin Beaver, John Hamilton (p. 444-447)

COLSTON, WILLIAM
Inventory & Appraisal. 4 Sep 1815
Appraisers: Henry Seever, Isaac Wood (p. 447-449)

PLUMB, VANCE
Inventory & Appraisal. 4 Sep 1815
Appraisers: William Denny, George Linn, Daniel Mytinger (p. 449)

GRAVES, CHARLES
Will. 15 Dec 1812/ 5 Sep 1815
Wife: Elizabeth
Children: John, William, Joseph; other inferred, unnamed
Exrs: Benjamin O'Rear, Henry Jeans, James Sowers, John Foster
Wit: James Stuart, John Montgomery (p. 450-452)

WOOD, JOSEPH
Inventory & Appraisal. 4 Sep 1815
Appraisers: Joseph Parrell, Wm. Tyler (p. 452-453)

SOWERS, DANIEL
Inventory & Appraisal. 14 Mar 1815/ 2 Oct 1815
Appraisers: J. Fauntleroy, Rich. Meade, Saml. Briarly
(p. 453-458)

SPIKENALL/SPICKNELL, JOHN
Inventory & Appraisal. 2 Oct 1815
Appraisers: Reuben Jordan, William Reed (p. 458)

WILLIAMS, JOHN S.
Inventory & Appraisal; Sale Account. 2 Oct 1815
Appraisers: Nathan Anderson, Edward Slater, Leml. Bent
Admr: Charles McCormick (p. 459-463)

SNYDOR, HENRY
Will. 29 June 1808/ 2 Oct 1815
Children: Frederick, Christiana; other children unnamed
Son-in-law: Jacob Rode
Gr. ch: Children of Christiana, unnamed
Estate to be sold and money divided between all my children and the children of my daughter Christiana to have equal share. To son Frederick, $50 over and above his share.
Exr: Son-in-law Jacob Rode, and Jacob Danner
Wit: Jacob Rhodes, Rhoda Rhodes, John Mastin (p. 464)

GANNTS/GANTZ, GEORGE
Inventory & Appraisal. 4 Nov 1815
Appraisers: John Barrow, William Barrow, Jonathan Hughes
(p. 465-466_

BELL, THOMAS
Inventory & Appraisal. 6 Nov 1815
Appraisers: John Wright, William Bailey (p. 466-467)

DESPONETT, BARNETT
Will. 26 Feb 1813/ 6 Nov 1815
Daus: Christine Houseman, Elizabeth Pollack, Mary Dunfield
Gr. ch: John Desponet
Exr: Henry Richards
Wit: Moses Russell, James Russell, Elias Kackney, Jr.
(p. 468-469)

MUSE, JOHN
Sale Account. 6 Sep 1815
Among buyers: Susan Muse, Robert Muse (p. 469-472)

BROUNLEY, BETSY
Inventory & Appraisal. 6 Nov 1815
Appraisers: Elias Earle, John B. Earle, Benjamin Elliott
(p. 472-473)

TRACEWELL, JOHN
Estate Account. 8 Nov 1815
Admr: William Reed (p. 473-474)

TAYLOR, BENNETT
Inventory & Appraisal. 4 Dec 1815
Appraisers: John Ship, Tredwell Smith (p. 474-480)

GLASS, PETER
Will. 7 Nov 1815/ 4 Dec 1815
Wife: Eleanor Mary
Heirs: Peter Glass, Catherine Griffin, Charity Rulet(?), Margaret McNut, Masy(?) McNut
Exr: Meredith Darlington
Wit: William Rinker, William Crumley
Sec: Archibald Robinson
[Catherine Glass m Richard Griffick(?), 2 Feb 1797; Fdk.Co.Marrs. Margaret Glass m David McNutt, 22 Apr 1797; Berkeley Co. Marrs.] (p. 480)

SPERRY, NICHOLAS
Inventory & Appraisal; Sale Account. 4 Dec 1815
Admr: Abraham Lauck
Appraisers: George Trister, John Shutz, John Sperry, Frederick Kurtz (p. 481-489)

CARPER, MARGARET
Inventory & Appraisal. 2 Oct 1815
Appraisers: Wm. Kerfoot, Michael Pierce, Saml. Drake (p. 489-490)

TALBOTT, JOHN
Orphan of Benjamin Talbott
Guardianship Account. Apr 1791/ 4 Dec 1815
Note: Clerk recorded part of this account as being of Benjamin Talbott, dec'd, by Elisha Phelps, Admr; part recorded as Elisha Phelps, dec'd, Benjamin Talbott, Admr. (p. 490-496)

GLASS, SARAH
Will. 6 Aug 1812/ 4 Dec 1815
Dec'd husband: Robert Glass
Sons: Robert D. Glass; Joseph Glass, now in Kentucky
Exr: Son Robert D. Glass
Wit: Andrew Shannon, Jos. Longacre, Joseph Glass (p. 496-497)

MARTIN, SNOWDON
Inventory & Appraisal; Sale Account. 1 Jan 1816
Appraisers: Wm. Kerfoot, Frederick Carper (p. 497-499)

DYER, JOHN
Will. 18 Jan 1815/ 1 Jan 1816
Children: Abraham, John, Jacob, Isaac, Israel, James, Rebecca Dyer, Selah, Mary Ann, Susannah Graves- Molly, Rachel Morgan, Betsey Timmons, Sarah Fridley, Peggy Welch
To sons Abraham, John and Jacob and daughter Molly, 1 shilling each as full share of estate. To son Isaac, $5. To son Israel, $25. Other children named.
Exrs: Son Isaac Dyer, son-in-law John Morgan, Benjamin O'Rear
Wit: Benjamin O'Rear, James Lyons, Dennice Lyons
[Sarah Dyer m Henry Friedly, 5 Dec 1803; Elizabeth Dyer m Peter Timmons, 5 July 1806; Susannah Dyer m Joseph Graves, 15 Jan 1793; Fdk.Co.Marrs.] (p. 499-500)

COOPER, FREDERICK
Will. 16 Nov 1815/ 5 Feb 1816
Wife: Hannah
Children: Jonathan R., Henry, Rachel, Isaac
Exrs: John Richards, Henry Richards, John Russell
Wit: Jacob Wolfe, John B. Dyson, Joseph Dyson (p. 500-502)

WILL BOOK NO. 9, 1810-1816

LOWRY, ROBERT
Inventory & Appraisal; Sale Account. Sep 1809/ 5 Feb 1816
Admr: Joseph Baker
Appraisers: Daniel Wade, Jacob Taylor
Among buyers: Agnes Lowry, John Lowry (p. 502-504)

PAGE, WALKER
Will. 9 July 1813/ 5 Feb 1816
Brother: John W. Page
Aunt: Judith White
Uncles: John Page, Robert Page
Sisters: Jane Byrd Page, Sarah W. Brook, Judith R. Page, Catherine Page, Molly Page
Legatees: Sarah Walker Page of Page Brook, Jack Andrews, John Page son of uncle Robert
Exrs: Wm. Byrd Page of Page Brook, uncle Robert Page
Wit: Wm. B. Page, Sally Page
Will proved 6 Dec 1813; further proved by oath of William Byrd Page, Sr., of Alexandria (p. 505-506)

GLASS, ROBERT
Appraisal of one slave. 6 Feb 1816 (p. 506)

GLASS, SARAH
Inventory & Appraisal. 6 Feb 1816
Appraisers: Robert Vance, John Hamilton, John Gilkison (p. 507)

COLVILE, JOHN
Estate settlement. 6 Feb 1816
Admr: John Adams (p. 507-510)

SOWERS, DANIEL, SR.
Sale Account. 5 Feb 1816
Among buyers: Catherine Sowers, William Bowers (p. 510-516)

DYER, JOHN
Inventory & Appraisal; Sale Account. 5 Feb 1816
Exr: John Morgan, Sr.
Appraisers: James Lyons, John Ferguson, James Marshall

DESPONETT, BERNARD (dec'd 23 Dec 1810)
Inventory & Appraisal. 5 Feb 1816
Appraisers: John Richards, John Russell, Elias Kackley (p. 520-521)

MARQUIS, WILLIAM
Inventory & Appraisal; Sale Account. 5 Feb 1816
Appraisers: Joseph Glass, Robert Glass, Nicholas Kern (p. 521-532)

DRAKE, JOSEPH
Estate Account. May 1809/ 6 Feb 1816
Admr: S. Drake (p. 532)

COCHRAN, JOHN
Estate Account. 6 Feb 1816
Admr: Robert Cochran (p. 532-533)

WALKER, LEWIS
Will. Signed "on this the 19th month" 1812/ 4 Mar 1816
Wife: Sarah
Children: Isaac Walker, now of Washington Co., Pa., Leah Steere, Sarah Walker, Surd(?) Walters
Gr. ch: Lewis W. Jackson, Joseph Jackson
Devises plantation where he now lives.

Exrs: Son Isaac, son-in-law Isaac Steer
Wit: James Mendenhall, Levi Smith, George Smith
[Sally Walker m Tobias Walters, 27 Aug 1804; Fdk.Co.Marrs)
(p. 533-535)

RICE, ELIZABETH
Will. 18 Feb 1816/ 6 Mar 1816
Daughter: Rebecca
Legacies to: Emila Rice, Edwin Rice Kiger, George Rice Kiger, "To my daughter Rebecca Kiger, wife of George W. Kiger" (only relationship shown)
Exr: Son-in-law George W. Kiger
Wit: Danl. Magruder, Eleanor Magruder, Jane Anderson, John Rice
(p. 535-536)

LOWRY, DANIEL
Inventory & Appraisal. 4 Mar 1816
Appraisers: George W. Kiger, John Bond, Robt. Bryarly, Danl. Magruder (p. 536-538)

CLARKE, MARY
Inventory & Appraisal.
Appraisers: Danl. Magruder, Henry Seever, Benjamin Harris
(p. 538-540)

ALDRIDGE, ADAM
Inventory & Appraisal; Sale Account. 4 Mar 1816
Appraisers: Saml. Bryarly, Ferguson Bell, James Bell
(p. 540-556)

LOWRY, DANIEL
Sale Account. 5 Mar 1816
Among buyers: Ann, George, Mary Lowry (p. 556-558)

McINTIRE, SAMUEL
Inventory & Appraisal; Sale Account
Admr: Charles McIntire
Appraisers: Peter Dick, F. Snydor, Wm. Trotten (Trotter?)
(p. 558-559)

BECKWITH, RICHARD
Guardianship Account. 6 Mar 1816
Guardian: James Roberts
Examiner: Lemuel Bent (p. 559-560)

INDEX